# *Riding to Jerusalem*

## BETTINA SELBY

Mountain House Publishing

2003

First Published in 1985

British Library Cataloguing in Publication Data

Selby. Bettina
    Riding to Jerusalem
    1.Europe. Overland travel to Jerusalem
    2. Middle East. Overland travel to Jerusalem
    1.Title
    914'.04558


**ISBN 0-9538007-2-5**

This edition has been revised and printed
Digitally  and been produced in a standard
format in order  to ensure its
continuing availability.

**To my son Jonathan, also a traveller**

Books by Bettina Selby

Riding the Mountains Down
Riding to Jerusalem
Riding the Desert Trail
The Fragile Islands
Riding North One Summer
Frail Dream of Timbuktu
Beyond Ararat
Pilgrim's Road
Like Water in a Dry Land
Two Cats Walking

These titles have now all been reprinted
and are available on demand
through bookshops

# Contents

Foreword 7

Chapter One 11
Chapter Two 25
Chapter Three 37
Chapter Four 51
Chapter Five 65
Chapter Six 79
Chapter Seven 91
Chapter Eight 103
Chapter Nine 117
Chapter Ten 130
Chapter Eleven 145
Chapter Twelve 160
Chapter Thirteen 175
Chapter Fourteen 191
Chapter Fifteen 207
Chapter Sixteen 221
Chapter Seventeen 236
Chapter Eighteen 255
Chapter Nineteen 270

# Maps

General map of the Journey 18/19
The Routes of the first Four Crusades 56/57
Turkey during the Roman Empire 82/83
Syria, Jordan and Israel 185

# Foreword

In the fourth century AD Constantine the Great became the first Roman Emperor to embrace Christianity. As soon as he had done so, his mother, the energetic Empress Helena, made a pilgrimage to Jerusalem, and travelled throughout the Holy Land identifying Calvary and other sacred scriptural sites in a great archaeological triumph. She also collected the objects of Christ's Passion, such as the wood of the True Cross, skulls and bones of saints and martyrs and other memorabilia, thus setting a fashion for souvenir hunting, rife to this day. From that time onwards there has been a steady stream of pilgrims converging on Jerusalem and the Holy Places.

By the Eighth Century pilgrims were even coming from as far afield as England. There is an account of a St Willibald leaving Hampshire with his father and brother in 720 AD, when he was just twenty years old. By this time the Holy Land was no longer under Christian rule because of the emergence of Islam, but although Jerusalem had become an Arab city and a great Muslim shrine, it was at that time under a benign rule which did not debar worshippers of other faiths.

As the power of the Byzantine Empire gradually waned, various waves of Turks began to move into Asia Minor and the Middle East, and the way to the Holy Places became more perilous for pilgrims. Nevertheless, apart from minor setbacks due to temporary outbreaks of persecution, pilgrimage continued to increase in popularity, and by the end of the Tenth Century the monks of Cluny were making a profitable business from organizing the traffic.

It was not until the late Eleventh Century, when a shift of power in the East made pilgrimage impossibly dangerous, that the West decided to take a hand. In 1095 Pope Urban the Second preached a Crusade to the whole of Western Christendom, 'The sacred right of all men to pray at the sites where Christ lived his saving life is denied... His Holy City is in the hands of Infidels, it is our duty to set it free... All men who take the Cross, their sins are pardoned... It is a glorious thing to die in the city where Christ died for us all... *Deus Vult* - God wills it.'

The First Crusade was full of enthusiasm, rushing through like a barbarous tide to take Jerusalem in 1099. The Christian princes then set about establishing the Crusader kingdoms of La France Outremer - France Beyond the Sea along the narrow coastal strip of the Middle East. Their courage and fighting skills were unfortunately not matched by any great ability in consolidating their positions. Very soon they found themselves hard pressed by the Saracens under Nur ed Din and a second Crusade was called.

The Second Crusade left Europe in 1145 under the leadership of Louis VII of France and the Emperor Conrad III of Germany. Louis took his dynamic wife Eleanor of Acquitaine along with him and the result of that was a divorce as soon as they returned home. The Second Crusade might just as well have remained in Europe for all the good it achieved, having quickly degenerated into separate sorties against all sorts of factions that had nothing to do with the main issue, and proved an extraordinary waste of money and effort.

Europe licked its wounds and Outremer muddled along as best it could on its own. In the meantime Nur ed Din's brilliant successor, Saladin, became ruler of Egypt, and having gained the ascendancy of the region, went on to capture Jerusalem in 1187.

This spurred on the Third Crusade which, had it been less tardy, might have arrived in time to save the Holy City, for its leaders had delayed their departure for years. It finally got away in 1189 under the English king, Richard Coeur de Lion, the Emperor Frederick Barbarossa of Germany and Philip Augustus of France. Barbarossa had the misfortune to be drowned in Asia Minor on the way, but his companions continued and fought some well-planned battles, performed some superb feats of strategy, and achieved absolutely nothing of any significance. Richard alienated the Austrians who kidnapped him on his return journey, but the rest of the armies returned home with less misadventure, leaving the few remaining Crusader strongholds to continue their slow decline.

A Fourth Crusade was launched between 1200 and 1204 under Boniface of Montferrat. This murderous collection of cynical self-seekers, inspired by the evil genius of the Doge of Venice, got no further than Constantinople, which they decided to attack instead of the Infidel. A Christian Crusade called to defend Christendom succeeded only in destroying the greatest Christian city in the world. The subsequent surge of Islam, sweeping unhindered through Europe to the Gates of Vienna, owed much to the perfidy of the Fourth Crusade.

There were a few more attempts to stir up public feeling over the fate of the Holy Places of Jerusalem, but the Crusades which were launched could not begin to come to grips with the barbaric chaos which had engulfed the Middle East by the middle of the Thirteenth Century with the coming of the Mongol hordes. The last of the Crusaders left Outremer in 1291 and Christians did not again exert any influence upon the affairs of Jerusalem until Lawrence of Arabia and General Allenby entered the Holy City in 1917 - on that day wreaths were placed upon the tombs of the knights in the Temple Crusader Church in London.

# Chapter One

*Whan that Aprille with his shoures soote*
*The droghte of Marche hath perced to the rote*
*Than longen folk to goon on pilgrimage*
*and palmeres for to seken strunge strondes*
Chaucer

It was in April, with the earth stirring again after winter, making me restless with thoughts of far countries, that I made a chance visit which was eventually to lead me to Jerusalem. The Church of the Knights Templars, a unique treasure of London's rich past, is hidden away among the Inns of Court behind Fleet Street, and was unknown to me until that particular Sunday afternoon in April.

Entering the church through a beautiful, ornate Norman doorway, I found myself in a world far removed from the

Twentieth Century. On the flagstoned floor, in the centre of the high circular church, lay carved effigies of accoutred knights, their hands folded on their breasts in attitudes of worshipful repose. Shafts of coloured light from the stained glass windows fell obliquely across their stone features. The atmosphere, though suitably hushed, was also charged with chivalry and high adventure.

The church had been built as the headquarters for the Knights Templars in Britain and was modelled on the Church of the Holy Sepulchre in Jerusalem. In 1185 it was consecrated in honour of the Blessed Mary by Heraclius, the Patriarch of the Holy City, in the presence of King Henry II of England. Beneath its pavement many of the nobles of Britain lay buried. There was also a chamber that had been the treasury of the order, a grim penitential cell for unruly knights, and a small hidden chapel where they had performed their secret initiation ceremonies and had kept their vigil before departing for the Crusades.

I went home determined to find out more about these Crusader knights and the motivation that had led them to Jerusalem. It took very little reading to dispel any romantic notions that I had held at the beginning. Endlessly fascinating they certainly were, but also brutal and ruthless. They were a sudden phenomenon which had arisen in response to Pope Urban II's call in 1095 to free the Holy Places of Palestine from the Infidel. Islam had actually been in control of that part of the world for the best part of 400 years, but a recent shift in power had barred the way to the Holy City for Christian pilgrims. So strong was the belief at that time in people's inalienable right to go on pilgrimage, in order to pray at the sites central to their faith, that thousands flocked to answer the Pope's appeal for a Holy Crusade.

The more I read about the period, the more interested I became in the pilgrims who had been so central to the Crusades. They had been travelling to Jerusalem from every part of Europe, singly and in small bands, since the Fourth Century. What had it been like to make such a journey, I wondered, a journey fraught with difficulties and uncertainties; a journey which might last for many years?

What of the innumerable dangers they had faced from pirates and shipwreck, avalanches and brigands, not to mention cold and hunger and losing their way in wild places? What, too, of the wonders they had seen along the way, of the impact upon them of the great cities they had passed through; coming, as they did, from the relatively barbarous West of that time to all the dazzling sophistication of the Greek and Byzantine worlds?

What, too, of Jerusalem? What had they found there when they had finally arrived at that strange city, which had drawn men to it even before King David took it from the Jebusites around 1000 B.C.

'Jerusalem the Golden', 'City of Peace', its name stirred the imagination as no other city has ever done.

Thousands had made the journey there before the Crusades, but only a handful left any written record of their experiences. One account we do have concerns a young man called Willibald who set out from England in 720 AD when he was just twenty, and spent eight and a half years getting to the Holy Land and back to Europe. He never returned to his native land, but finished his life as St Willibald, a missionary bishop in Germany. Several such accounts exist; some of them give fascinating snippets about identifiable places which were visited on the way. Others are frustrating because they reveal so little. St Jerome's book states at the beginning that he is setting out more with the  intention of edifying the reader spiritually, than of  providing him with a guide book.

Nothing, however, that had been written by or about these early travellers could really tell me what their experiences had been like. To attempt to get some flavour of their extraordinary journeys, I would need to follow in their tracks and make my own odyssey, and this I decided to do. I would travel the old pilgrim and Crusader routes, through Europe, Turkey, and the  Middle East, and see what those parts were like now and whether it was possible to obtain some apprehension of the world that the early pilgrims had seen.

Travelling by bicycle seemed to me the ideal way to make such a journey. On a bicycle I am exposed to all local experiences as no modern traveller, other than a walker, can hope to be. Moving quietly along at gentle speeds allows me to see, hear, and smell the country, in a way which isn't possible encapsulated in a motorcar or a bus. Unlike the motorized traveller, I am not cut off from the people around me either; I can stop wherever and whenever I want to, and respond to the greetings of workers in the fields, passers-by, or friendly villagers. Equally, I am as dependent on local goodwill as were the early pilgrims. When, at the end of a long day's ride, darkness approaches - and maybe the area is plagued with bandits or terrorists - I can't start picking and choosing my accommodation. I must stay in the first available safe shelter that presents itself. If there is no hotel, then I must seek help from local people. But there also seems to be a built-in safety factor when travelling by bicycle which I think has some thing to do with its totally non-aggressive image. No one sees the perspiring cyclist as a threat, nor their dusty cycle as a symbol of unattainable wealth. Both present an image essentially as humble and as innocent as a pilgrim's staff.

I set out for Jerusalem on a delightful, cool morning in late July, and within an hour I had left London's murderous rush-hour traffic and was riding through steep Kentish lanes, under a canopy of beech trees. It was difficult to believe that after all the months of preparation I was at last really on my way, or that I could be starting on a five-thousand-mile journey with so little fuss and formality.

The leafy tunnels through which my route began are ancient ways, worn down by the feet of countless travellers before ever the wheel was invented or roads were paved. They were once the highways of England's history; thoroughfares of kings, merchants, soldiers and peasants. Crusaders of all degrees had ridden along them. Some had been proud knights, the elite of the shires, riding fine horses; their well-greased chain mail wrapped in a linen cloth and carried by squires riding on lesser mounts behind them. Others, of humbler birth, were identifiable as part of a crusading army only by the cross sewn on the shoulder of their coat. Long before the knights, however, and long after them, these lanes had been host to a thin but constant trickle of anonymous pilgrims.

When I emerged from the shade of the beech trees into the bright sunlight at the top of the North Downs, I stopped to rest and regain my breath after the long haul up, as most people travelling this route under their own steam would always have done. It was almost impossible not to pause here for the view over the wide rich acres of the Weald of Kent is one of the loveliest in England. I wondered if departing pilgrims gazing at the prospect had felt, as I did now, a momentary pang of sadness for what they were leaving behind, as well as a degree of apprehension about what lay ahead of them. It is the sort of place that invites such thoughts, for beyond the orchards and meadows and the dark green woods rise the distant blue uplands of the South Downs, and beyond them lie the Channel ports with ships for France.

I sat there thinking about the reading and the planning that had occupied most of my waking moments over the past few months. Working out a route had been a major consideration.

There were many possible ways to come to Jerusalem by land. The one I had finally chosen was a mixture of several different historic routes taken by crusading armies and by individual pilgrims. I would begin by following the southern route of the First Crusade through France and Switzerland. Then, once over the Alps and amongst the Italian Lakes, I would swing eastwards across the Lombardy Plain and make for Venice. Venice had been the assembly point for the armies of the Fourth Crusade, and like them, I would take a ship from there to Istanbul - Constantinople as it had been then - the greatest Christian city, and possibly the greatest city ever to have graced the world. I particularly wanted to arrive there by ship in order to see its famous domed and pinnacled skyline from the sea.

Across the narrow waters of the Bosphorus lies Asian Turkey, and from there I had a choice of many historical routes. The one most frequently used by pilgrims and

Crusaders went directly south-eastwards, across the vast central plateau and down through the Cilician Gates to the fertile plains around Tarsus - the birth place of St Paul. I was very tempted to go this way too, because crossing the inland mass of Asia Minor would make a splendid and exciting journey, and there is so much that would be fascinating to see there, especially the strange, eroded area of Cappadocia. But after weighing up the advantages, I settled for the much older and considerably longer coastal route, which would take me through the area of the Seven Churches of Asia - the scenes of St Paul's journeys, and places of pilgrimage in their own right. If I found myself with time in hand, I could always make a detour into the interior of Turkey on the way.

The Aegean and Mediterranean coasts also drew me because of the sites of the ruins of ancient and classical Greece - fabled cities like Troy, and Pergamon, Ephesus, and Miletus, which I had wanted to visit since I first knew of their existence. And further on, the steep slopes and wooded shores of Rugged Cilicia are dotted about with the ruined castles and cities of the vanished kingdom of Armenia. Added to the prospect of all these delights was the fact that travelling by bicycle in summer, in hot southern climes is very hot work, and on the coast I should at least be able to swim sometimes - that is if the Turk was not as censorious about female bathing as so many Muslims tend to be.

After Turkey, my plans were somewhat fluid, as I would be travelling through the Middle East, an area notorious for unrest and sudden wars. It seems to have always been that way since the dawn of history and the coming of the Sumerian culture six thousand years ago. My preference was to continue on round the coast of the Mediterranean, along the ancient Roman road, the Via Maris, through Syria and Lebanon, and so eventually, by natural progression into Israel. However, with  Lebanon still occupied by Israeli troops, and with various Muslim extremist groups active in the North Bekaa Valley and elsewhere, the Via Maris it might well prove far too dangerous. I could only decide that nearer the time, in the light of local intelligence. This made me feel very close to my pilgrim predecessors who had also faced such local uncertainties throughout their journeys.

The problem of Lebanon could have proved purely academic anyway, since I could reach Lebanon only through Syria. And although dangerous war-torn Lebanon willingly granted me a visa - it's another $20 in their exchequer, after all, and they don't have to guarantee anyone's safety - Syria steadfastly refused me one; not because of anything to do with my safety, but because I might be a spy. Apparently the Syrians consider all writers are spies, and it is up to the person applying for the visa to prove that they are not. I was eventually able to do so by producing a passport which claimed I was a teacher. Again things were reminiscent of earlier travellers who, even in the Sixth Century AD, had encountered problems in Syria over visas.

Getting into Israel was posing another problem, or rather the bicycle was. Both of us could fly in; this would upset no one. But ride in under our own steam, it seemed, we could not. In any event we could not enter from Lebanon but would have first to come inland to Jordan. There is a single frontier open between Israel and Jordan - the Allenby Bridge. Buses and trucks continually use it, in both directions, but not bicycles. 'Why not?' I asked, when finally I got through to someone at the Israeli Embassy in London - even this had been tricky as the Embassy was officially on strike and remained so for five months. The person on the other end of the line (I think it was the Ambassador himself, as he was the only person there not officially on strike) was most apologetic and could not at all understand why there should be this embargo placed on a humble, harmless machine like a bicycle. It didn't make sense, he agreed, and at first he had not believed it, but the reply had come back from Tel Aviv: No bicycles!

Feeling by this time something of a crusader myself for 'justice for bicycle riders', I took my problem to the Foreign Office, who, I am pleased to say, were on the side of justice and the individual - though they called it 'common sense'

London
Folkestone
NETHERLANDS
EAST
GERMANY
P
BELGIUM
WEST
GERMANY
CZECH
Guise
Verdun
Metz
Nancy
Basel
Zurich
Douremy
la Pucelle
SWITZERLAND
AUSTRIA
FRANCE
Pass...mine
Verona
Vicenza
Padua
ITALY
Venice
YU
SPAIN

------- Bettina's route
------ by sea

Kilometres
0        500

A
F

when they attempted to get me special permission through diplomatic channels.

'Who ever heard', they said, 'of a middle-aged kamikaze female bicyclist, panniers stuffed with explosives, riding four thousand miles to blow up an Israeli frontier crossing post - a bridge, moreover, which we British built?'

Apparently the Israeli diplomatic had not heard of such a phenomenon either, and when it was put to them like that they were all for removing their objections and welcoming both me and the bicycle across the River Jordan. Alas for intentions, jurisdiction over the Allenby Bridge rested not with the Israeli diplomatic, apparently, but with the military, in the person of the Mayor of Samaria and Judaea.

The Foreign Office, bit between teeth, were currently seeking this person's permission and were `cautiously optimistic that there might be 'a favourable response' before I actually reached Israel in about four months' time. I could do nothing more and left the worry to them. There comes a point in the planning of any journey when one realizes that some things cannot be settled in advance; there must always remain areas of uncertainty. This really is no bad thing, for if nothing is left to chance, the unexpected has no opportunity to break through, and when that is the case much of the purpose of travel is defeated.

On this philosophical note, I got back on my bicycle and sped down towards the Weald. Any sad thoughts melted away, and I was conscious only of the wind in my face and the exhilarating sense of freedom at having my burdens limited to what could be carried in the panniers of my bicycle. The sense of the adventure suddenly struck home. The months of preparation were finally behind me. The journey had well and truly begun.

For the rest of the day I rode through the intricate maze of Kentish lanes, which reveals another England from the one seen by the motorist on the major roads - an England of oasthouses and hopfields; pretty villages with ancient inns and gardens full of old-fashioned flowers; tiny hamlets with thatched cottages, and the occasional proprietorial dog. I know this countryside well; its lush greenness is what comes to mind when I think of home. In the months ahead, riding through the Syrian deserts, or the hot, dry mountains of Turkey, it would be a comfort sometimes to remember that such a land existed.

I arrived at Folkestone in the early evening and found a ferry ready to depart for Boulogne. Once I had taken the traditional farewell of England's white cliffs, I went down below to check over the bicycle after its maiden voyage. It was still so new that I enjoyed just looking at it and wondering if I had got the design of it right; though at this point, it was more important to make sure that nothing had worked loose, or fallen off, nor anything vital been left behind.

Having come to discover the incomparable joys of cycling somewhat late in life (practically forty), ten years later I am still bowled over by the infinite possibilities it affords to experiment and innovate.

To the layman, a bicycle is just a bicycle. It has two wheels, large or small ones, and is either a sedate, sit-up-and-beg model- heavy and upright and usually ridden by policemen or old ladies - or it is a 'a racer', which is to say shiny, with drop handlebars and lots of gears. My bicycles would be classed as a racer, though I would never dream of doing anything so violent as competitive cycling. What interests me is achieving the greatest return for my invest-ment of effort and energy. I want my cycling to be as effortless as possible. I want to able to go on long journeys, often through mountainous country, carrying the equipment I need, without being too exhausted to enjoy the experience. I soon found that in order to do that I had to have a very good machine. Moreover, as most women have different physical proportions to a man's, and bicycle manufacturers cater almost exclusively for men, it was necessary to have a frame made to measure, and to carefully select all the various working parts to put on it.

I would like to get it straight at this stage that there is no such thing as a 'man's bike' as opposed to a 'woman's bike'. The constant query of 'Why do you ride a man's bike?' becomes curiously irritating after many hundreds of times of asking. A bicycle frame is basically composed of two triangles which form the 'diamond frame'. Remove one side of a triangle and the strength, rigidity and responsiveness of the machine is seriously compromised. The fact that some bicycles are designed with an 'open frame' is to accommodate the rider's wearing of a kilt, a cassock, a long evening dress, or the robes of a High Court judge, and is a triumph of ingenuity and adaptation. But it is at best a compromise. To call the resulting hybrid a 'ladies' model is to imply that 'rational cycling dress' had not been invented by our Edwardian sisters, and that all women are still compelled to go about out in long skirts and bustles. Certainly no serious cyclist would consider setting forth on a lengthy journey upon a 'ladies bicycle', unless forced to by penury, or by the deep-seated conviction held by some religious sects that the wearing of trousers is sinful and contrary to Holy Writ. It would be like a knight riding to the Crusades on a donkey.

It was due to revolutionary advances in tyre technology that I had a new bicycle built for this journey. One of the nightmares of extended cycle travel abroad had been the replacement of tyres. As many as half a dozen replace-ments might be needed on a journey such as this one. Too heavy to carry, impossible to buy on the way, because of differing wheel sizes, they had therefore to be sent on ahead, at enormous expense and with no guarantee that they would arrive safely. The recent advent of cycling mania in America had led to all sorts of advances in equipment, including much improved tyres. These were reported to have at least three times the life of conventional ones, but they were not made to fit the size of my wheels. I therefore decided that it was worth having a new bicycle made to accommodate the slightly larger wheels that these revolutionary new tyres did fit.

The new bicycle was black and very shiny, with the maker's name, Evans, in gold lettering on the down tube. Every bicycle has its own peculiarities and it takes time to adjust to them. I was still treating Evans with some caution; it was not yet, so to speak, a tried and trusty friend.

The sombre black of Evans' livery was offset by four bright red pannier bags in which I carried all the worldly goods I should need for the months ahead; together with some camping equipment which I should not be using after leaving Europe. I had been advised that it was not safe for women alone to camp in Turkey and the Middle East, so I would try to send that equipment back home from Istanbul to lighten the load. As always, tools for repairing the bicycle made a weighty item, as did the collection of medicines and unguents for repairing me. The books and maps I was carrying weighed even more, as the historical complexity of the lands I was to travel in made it necessary to carry several guides and reference books, and of course, a bible, which is the number-one reference source to the whole area east of the Aegean. Sea

Notebooks, pens, camera, film, safety pins for hanging up washing, and a length of thin nylon line to hang it on, a compass, a torch - .the list was seemingly endless. Those who are interested in these minutiae are directed to the last pages of the book where I shall set it all out, together with other technical details.

There were so many things that I considered indispensable that very little room remained for what I find is the most difficult and time-consuming area of my luggage - clothing. What to wear on a bicycle so as to be both comfortable and socially acceptable in the many different situations in which I find myself, is something I have not yet managed to discover, although I have given the matter a great deal of thought. In Europe it is perfectly alright to ride in a vest and a pair of shorts, with a track suit handy for slipping into, when visiting churches or suchlike. Track suits don't do for more formal wear, however, and shorts are simply not worn at all by men or women in any Muslim countries that I have previously visited; so compromise and inventiveness are called for.

What I settled for finally were baggy, cotton trousers; two pairs, one of very flimsy material and the other more robust.

Both had elasticated ankles so that they could be hitched up to the knee and worn as plus-fours, which is more comfortable for bicycling, especially uphill. Two long-sleeved, loose-fitting shirts would combine with the baggy trousers and allow for maximum air flow and minimum exposure - I could expect very high temperatures and burning sun for most of the way. I hoped that these two outfits, negligible in weight, would also serve as suitable attire (perhaps with the addition of a belt and a silk handkerchief) for any social occasion or function I might be invited to attend. I also took an old cashmere sweater, a pair of woollen tights and a Goretex jacket to combat the possible cold of nights in the desert. This, with the addition of a pair of sandals, a sun hat, and a minimum of underwear, was to be my wardrobe until I returned; though the tally did not include the shorts and short-sleeved shirt in which I was currently riding and which I felt I could wear with impunity until I was beyond the limits of Christendom.

I finished checking over my gear and re-stowing it as the ferry slid into Boulogne harbour and tied up at the quay. With a screaming of motors and a juddering of metal the great doors gaped open and I was directed to lead the queue of vehicles up the metal ramp, onto French soil.

# Chapter Two

*And Frensh she spak ful faire and fetisly*
*After the scole of Stratford atte Bowe*
*For Frensh of Paris was to hir unknowe*
Chaucer

Arriving in France, I always feel as though I have strayed onto a stage and am acting in a play where I haven't quite finished learning the lines. The words have a familiar ring to the ear, but I am not totally sure of what they mean, and even less sure that the words I use in response convey anything but confusion. The close proximity to Britain makes it difficult for me to believe that I am in a foreign country, and I imagine that soon everyone will stop pretending and begin to speak good, plain English once more.

Perhaps the knights who assembled here in 1097 to join the first Crusading armies felt much the same; certainly the 'savages' from Scotland must have done so. They are reported to have arrived 'speaking no known tongue' and making their intentions understood by holding their fingers in the shape of a cross.

My French, however, is quite adequate for asking directions to 'le camping' and, thanks to the admirable French habit of using a good deal of gesticulation to accompany words (did the French perhaps learn this from the savage Scots?), I was able to reach it with only one or two wrong turnings. But, having got there, I rather felt that it had not been worth the effort. It was possibly the same campsite as Napoleon had used for the army he assembled to invade Britain in 1805. If it was, and if it was then as dirty, overcrowded and  depressing as it is now, I'm not at all surprised that he gave up the whole enterprise and went off to camp elsewhere. This was a great misfortune for the Austrians, for he attacked them instead. I might also have sought alternative accommodation, had it not been just half an hour from sunset.

I managed to find a small spot to pitch my tent, protected on one side by the tent of a couple of young Dutch girls, and on the other by a very large refuse container. My tent, being a coffin-sized scrap of  material, the shape of a windsock sliced down the middle, I was rather afraid that someone might fall over it in the dark if I was in a more exposed position - not that there was a lot of choice.

The Dutch girls declared themselves intrigued by the dimensions of my tent and asked me how I managed to get myself into it. This was something that I had taken the trouble to discover before I left England; actually there were two ways, and the one that worked best was to lie on my back and do a sort of feet-first shuffle backwards into it - like a very low-slung limbo dancer who was cheating by using hands.

Once inside, other possessions could be dragged in after me, that is if I didn't mind them sitting on my chest all night. The compensations of the design were that it weighed only a couple of pounds, was superlatively easy to erect and was a very pretty buttercup-yellow, which is a more cheerful colour to awake to than the usual drab green. The Dutch girls had kindly invited me to take a cup of soup with them, but after I had demonstrated my means of entry into the tent, the cup was passed to me where I was, since it was clear that such a performance could not be repeated too often in one day.

The next morning I was up and away before the camp was stirring, glad that my route lay south-eastward, away from the crowded coast. Within a short time, I was among fields of heavy-headed grain, ochre-coloured and nearly ready for harvesting. Dotted about, here and there, were strange shaped hillocks, rising abruptly from the flat plains - grassed-over slag heaps from either defunct or well-hidden coal mines. This was not a tourist area, but real provincial France, substantially unchanged for centuries.

One of the great blessings which France has to bestow upon cyclists is a network of roads seldom frequented by anything other than cyclists. Faster road users have separate road systems, more suited to their needs. On these 'D' and 'C' roads I cycled right across the eastern border lands of France, almost entirely free from the noise and pollution of traffic. The villages I passed through were usually too insignificant to have a bank, and on the day I made a detour in order to cash a traveller's cheque, the small town bank was quite suspicious about it, as though they had never seen such a thing before. They suggested that I take it to some larger town, but someone who came in after me said that Madame was travelling '*à vélo*', so that was all right; my cheque was changed without further hesitation. Bicyclists are respected in France - even by car drivers, who normally give them a wide berth and never 'cut them up', as happens all the time in England.

Rich farm land spread away in all directions as far as the eye could see, lands whose ownership had never stayed in the same hands for long, as national borders had shifted to and fro. Only the peasants who worked the fields have remained substantially unchanged, carrying on more at the dictates of the seasons than the whims of whoever happened to be in power. Some of these lands of Lorraine had been the fiefdom of Godfrey de Bouillon. With his older brother Eustace, Count of Boulogne, and his younger, landless brother Baldwin, he had set out from here for the First Crusade. Godfrey had sold the town of Metz, which was just out of sight over a hill, in order to finance the journey. Baldwin had taken his wife and family on the Crusade with him; clearly neither of them intended to return. Both were ambitious men and both achieved the most glittering of the prizes. Godfrey, modestly declining the crown, had become ruler of the Holy City under the title of Advocatus Sancti Sepulchri. After Godfrey's early death, Baldwin, with no such inhibitions, became King Baldwin I of the new Crusader Kingdom of Jerusalem.

The brothers, with their considerable following, had not ridden to Constantinople with the rest of the Crusaders on the route which I was pursuing. They had instead taken a more easterly course, through Hungary, following in the footsteps of the peasant army led by Peter the Hermit and Walter the Penniless. This terrifying rabble of upwards of twenty thousand men, women, and children had preceded the main army and was the first taste of Western Christianity's two hundred years of crusading which were to follow. The effect of such a horde moving through medieval Europe, living off the land, could be more devastating than a plague of locusts. Godfrey's army had a lean time following in their wake..

The Crusaders were never far from my thoughts as I rode through this area, where every place name was associated with some knight who had taken the Cross. Like them, I camped every night and the weather was as ideal as is possible to imagine. Each morning I awoke in my small, yellow tent as early as five or half-past, and wriggled out to find no dew at all on the grass to chill my feet as I brewed up the first drink of the day. It is a great blessing to be a natural early riser, I think, for there is no other time in the whole day which seems so fresh and full of promise. I would sit there drinking my coffee surrounded by a sleeping tented village which had sprung up overnight and which would disappear in an hour or two. France in summer is full of these camp sites. It made it seem as though once again all of Christendom was on the move; armies with banners marching to the Crusades.

The pattern became so fixed that it was a shock when one morning broke quite differently and I awoke to a grey persistent mist. It was a day when I became less aware of the larks ascending from the endless rolling fields of grain, and more conscious of the vast extended battlefields of the First World War, through which I was now riding. In this strange new world of swirling mist, Picardy took on a sinister aspect. Grey, featureless plains were edged in the far distance by ranks of tall, uniform trees, which might equally have been a line of sea defences, or strange, science-fiction creatures keeping watch over the land. Hundreds of war cemeteries were filled with rows of sharply-cut, very white gravestones, arranged with geometrical precision. It all looked newly-made and totally inhuman - like an exercise in surrealism. I thought how much better it would have been to plant forests as a memorial, but perhaps these chilling acres of cold, white stone serve as more poignant reminders of the shameful wastage of a generation of young lives.

Because this was not a tourist area, camp sites were rather sparsely scattered and this day I found none at all. By early evening, the mist had cleared and a fine sunset promised fair weather for the next day. The gloom I had been feeling, riding through the endless sad war cemeteries, had also lifted, but I was tired, having cycled much further than my sixty-mile daily quota. The evening wore on, still no camp site appeared and no one I asked knew of one thereabouts. So, at the next farm I stopped and enquired if they had somewhere I could pitch my tent. After the initial surprise I was welcomed very warmly by what seemed at first a very large extended family, but which turned out to be three couples, each with three children and a grandmother, who were all spending the day together. The couple who owned the house were farmers and obviously wealthy. They wouldn't hear of me putting up the tent, but insisted instead that I spend the night on a camp bed in their enormous games room, which had been converted out of the old stables.

I dined with them too; we were ten adults and nine children, and even with this number there was still room for more around the elegant mahogany dining table. Everything about the house spoke of the same quiet elegance. The work of the farm did not intrude at all, but was kept well beyond the confines of the neat courtyard and pretty gardens. Once a little wine had removed people's inhibitions about speaking another language, we all got along famously in a kind of polyglot tongue, discussing such subjects as the Common Market, Mrs Thatcher, and the British Royal Family. These are subjects about which I know little, but the French feel passionate about all three, as can be seen from their magazines and television programmes. My host kept leaving the table to fetch various journals, to show me scurrilous cartoons of prominent British people. I was impressed that they took so much interest in foreign affairs; it made me realize how very insular the British are in comparison. They also expressed a lively interest in my journey and I had to try to explain why I was undertaking it. They found it difficult to accept that a woman would want to travel on her own, but were enthusiastic that I was doing it by bicycle.

After the visitors had all left, the children of the house were brought into the games room to bid me a formal farewell, as I would be away before they were awake. I had already been provided with a thermos flask of coffee for the morning by my kind hostess. The older children shook hands shyly, but the youngest, a little boy of four, threw his arms around my neck and kissed me. While I was still recovering from the shock (most four-year-old boys I know need to be bribed to kiss anyone) he darted off and returned clutching a small toy St Bernard. This he thrust into my hands and, despite his mother's protestations and mine (about weight of luggage, etc.), he insisted that the 'English Madame' had to have the dog, to keep her safe over the Alps.

Because of this touching little incident, or because I had grown unused to sleeping indoors, that night I slept badly. I dreamed about the two Children's Crusades of 1212 AD, when Pope Innocent III had preached for a Fifth Crusade to try to retake Jerusalem, once again conquered by the Infidel. Response had been minimal from a war-weary Europe, except, unaccountably, from the children. A French shepherd boy, Stephen of Cloyes, believed that God had called children to succeed where adults had failed. He preached Crusade with all the eloquence of the earlier Pope Urban II, and children from all over France flocked to his banner. The old Crusader cry of *Deus Vult* -'God Wills It' rang out again, this time from children's lips. Stephen, riding in a flower-bedecked cart, with a few noble boys on horses riding beside him, led the huge army to Marseilles. Many of the younger children died on the way, for it was a very hot summer and few of them were more than twelve. At Marseilles, they expected that the sea would divide for them, as it had done for the Children of Israel, so that they could walk dry-shod to the Holy Land. No such miracle occurred. Instead two opportunist merchants, Hugh the Iron and William the Pig, offered to transport all of them by ship to Palestine, free of charge, for the glory of God.

It was eighteen years before news of the children's fate was known. Of the seven ships which had left Marseilles, two sank in a storm with all hands drowned. The other five kept a rendezvous with Saracen slave traders off the Algerian coast and the children were sold into slavery, most of them spending the rest of their lives in captivity there. A handful were sold in Baghdad and suffered martyrdom for refusing to accept Islam. Some few who were literate - not a common accomplishment in those days - were bought by the Governor of Egypt and kept as scribes and translators. It was one of these who had somehow escaped, who found his way back to France to tell the awful story.

The German crusading children were slightly older than the French, and were led by a boy called Nicholas, whose father was later hanged for encouraging him. They set out from Cologne and headed for Italy, over the Alps. Only a third of them survived to get as far as Genoa. Like the French children, they expected the seas to divide for them and, when this did not happen, many lost heart and turned back. The rest struggled on as far as Rome, where Pope Innocent, embarrassed by this response of youth, ordered them to return home. Very few survived the terrible journey back across the Alps.

In these Children's Crusades, 30,000 French and 20,000 German children were lost. It seems too terrible and pointless a tragedy to comprehend.

I resumed my pattern of camping at small-town, municipal camp sites each evening; eating my only cooked meal of the day at whatever local *auberge* or restaurant was recommended by the camp guardian. I ate reasonably and well, sometimes even memorably, as at Domremy-La-Pucelle - the birthplace of Joan of Arc. The camp site there was just a bumpy field from which the cows had been temporarily driven out, and the church was a horribly-restored, touristy place, full of labels pointing out where Joan had prayed, taken her first communion, confessed her sins and so forth. It seemed a rotten sort of shrine for such an indomitable spirit.

I've always felt a great deal of sympathy for Joan, especially when everyone was bullying her in prison about wearing 'men's clothing'. All the poor girl was trying to do was to defend her honour against the brutal and licentious soldiery, so that she could concentrate on the more important matter of whether to recant or burn. Yet this question of what is seemly or modest for women to wear, still seems to vex people. Trousers particularly appear to present an insuperable problem. In the West they are still considered by some to be both an unsuitable and even an ungodly garment for women, while in the Muslim East it would be unsuitable and ungodly for a woman not to wear them. I would have thought that males and females, being of a roughly similar shape, would need similar garments for the same pursuits. The sort of mind that wants women back in voluminous skirts, riding side-saddle, would certainly meet the approval neither of Joan of Arc, nor of this expedition.

The restaurant at Domrémy is squashed between two souvenir shops, each vying with the other as to which can sell the most repulsive mementoes of 'The Maid'. Certainly not an auspicious place; but once seated at a table with a blue-and-white checked tablecloth, sniffing the aroma delicately wafting in from the kitchen, and I knew I had hit pure gold.

'French lamb, it is not like your English with all the fat,' said the extremely rotund patron, recommending the *côtes d'agneau.* It came roasted in parsley and rosemary, accompanied by new potatoes and dark-green french beans tossed in garlic and a little butter. The keen appetite cycling encourages might have helped, but I felt I had never before eaten such succulent and well-cooked lamb. With it I drank a half-bottle of good local Burgundy. I had an excellent vegetable soup to start, and for pudding an orange which had been scooped out and the inside filled with icecream and then frozen until some of the bitter flavour of the skin had permeated the filling - quite delicious, and it all cost less than ten pounds.

Breakfast and lunch I mostly had alfresco, brewing up coffee or tea on my small gas stove and eating bread, fruit, and whatever cheese or *charcuterie* I found in the small shops along my rural route. As I was in the saddle by six-thirty, or at the latest, seven each morning, I liked to find some shade and relax for a few hours in the middle of the day, eating and reading, or just looking at the view. I tried to resist the temptation of drinking any of the delicious local beer or wine at lunch, as it had a disastrous effect upon my impetus for the rest of the day.

Although I kept detailed notes, a great deal of this part of the journey has merged in my mind, into an overall idyll of winding rivers and low hills; fields of wheat and hedgerows thick with more varieties of wild flowers than I had ever seen together in one place. The incidents which detach them-selves from the background of quiet contentment have no particular significance, but are remembered for the way they caught the mood of that time.

There was an afternoon when I sat on an ancient stone bridge and gave the heads of the shrimps I was eating to a thin ginger tom cat who sat beside me, pretending that he was really interested in watching the river flowing gently below, and was only eating the scraps to be obliging. I can see him still and marvel at the lightning speed of his paw, darting out to capture a shrimp head, while all the rest of him seemed to remain relaxed and motionless.

The idyll ended when I began to ride through the Vosges, an area more suited to walking than to bicycling, for fewer roads run through this dramatic mountainous region, and I had in consequence to travel on the *camion* routes. It was still lovely country, but now I needed more of my attention for coping with the traffic. High wooded ridges culminated in peaks called Ballons - very festive sounding - and between these were dramatic descents into deep valleys. The high temperatures of the past weeks dropped several degrees and a cool wind sprang up, at my back - a rare occurrence and one I made the most of, rushing along at great speed, enjoying every moment. With the wind behind, every cyclist feels like a champion.

I stopped in a small mountain town in this region to have coffee, and while I was deciding which of two cafés looked the nicer, it came on to rain with a sudden and startling ferocity. My choice was made quite simple now, because one of the cafés had an awning under which Evans could shelter. At first everyone in the café seemed happy to see the rain. 'The first we are having in six weeks, very much good for farmers,' the proprietor told me. Soon, however, when the rain showed no sign of lessening its vigour, and the water level in the street rose to halfway up the wheels of cars and started to enter some of the shops and houses, pleasure began to turn to consternation. The proprietor was busy pushing a broom against the underside of the awnings to spill the lakes of water which had formed there. He was too late with one and it burst, scattering great chunks of water all over Evans. *Sapeurs-pompiers* in World War 1 helmets charged up in an antique open fire engine, brass bell ringing wildly, and out they leaped, to poke about in the gutters with long metal rods.

Such a ferocious downpour could not persist for very long; by the time I had added a light lunch to my earlier coffee the pavements were beginning to steam, and the proprietor was able to relax and practise a little more English. Having ascertained that I had ridden all the way from England, he said, quite seriously, 'Aren't you a clever girl.' And I got the giggles for the first time in years.

No sooner was I back in the saddle than the thunder started once more to roll around the hills, and in every direction I looked, towers of black clouds were building up. It was not at all suitable for my frail, fair-weather tent. I thought of a prayer in the Pilgrim's Itinerary I had with me, a form of service which dates back to the Fourth Century and which I'd copied out to bring with me. It asked, among other blessings, for a covering in the rain and cold, and I thought this was a most appropriate prayer in the present circumstances.

And the prayer was answered before the next inundation, in the shape of a sign pointing the way to an *Auberge Jeunesse.* By that time, I had wound my way down through the last of the hills and was at the border town of St Louis, just a mile or so from where Germany, France, and Switzerland meet. There was no question of exploring the town in the steady downpour which seemed to have set in for the night. 'English weather,' said the hostel warden, which was not true, as I had heard on the radio that England was sweltering in a heat wave, while a deep depression had extended over the Alps and the areas around it. I stayed in and checked over my equipment, ready for the crossing of the Swiss Alpine passes.

I had wanted to find out why this small place was named after the last of the Crusader kings, Louis IX, known even in his lifetime as St Louis. He was a humourless man who had, nevertheless, inspired great devotion in his followers. Both the Crusades he led had proved disastrous, achieving nothing, except the loss of two huge armies and the surrender of further territories to the Infidel. In fact, it would not be unfair to say that he did more harm than good to the Western cause in Palestine. But in an age when the ideals of chivalry were admired but seldom practised, St Louis was the epitome of the 'verray gentile parfit knight' and as such he was loved and honoured.

As he lay dying - typically it was in the wrong place and at the wrong time - he was leading another Crusade. In the terrible heat of an African summer, encamped outside the walls of Carthage, the flower of Europe lay dying all around him. Smitten with disease, the last of the great crusading armies of the West was expiring without a fight.

In spite of all his years of crusading, Louis had never seen the Holy City. Perhaps at his end, in 1270, he was granted a glimpse of it, or of its heavenly counterpart, for his dying words are said to have been, 'Jerusalem, Jerusalem.'

I did not manage to find out why this small border town was named for him, but often on stretches of the journey ahead, when the going became somewhat rough, those last words of his would come to mind and provide the necessary spur to carry me on.

# Chapter Three

*And fyry Phebus ryseth up so brtghte,*
*That all the Orient laugheth at the lighte,*
*And with his stremes dryeth in the greves*
*The silver dropes hanging on the leves.*
Chaucer

Climbing up to the summit of a high pass, in the flat light of early morning, the great peaks of the Swiss Alps appear insubstantial, lacking the detail they will acquire later in the day, when the light hardens. They rear up all around, silhouettes on an awe-inspiring scale; fantastically pinnacled, like backdrops to a giant's fairy tale. The air at this hour is full of moisture which clings to eyelashes and beads the grass, clothes, animals, and cobwebs. For a very short time, the rising sun shining on all these droplets creates a world of crystal, chill and very beautiful.

Having reached the summit, I liked to wait until the sun had time to warm the air, postponing the moment when I began the glorious swooping descent of the mountain-side, winding my way down, through an intricate succession of hairpin bends, the valley floor rushing up to meet me. I know of no sensation so thrilling as riding a well-balanced bicycle down the steep roads of high mountains. The sheer economy of movement needed to lean into the corners, at speeds which I could not hold in a car, makes me realize afresh, each time, what a marvellous thing is a bicycle. At such times I find it impossible not to break into song; it's a kind of spontaneous thanksgiving for the glory of being alive; primeval worship perhaps, as natural as breathing.

Not that Switzerland had been unalloyed joy. I had crossed the border at Basel in dull weather, and had not found that this town had a great deal to recommend it, apart from the industriousness of its inhabitants. By eight o'clock, they were all either already at work, or scurrying along to get there. They had no time at all to answer queries from an English-speaking cyclist, who could not find the Zurich Road. Like so many White Rabbits out of *Alice in Wonderland,* the ones I approached ran off in the opposite direction with pained glances at their wrist watches, muttering in German. Even the girl in the post office, who spoke good English, claimed not to know the way to Zurich; for, she said, she had never in her life been outside the city! Had it not been for two young German cyclists, also bound towards the high passes, I might still be circling the inner ring road of Basel.

It rained on and off for most of the first three days in Switzerland, which is not a good introduction to a country. Camping was out: I don't mind riding in the rain, but at the end of the day I like to be somewhere warm and dry. Fortunately there are plenty of youth hostels, though these are more luxurious and considerably more expensive than in most other countries. They are also equipped with fall-out shelters, as all new buildings must be under Swiss law. The war-lords of the East and West might be threatening to bring the world to ruin, but if there is anything left after the nuclear holocaust, then the Swiss are making sure they will be around to inherit it.

I quite enjoy staying at youth hostels; I like the informality, the simple accommodation and the friendly people one normally finds there. Although youth hostels were founded primarily to encourage young people to explore the country-side, all ages now use them and the mixing of the generations is part of the charm. They seem to me to be the closest thing to pilgrim hostels of earlier times which were run by the monastic orders, particularly by the Cluniacs. By the Tenth Century a chain of these hostels stretched from France to Jerusalem, one for the end of each day's march - twenty-five miles in good easy conditions, much less in rough mountainous places. I like to think that pilgrims exchanged notes and experiences with other pilgrims, much as modern hostellers do.

In those days, Switzerland was one of the poor areas of the world; few roads traversed it, and bears, avalanches, and brigands lay in wait for the unwary. Few people would have dared to travel through it alone, and well-armed guides escorted the pilgrim bands. Now Switzerland is one of world's richest countries, and that is not just because of cuckoo clocks and tourism. Banking other people's money in the safety of neutrality is one of today's big businesses, one in which Switzerland gained a head start while most of the rest of Europe was involved in World War 2. Doubtless there are moral issues involved in the source and legitimacy of some of the money in foreign bank accounts, but what the traveller passing through Switzerland sees is a country which is probably safer than any other, and where litter and vandalism seem non-existent.

One wet night I was heading for a small hostel in the hills, but, due to the rain, I had not paid enough attention to the contour lines on the map. After struggling twenty kilometres up the most frightful gradients, and not even compensated by pretty views, I took advantage of a temporary dry spell to take a closer look at the map. What I had though was a short detour from my route was going to turn out to be a full day's journey, and there were still some thirty kilometres of these impossible gradients to ride up. It would take me another three hours at least.

I had stopped by a sort of island formed by a U-bend in the road, where a small, old-fashioned Swiss chalet stood, all carved shutters and balconies. Alongside it was a two-tier wooden barn, its upper part half-filled with newly cut hay. Just the place, a real port in a storm, I thought, and wondered if the occupants of the chalet would let me stay there for the night. A man and two teenaged boys were outside in the garden, picking cherries during the lull in the downpour. One of the boys spoke English and acted as interpreter. The fact that I was a non-smoker settled the matter in no time; since there was no danger of my setting the barn on fire, I was welcome to stay there.

However, it was in the chalet that I finally slept, in a room which could have been used for filming *Heidi*. The couple who owned the place were going out for the evening and were rather glad to have found a 'baby sitter' for the boys. It was the wife's family home, and they used it now just for holidays, as they lived for most of the year in the Canary Islands, where the husband was a tennis coach. Their thirteen-year-old son, Roman, was at an international school there, which was how he came to be the only member of his family to speak English. His friend, Pablo, was Spanish and spoke no other language.

The earning of bed and board turned out to be anything but onerous. Roman made a charming host, only too pleased it seemed to have someone different to talk to. He didn't really like living in the Canaries, he told me, and was not at all impressed with the climate there; it was always the same, just sun. That was what his parents liked, but he preferred to have variety, as in Switzerland, and if he could choose, he would live here always, climbing the hills in summer and skiing in the winter. While he chatted, he organized a filling supper of boiled eggs, fruitcake, and salad, and was adult enough to make me feel useful by allowing me to wash up.

After supper we all sat around a log fire, the boys playing chess while I wrote in my journal. Everything in the construction of the chalet was of wood and it glowed with age and polish. It had been built, Roman said, by his great-grandfather, who had even felled the trees and shaped the planks himself. One day it would be his, and then he would live here all the time and maybe earn his living as a ski instructor.

The depression had lifted in the night, and in the morning I dropped swiftly down the painful miles of yesterday in an altogether different landscape. I could understand why Roman was so keen to return to his native land. Shapely, white-clad peaks lined the valley on either side, sparkling under blue skies, which looked as though they could never have harboured a grey cloud. The Alpine meadows were lush with thick grass and wild flowers waiting to be cut and stored in the wooden barns with shingled roofs which were dotted around the slopes. Everywhere I looked would have made a suitable picture for a calendar.

I had no more rain after that in Switzerland; instead it grew hot, and as I came to the high passes it became even hotter. I had chosen to cross as far to the east as was feasible, so as to avoid descending into Italy too close to the industrial environs of Milan. I also wanted a route which would be as free as possible of the busy summer traffic. The best way seemed to be over the little-used Passo Bernina; and to get there, I had first to climb the Lenzerheide and Albula passes.

Because of all the rain, I had neglected to have a rest day since leaving England and had got over-tired. As a result, the first pass went very badly. In fact I walked almost its entire length, thinking sad thoughts about being too old for this sort of activity. Walking a heavily laden bicycle uphill is very hard work, and it is really easier to ride it if the gearing is low enough, which mine certainly is, for it was the same gearing as I used in the Himalayas. But once the energy has fallen below a certain level, cycling is no longer possible. I crawled along, perspiring so much that my navy blue shirt eventually turned grey with the sun's action on the sweat. To make matters worse, it was Sunday, and the narrow road was full of cars out for a drive. As this was a relative backwater, all the cars were Swiss and were driven in the Swiss manner; that is to say, the drivers appeared to think they were at the controls of trains rather then cars. They were driven with precision along a totally undeviating course. Nothing, it seemed could persuade them to leave their imaginary rails and allow enough road to a humble bicycle, so perhaps it was just as well that I was walking that day.

After the Lenzerheide, I rested up for a day, lazing beside my tent and talking to some of the other campers in a beautiful wooded valley with a shallow river flowing through it and white-capped mountains rising above. I was invited to a meal there by a Tibetan couple with whom I had got into conversation. I had visited many parts of Nepal and India through which they had wandered after their escape from the Chinese take-over, and we all three found pleasure in recalling these places. It was a great delight to meet Tibetans in Switzerland; their warmth and humour contrasted so beautifully with the reserve of the Swiss. Tibetans are real survivors and I admire them very much; these two were typical of the many I have met. In the ten years since they had fled the Chinese, they had passed through many countries  before finally becoming Swiss citizens. They spoke four European languages, as well as Tibetan and several Indian dialects, and still tried to keep alive the important spiritual aspects of their culture in order to pass them on to their two young sons, who would probably never see Tibet.

I asked them if they found Switzerland a particularly difficult country in which to maintain spiritual values. They thought that it was, mainly because it was such a materialistic society and this was very apparent in the education. Unfortunately there were too few of their fellow Tibetans in Switzerland to form a community and provide alternative education for their children. The main compensation was the mountains; they didn't think they could ever be happy away from those. They only hoped that the Swiss would not eventually build all over them, for at the present time, they told me,  mountain pastures were being converted at an alarming rate to provide the Swiss with second and even third holiday homes.

Following my Sabbath, the Albula Pass went much better, though it was extremely hard because I had reached the steepest gradients in the hottest part of the day. I toiled up and up, passed at intervals by solitary Swiss cyclists in fashionable cycling gear, followed by an attendant in a car (often their mother) carrying fresh 'skinsuits' and other comforts. They never wasted their breath on a greeting as they passed me - perhaps on the laden Evans they didn't recognize me as a fellow cyclist. Sometimes I would come upon them again at the top of some col, where they had stopped to rest. They would be looking fresh and relaxed as they posed for photographs, leaning elegantly against their shiny unladen bicycles, in their shiny, sweat-free clothing, just like modern-day knights. I envied them the delicious cold drinks that had been brought up in the cars for them, for it was difficult to carry enough liquid and the plastic bottles certainly did not stay cool for long. Sometimes an admiring mama would remove her eye from the camera as I passed between the lens and her son, and would cast me a pitying smile, but no one offered me a cool drink, alas.

I don't know why there seems a sharper pleasure to be gained if one has had to work for it, but if I arrive at some famous view by motorcar or bus, I never seem to be able to respond to it in the way I can when I have got there under my own steam. Mountain scenery remains indelibly with me from the ascent of the Albula; and I remember the clumps of Alpine flowers as clearly as if I had them still before me. They seemed so extraordinary, growing out of the bare rock - trumpet-shaped flowers, deep, deep blue and the softest of pinks. The higher I climbed the thicker the flowers grew, even in the loose gravel at the very edge of the road.

Then came the day when, well run in at last, I topped the Bernina Pass and all that was left of Switzerland was a long downhill swoop to the border. Thirty kilometres of plummeting descent I dropped, passing the Italian border where the guard, lounging in the shade, cigarette stuck to lower lip, waved me through with a barely perceptible movement of the head. I had shown no one my passport since leaving England, and this was now my fourth country.

On down I went, through the medieval streets and squares of Poschiavo and out through the remaining fragments of its southern gate. This marked the end of the hairpins; the way was still steeply downwards but straight enough now to relax and take in the changed landscape.

I had passed a more significant border than a national one, and was now in southern climes. The air was full of different scents and the shrubs were familiar only from books. Hillsides, cunningly terraced, were clothed in trellised vines, bordered by neat, round-topped trees. Here and there a cluster of terracotta roofs announced a perfectly sited village on a natural rise. It was a landscape I recognized immediately. It had supplied the backdrop for untold numbers of Italian paintings; Annunciations, Nativities, Crucifixions, Depositions, Transfigurations, Assumptions: all the central events of the Christian Gospels had been depicted against such a landscape. Seeing it just on its own was curiously unreal, like entering an art gallery where all the figures had disappeared from the canvases.

The descent ended and I arrived at last at the bottom of a deep gorge that sheltered Tirano, a town which had played a significant role in the religious persecutions of the Fifteenth Century and had done little of note since. The way out of it to the south was upwards, over the Passo d'Alprica, almost as steep and as high as the pass I had just descended. I postponed the battle by ordering a plate of spaghetti and a carafe of the local wine and sat enjoying them in a café in the main square.

The outlying spurs on the Italian side of the Alps provided a fine route down to the Italian Lakes: dramatic scenery on either hand, where nature - working with just two elements, rock and water - had achieved extraordinary variety. Man had added his share of creativity further down among the foothills, where the rock gave way to pockets of fertile soil. It was a lovely ride and, had I realized the very different sort of drama which awaited me once I had descended to the level of the Lakes, I would have relished it even more than I did. For, after Brescia, the enjoyment of cycling through Italy was finished for me.

I have looked up many guide books to see what is written about what I consider to be the curse of Italy, namely its drivers. All the books have something unfavourable to say, from the mild 'Italian drivers tend to be rather selfish' to 'Only those of an extraordinarily unnervous temperament should attempt to share the road with Italian drivers', but I found nothing to equal the strength of my own feelings in relation to them. In the two hundred miles I rode across the plains of Lombardy, I must have had more narrow escapes than in the several thousand miles I ride each year. To make it worse, while I was dicing with death on a narrow road, with cars and juggernauts fighting each other and Evans for every inch of space, a stone's throw away was a six-lane *autostrada,* virtually empty because of the prohibitive tolls.

Every forty miles or so, the horrible road would pass by one of the exquisite Northern Italian cities - Verona, Vincenza, Padua - and for a few hours I could forget about my grim struggle with Lucifer's minions, and recover among Roman theatres and Renaissance palaces. I saw Juliet's balcony and her supposed tomb at Verona; Palladio's majestic Basilica in the Piazza Dei Signori at Vincenza; and Giotto's famous frescoes in Padua. But as for whatever else I saw or did not see, that has all now merged into a general impression of vast squares and elegant buildings; Romanesque and Gothic churches; and paintings whose backgrounds were the lovely landscapes I had so recently ridden through. Each of these splendid cities would repay a week's dedicated sight-seeing, but I had a boat to catch and could not linger long enough to do them justice. One day, I promised myself, I would return and spend a leisurely holiday there.

I did not know where I would stay in Venice, since, being built in the middle of a lagoon, it was unlikely to have much spare space for tents. So when I spotted a sign some ten miles before I got there, which read 'Serenissima Camping', I thought that I might stay there. It was not to be, however, for no sooner had I wheeled Evans in through the gate, than I was attacked by a small, unshaven young man who obviously hated bicyclists. He rushed up to me and looked uncertain as to whether to grab me or Evans first. He compromised by shaking his fist under my nose.

'Why you ride into my house?' he screamed, in what I thought was very stagey Italian. 'I not come into your house. This is my house. Why you not wait till I tell you come in?'

Plainly I had crossed some invisible line and broken an important taboo. I made apologetic gestures and smiled placatingly. This seemed only to enrage him further and I rather feared he might actually let fly with his menacing fist.

'Shouldn't tangle with him, mate,' said a voice behind me. 'Hates the Brits, he does. We're only here 'cos he thinks we're Aussies. I'd go on to Fusina, mate, plenty of camping there.'

'Fusina!' screamed the enraged Italian, turning his attention on the helpful adviser. 'Why you say go to Fusina?' Another taboo had been broken, and while his attention was distracted I seized my opportunity to depart and go in search of this, hopefully more accommodating Fusina.

When the Fourth Crusade assembled at Venice in June 1202, to await the ships to the Holy Land promised to them by the city councillors, they were billeted in camps on islands in the lagoon — no city wants an army, however holy, too close to its doorstep. Fusina was on the edge of the lagoon, not on an island, but in other respects it was probably quite like the Crusader camps. It was a very large site, used by a wide variety of nationalities, in small and large parties. One tour company which took double-decker bus-loads of young people overland to India habitually called here *en route.* Similar tours by lorry disgorged their passengers to set up clusters of tents. So the place was a confusion of camps within camps, all higgledy-piggledy, with camp fires and barbecues all over the place. But it possessed its own unobtrusive order and discipline, and worked well I thought, and I liked the easy camaraderie.

In other ways, too, the Crusader camps were probably not unlike Fusina. The mosquitoes must have bitten just as relentlessly, and doubled their attentions when it rained, which I suppose it must have done on the crusaders as well as on me. If it did, I can only hope that their tents were more efficient at keeping water out than mine was. Not that I had much cause for complaint because far from being *persona non grata* ('Brit' variety), at Fusina I had been most warmly welcomed as something of a novelty. They seldom saw lone cyclists, especially not middle-aged female ones. So when it rained, people kindly invited me in to share the shelter of their more efficient roofs. Thus one night I spent under the awning of a caravan extension, the owners of which were on a working holiday, photographing major works of art in Northern Italy for future lectures.

Another night I was the guest of a large party of eager young Americans who were combining a summer tour of Europe with a mission to tell people of how Jesus had changed their lives. Their leaders, whose tent I shared, said that the young people were probably spending more time enjoying the trip than 'bearing witness'. I hoped they were, for I thought this would probably be a better use of their time, and arguably just as good a way of 'bearing witness', but since I was their guest, I resisted the temptation to air this view.

The final night I bedded down in the hut shared by some of the girls who helped to run the camp; many of them belonged to that wandering army of casual young labour from Australia, America, Europe, and Britain who tramp through the world, prepared to do almost any job in order to go on travelling.

Even with all this kindness, and with interesting people to talk to, four days of rain and mosquitoes had me eager for departure. The wretched Crusaders, stuck on their islands, unable even to wander around the glories of Venice, must have been quite desperate after a few months of it. That of course was the whole idea. The rapacious Doge of Venice had laid his plans carefully. Blind and old he might have been, but Henrico Dandolo, as venal a man as the corrupt 'Serenissima' ever produced, was also very active in laying his plans. By keeping the crusading army waiting for its transports, and eating its head off the while, of course, he forced the leaders into such debt to him that he was able to turn them from their original purpose, and use them for his own ends.

What Dandolo had in mind was no less than the conquest of Constantinople - the richest city in the known world; where the plunder would be worth more than in all of the cities of the Infidel put together. The fact that it was a Christian city deterred him not at all. Venice owed allegiance to the Church of Rome and the hatred of the Roman Church for Eastern Christianity was well established, motivated as much by envy as by theological differences. Venice was also a trading state and as such was in deadly rivalry with the whole Byzantine Empire.

So when the Fourth Crusade eventually set sail, on the eighth of November 1202, it had as its immediate objective, not the 'Liberation of the Holy Land', but the destruction of the only Christian power which stood between Europe and invasion by the Muslim Turks. And *en route,* as though they needed a rehearsal, they destroyed another Christian trading rival which had been a thorn in the Venetians' side. Zara, an Hungarian port, fell to the Crusaders with very little trouble. After they had pillaged it, they wintered there before continuing, excommunicated but unrepentant, to the sack of Constantinople.

While I waited for my ship, also bound for Constantinople - or rather Istanbul now, for of course the Ottoman Turks did eventually overrun Byzantium and huge areas of Europe besides - I wandered around Venice where the comparative emptiness of the streets compensated for the rain which kept the holiday makers indoors. There is no off season in Venice; tourists flock there all the year round, and small wonder, beautiful as it is and filled with so many beautiful looted marvels. But August brings the greatest crowds, as it does to most of the Mediterranean.

It is the limitations of its situation which make Venice so uniquely beautiful. With no roads, only pavements and canals, the buildings can be seen as they were meant to be, and not through a tangle of noisy, honking cars. It is a treasure trove, a pirate city full of wonderful things, stolen from every corner of the globe. Even the glorious basilica of

St Mark's itself was built to house a stolen holy relic - that of the body of the Apostle Mark taken by Venetian merchants from Alexandria in 828 AD. On a balcony of the façade facing St Mark's Square stand the incomparable bronze horses, part of Venice's share of the loot from the Fourth Crusade's sack of Constantinople.

It is hardly possible to get near St Mark's in August for the crowds, but even at its busiest there are alleys and backwaters - the linings of the city - seldom visited by most tourists, and these I know from previous visits. Through one of them I can get easily to the small Scuola di San Giorgio degli Schiavoni, which houses some of the most delightful pictures in Venice. They are scenes from the lives of St George and St Jerome, painted by Carpaccio, and so lively and full of strange detail that I find myself returning there again and again. St Jerome had a particular significance for my journey, because he had been one of the very first pilgrims to the Holy Land and had eventually settled there, in the monastery he founded at Bethlehem. He had lived at a time when women were regarded more favourably than in later, less enlightened ages, and he was often accompanied by devoted female followers. Amongst his many writings and translations is a book about a journey he made around the Holy Places, in the company of two noble Roman ladies, St Paula and her daughter Eudocia. I would have welcomed a little more detail about the route he took on this tour, and descriptions of the countryside, but he states at the outset that he was not writing a travel book, but showing Paula's proper and devotional responses to the places of Holy Scripture. There is none of this somewhat straight-laced attitude in Carpaccio's portrayals of him. The painter concentrates far more on the everyday human life of St Jerome, especially on how good he was with lions.

My ship arrived punctually, flying the flag of the Union of Soviet Socialist Republics and looking enormous against the ancient quay. Evans was stowed away in an empty cabin, deep down among the engines: I felt a little sad at leaving him there in all the stink and clatter, so I suppose I was beginning to think of him now as a friend. I climbed up to the top deck to watch Venice sink down into the lagoon. There was a red sky behind her, promising a welcome break in the spell of wet weather. But I was no longer concerned with Europe's weather. I was bound eastwards, and, hopefully, would not see rain again before I reached Jerusalem.

# Chapter Four

*Now longe moot thou sayle by the coste,*
*Sir gentil maister, gentil mariner.*

Chaucer

One of the first things I did aboard the SS *Azerbaijan* was to unscrew the plate over the loudspeaker in my cabin ceiling and disconnect a wire. This could be seen as an act of vandalism, I admit, but it was done in order to preserve my sanity, and I did reconnect it before I left the ship. Had I spoken Polish, Russian, or even German - which tongues had poured out of this loud speaker in frequent spates - or been addicted to jolly music at dawn, I might have left the device intact in the interest of safety. But I knew that if the ship was about to founder, no one would bother to announce the fact in English. Only four other people aboard spoke English: a Jewish couple, psychiatrists from Venezuela who were fluent in six or seven tongues; a young Englishman from Pinner who was the ship's photographer;- and a girl from the Mile End Road who looked after the ship's boutique, and who was suffering withdrawal symptoms brought on by life aboard, aggravated by the constant problem of keeping unattached females away from the photographer - who was tall and presentable.

I had not known that it was a Russian cruise ship that I'd booked on for the four-day journey to Istanbul. It was run by a company called the Black Sea Line which I'd assumed was Turkish. The Hammer and Sickle fluttering from the stern had given me quite a shock when I'd seen the *Azerbaijan* alongside the Venetian quay and realized that for the first time in my life I was about to enter communist territory and place myself on the wrong side of the 'iron curtain'.

My experiences on the *Azerbaijan* did nothing to make me want to have any further excursions on Russian ships. But then I am no authority on cruises, having seen glamorous life aboard Cunard and P& 0 liners only on cinema screens. It certainly wasn't like that on the *Azerbaijan*. The Venezuelans, Reuben and Elaine, said that for the money you couldn't complain, except about the food. The ship was seaworthy and that was the most important thing. The two English, Debbie and Wayne did, in fact, complain quite a lot, particularly about the food: but then they were living on board, not taking a two-week cruise to Odessa and back to Venice, stops at Dubrovnik, Athens, Istanbul. When the ship spent a night in port they said they took the opportunity of staying at a luxury hotel ashore; to remind themselves that there was more to life than the *Azerbaijan.* I was glad that my trip was to last only four days because I began to share the prejudices about the food as soon as a day's inactivity had blunted my normal healthy cyclist's appetite. I also suffered from boredom.

Perhaps food was in short supply behind the 'curtain' because the Poles and East Germans seemed to have no problems at all with their meals, and got through very large helpings. I don't know about the Russians, as they were kept closeted away in their own dining room on a lower deck, but judging by their generous proportions I think they too probably enjoyed the meals. The Russians' visits ashore were also kept separate from those of the other passengers, and carefully controlled, in case, I supposed, they should take it into their heads to defect to the West. There were four meals a day, five if you counted tea. The last meal was a substantial buffet supper, served several hours after the substantial dinner, and this last chance of the day's gorging I did not discover until my final night aboard. It is not easy to explain what was wrong with the food. The menu always sounded most promising, exotic items like blinis, steak Marie Thérèse, chicken à la duchesse, etcetera. But when it came, it tasted as though whoever had cooked it was still in the rudimentary stages of his or her career, and would probably never achieve the Order of Lenin for Soviet Chefs. Everything managed to be very heavy and quite tasteless at the same time, and either cooked to a cinder or almost raw. One light note in all this weightiness was that every dining table on this communist ship was graced with a bottle of H.P. sauce, each bearing its proud symbol of democracy - a picture of the British Houses of Parliament. Between meals the passengers lay about the decks, like so many seals soaking up the sun. And that was what the cruise consisted of really, just food and sunbathing. Sight-seeing was minimal, shore-going expeditions being organized strictly around the necessity of returning aboard in time for meals. There was entertainment in the evenings but not of the romantic or decadent sort I had been led to expect from my cinema-going. One night there was Bingo; another evening we had a fashion show of the clothes available in the ship's boutique; with the over-worked waitresses and the more virile of the ship's crew doing the modelling. If one wanted a change from lying in the sun there was a swimming pool the size of a playpen and a library full of free communist literature in many languages. Only Reuben and I frequented the library, although it was the pleasantest room aboard. But I suppose everyone else on the cruise, apart from the five English speakers, was already living the communist ideals and did not need to read about them; in fact, they were probably model party members, for how else could they have afforded a place on such a cruise? There was also a small netted area for playing deck games, but this too was not used, which was very sensible, since violent exercise would have probably resulted in a rash of heart attacks on top of all that food.

The Dalmatian coast slid slowly by, then Corfu and the rugged and forbidding shores of Albania, where the majority of the First Crusade had landed in 1097. It was all Byzantine territory then, and the Empire, under Alexius Comnenus, was still strong, and could provide enough armed guards to keep the 'Western barbarians' in order on their march to Constantinople. Anna Comnena, the Emperor's daughter, who was a gifted and civilized young woman, wrote a history of the times in which she gives us an idea of the sheer size of the First Crusade and the effect it provoked:

*'All the West and all the barbarian tribes from beyond the Adriatic as far as the Pillars of Hercules were moving in a body towards Asia, bringing whole families with them.'*

I am glad that Anna lived then and not a hundred years later to witness the sack of her city by fellow Christians. Not that I think it would have surprised her, for she makes it abundantly clear that she feels no good could possibly come through these violent and ungodly adventurers. The hope of the Byzantines that the West would send troops to fight under the Empire's banners for the return of their territories in the Middle East and Palestine were quickly dashed. These land-hungry Western hordes would fight only for their own profit and would never surrender what they captured. Yet, perhaps that is not altogether fair, at least not in relation to the First Crusade. Many of the early Crusaders went for what they thought was the Love of God, no matter how misplaced or misunderstood that concept was. What is certain is that such motivation quickly became rare as the Crusades proceeded, to be replaced by pure greed and by a brutal cynicism towards human life and religious principles.

The terrible dehumanizing consequences of warfare can be seen to be as real for soldiers today as they were in the Eleventh Century. South East Asia, the Lebanon, Rhodesia, there are countless examples of modern conflicts where ordinary soldiers, who would normally never step outside the bounds of common decency, have committed dreadful atrocities. Even so, there seems an essential difference between modern warfare and that of the Eleventh Century. Death inflicted at the distance of a bullet, a bomb, or a grenade can be an almost impersonal thing. The opponents are not face to face, sword to sword, in an immediate kill-or-be-killed situation, but targets, often discernible only through the rifle's telescopic sights or as a mark on a bombing schedule. The trauma of warfare must have affected everyone engaged in the Crusades, men, women, and children; for apart from the off season of the winter rainfalls, battles and sieges were an almost continuous state of affairs for the two hundred years that they lasted.

For the urbane Byzantines, fighting was at variance with Christianity; certainly you went to war if you must, but only when diplomacy had failed and you had no alternative except to defend your territory by force of arms. Western Christianity took many more centuries to arrive at the same theological position and, in the interim, awful things were done in the name of Christ, and with the sanction of Pope and Church. Even the concept of a Crusade runs counter to Christianity. There is no basis at all for it in the Christian Gospels, and many people argued against it throughout the period of the Crusades, including St Francis of Assisi, who went himself to the Holy Land in 1219, to try to bring about a peace.

The enemy - the 'infidel' - was in no such dilemma. Islam has Jehad at its very roots. Mohammed had himself both preached and fought Holy War. 'Better dead than not a Muslim' is a tenet of the faith, and Islam was established as much by the sword as by the book. The moral strength of the Muslim fighter, who is doing 'the will of Allah' in his battles against non-Muslims, can perhaps be seen in the

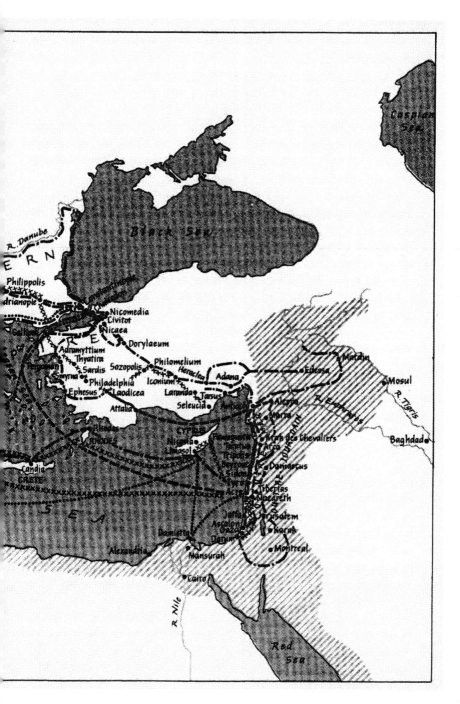

tenacity with which Afghanistan resisted the Russian take-over.

I thought it might be interesting to talk over this idea about Afghanistan with the Russian librarian, whom I discovered to be the sixth English-speaking person aboard, but he proved gifted in the art of not understanding difficult questions. He pointed me towards the free literature on Marxist principles and I gave in and went back to watching the endless hazy shoreline.

Because we kept well out to sea, we seemed to be moving down the coast at barely perceptible speed, and yet in three days we had covered as many miles as I had done on Evans in three weeks. I found the thought disorientating, and the two short trips I made ashore, one in Yugoslavia and the other in Greece, had been more disorientating still. I was used to a steady sixty miles a day, and the slow assimilation of new cultures, rather than disconnected arrivals with nothing in between. So although the cruise seemed boringly long, it also seemed to be no time at all before we were steaming through the narrows of the Dardanelles, with Asia to starboard and the long peninsula of Gallipoli to port - another of the sad slaughter-fields of the youth of the First World War.

The Hellespont, as the stretch of water was called in antiquity, was always a battlefield, since it provided a natural route from Asia into Europe, with only 1300 metres of water to cross. The great Persian King Xerxes brought his vast army over it on a bridge of boats to attack the Greeks in 480 BC. A few decades later, the Greeks, who had united to defeat Xerxes, were fighting each other and many of the naval battles of the Peloponnesian War raged up and down these straits, including the final one, in which a Spartan force led by Lysander decisively defeated the Athenian fleet commanded by Pericles. Here, too, Leander made his nightly swim to visit Hero until the fateful night of storms, when the lamp which she always placed in her window to guide him blew out, and he lost his way and drowned. His swim set a precedent for romantics who through the succeeding centuries have attempted the Leander swim with varying degrees of success.. Hero drowned herself when the body of Leander was washed ashore - which is, after all, what legend expects of a faithful woman.

The Sea of Marmara, which looks so very small in the atlas, swells out to a width of twenty miles or so after the Dardanelles. Apart from some islands, which I discovered later provided quantities of marble for the building of Constantinople, and also provided useful prisons for the more unruly of the Sultans' sons, we saw no land all day until just after three o'clock. when we began to approach the Bosphorus. This was a moment I had been eagerly anticipating for many months.

The famous skyline of a thousand minarets came slowly into focus. There was a blue heat haze, which veiled the seaward slopes and softened the outlines of the city. Three domes gradually stood out above the rest. On the left was the Blue Mosque, unmistakable with its six minarets. The last buildings before the land dropped down to the Bosphorus had to be Mehmet the Conqueror's Topkapi Palace. That left the great dome in the centre as Haghia Sophia, Church of the Holy Wisdom - Justinian's great masterpiece, still standing after fourteen hundred years. Once the centre of Christian worship, when Europe was still a barbarous wilderness, Haghia Sophia had stood in proud isolation on the ridge. Now it is just one dome among many, disguised as a mosque, with a minaret at each corner.

I hardly had time to take in what I was seeing before the *Azerbaijan,* closing fast with the land, had swept round Topkapi Point and the Golden Horn came into view to port. All was suddenly noise and confusion, as the stern swung around, and the ship moored against the Galata shore, looking enormous beside the black tugs and ferry boats which thronged the crowded waters, hooting loudly and belching forth enormous columns of thick black smoke.

All was confusion aboard too as I tried to organize my departure. It was already five o'clock and, as I had no idea where I would sleep that night, I was eager to get started. I had my four pannier bags packed and ready, but Evans was still down in the bowels of the ship (at least I hoped he was.

I hadn't seen him since Venice). I did not have my passport either; the ship's commissars had, from the moment of my coming aboard, a curious desire to hang on to it, which made me nervous. On the two occasions I had gone ashore, I had had to go through the same procedure of trying to get my passport from a reluctant purser. When I'd returned, someone had managed to persuade me to give it into their keeping again. I had tried to pretend that I didn't understand their gestures and the one English word 'passport', but reinforcements were called, and under the increased intimidation I'd weakly capitulated.

I tracked the purser down eventually; he was in the bar giving the Turkish customs officials hospitality in the form of vodka and pickled fish. My passport was no longer in his possession, but had been passed on to the Turks. I thought this was all a bit high-handed, but as there was nothing I could do about it, I could only hope that the vodka didn't unsettle them, making them careless with this essential document. After all, alcohol is expressly forbidden in the Koran and, as Turkey is almost one-hundred-per-cent Muslim, I assumed they were not used to strong drink. I was, in fact, soon disabused of this notion; there is a very relaxed attitude to alcohol in Turkey, which is convenient for natives and visitors alike.

The Turks instructed me to gather my luggage and join them on the quay in five minutes. I explained that I had a bicycle which I didn't know how to recover. 'No problem', said the Turks (strange how universal this expression is), 'he will help you'. 'He' was the purser and by far the least helpful person I had met aboard. Helping wasn't something he believed in and now he simply turned his back and downed some more vodka. I could have done with a shot of it myself by this time, but I thought I'd better go and try to find Evans by myself.

The only way down I could discover was from the foredeck, amongst the hawsers and mooring lines. A succession of metal stairways led from there, down and down to the car deck. Nothing looked familiar and a terrible booming and clatter from the engines was making it difficult to think. I'd entered the ship originally through the open car deck door at Venice, and I thought the cabin where we had put Evans was near the stern. But with it all closed up and the ship stationary, I'd no idea which end was the stern. A fierce, fat man, naked to the waist, came running fast towards me, waving his arms and shouting something incomprehensible in Russian above the din. For some reason he made me think of Mr McGregor bearing down on Peter Rabbit crying 'Stop thief! Stop thief!' while trying to pop a net over him. It was such a silly thought in the circumstances that I stopped feeling intimidated and harassed and was able to identify the door which led to the right cabin. The fat man, who hadn't really been fierce at all, or at least not when he'd realized that I wasn't a stowaway or a defector, kindly carried Evans up all the steel steps and down the gangplank and onto the quay.

The Turks were waiting for me, but they said we could not go yet, because the ship had berthed a long way from the customs; we would have to wait for an escort to conduct us there. The escort, a large Turkish lady, arrived after a half-hour's wait. I suppose we needed her there in case I tried to make off without going through the official formalities, in which case it wouldn't be proper for me to be restrained by a couple of men. But it was not I who needed restraining; it was the man who had my passport and who kept wandering off in order to have conversations with friends he met along the way. He kept my passport in his hand and waved it around a good deal while talking, and I continued to be worried for its safety, for if not exactly the worse for the vodka he had drunk aboard, he was certainly what could be termed 'mellow'. So it seemed safer to me to wait for him to finish his conversations, although the rest of the escort was all for leaving him and going on. Half an hour the slow amble took, and it seemed an odd sort of introduction to Turkey.

The formalities on the other hand took little time. The only thing the officials were concerned about was whether I was planning to sell Evans in Turkey and thereby contravene import regulations. To prevent this happening they entered him as a person in his own right into the back of my passport and he eventually collected more stamps on his page than I did on mine. I was told that I must not try to leave the country without him; and should he be stolen, I would have to prove that I had not secretly sold him. On this sobering note I was wished a pleasant journey and sent off into the lunatic rush-hour traffic of Istanbul.

Arriving as an independent traveller in a strange city is one situation I dread: it is a time when the simplest things assume their greatest degree of difficulty. I know that the first priority is to find somewhere to stay, but how to set about doing so can present insuperable problems. There are various lines of approach which sometimes work, like tourist offices, guide books, helpful taxi drivers. Standing beside the Galata Bridge at six o'clock in the evening, watching an endless stream of traffic weaving in and out of their lanes like low-flying swallows, was one of the occasions when none of these aids was available. I was on my own, and at some point I was going to have to wind up my courage to the point where I lifted Evans down off the pavement and joined the snarling tangle. There were solid, foot-and-a-half-high kerbs too, against which we could both be crushed to pulp; it seemed a suicidal undertaking.

It wasn't possible to choose a route. I rode at the dictate of the other road users, at the same time trying to avoid the worst of the gaping holes and huge corrugations of melted tar in my path. At the first opportunity I turned off, out of the maelstrom, and found myself riding in my lowest gear, up a steep hill with cobbles under the wheels and sleazy, tall buildings on each side. The hill ended at the top of a ridge and I had, by sheer good chance, arrived at the heart of Constantine's Empire in the blessedly traffic-free gardens between Haghia Sohphia and the Blue Mosque.

Later, when I'd purchased a guide book and begun to orientate myself, I discovered that the tourist hotels were all back on the other side of the Galata Bridge. Here in old Stamboul, there were just cheap, student-type hotels. Since that was exactly the type of accommodation I was seeking, and since most of the places I wanted to visit in Istanbul were right here,

I could not have arrived at a more appropriate spot. At the time, however, I was still reeling from the plethora of new impressions and was not really able to take in anything properly. I was just thankful to be out of the nightmare traffic with a park bench to sit on, and so I didn't really notice much about the young man who    approached me. Looking back at the incident, I am convinced that he was part of the Caring Providence that had me under its wing that day. At the time, I saw him simply as a souvenir seller, out to earn a bit on the side, by directing a tourist to an hotel in which he had an interest. Having politely enquired if I was a hippy or not, and receiving the answer that I didn't think I was, he explained that hippies want a room for too little money. If I could afford - and he named an amount which was the equivalent of about two pounds - then there were good, clean rooms available, and he would take me to an hotel where I could find one.

That was how I came to spend my first night on Turkish soil, not in a room (they were all full and I was too tired to look further), but on the roof, under the stars, together with a dozen or so young people of various nationalities. Our bodies, shrouded in sleeping bags, were laid out in decorous rows, like a collection of Egyptian mummies in a museum. I was very comfortable on a lilo lent to me by an Italian boy, who was also making a journey to Jerusalem on a motor scooter, and who had arrived early enough to obtain a room, and therefore had no need of his own mattress. I lay there with the dome of Haghia Sophia almost close enough to reach out and touch, and a warm sense of contentment and happiness spread over me as I sank into a dreamless sleep.

# Chapter Five

*That in this world ne was ther noon it liche*
*Of which I shal tellen al th'array*
*Than wolde it occupye a someres day,*
*Ther nis no man that may reporrten al*

Chaucer

Some of the most intense experiences in life exert such an overwhelming impression upon the senses as to be almost painful. Certain paintings can do this, music, perhaps, even more so, while great church architecture was designed to have precisely this effect. Obviously, the same things do not affect all people in the same way. Yet it seems curious when one has had just such an experience, to find other people who are totally unmoved by it. So it was with Haghia Sophia. A third of the people I met in Istanbul thought as I did, that it was the most marvellous building there, a third were indifferent to all ancient edifices, and the remaining third had given their allegiance to the Blue Mosque and tried to convert the rest of us to their way of thinking. Had the Blue Mosque not had such a rival in such close proximity, I think I would have enjoyed it more, but as it was, it seemed a trifle boring, a touch banal in comparison.

The exterior of Haghia Sophia is rather lumpish on account of the huge buttresses which were built onto it in the Fourteenth Century, to keep it from collapsing after various earthquakes had weakened the structure. But once inside, the brilliance of the design is immediately apparent. From every part of the immense nave the central dome is visible, because it is flanked by two enormous semi-domes, almost as high. This creates the effect of limitless space, and the dome seems to hover rather than to rest upon its piers. Four vast seraphim fill the pendentives; not pretty, Western angels, but the awesome Old Testament kind - huge featureless, whirling masses of feathered wings, and these add considerably to the unearthly, hovering effect. Light from the pierced tympanum walls, and from a circlet of windows below the dome, comes down into the interior in oblique shafts, like fingers of sunlight through cloud.

Once, all the interior surfaces shone with gold and figured mosaics, some of which still remain, uncovered again after centuries under the whitewash with which the Ottomans concealed them when they turned Hagia Sophia into a mosque. The most immediately striking of these mosaics is in the conch of the apse, where, against a golden background, the Mother of God sits enthroned with the Christ Child in her lap. An even more magnificent mosaic is in the gallery - the remaining top section of an enormous Deesis, depicting the Virgin Mary and John the Baptist pleading with Christ for the salvation of mankind. In this work the artist has somehow transcended the limitations of mosaic and achieved an extraordinary intensity of expression in the three faces. It was made in the early Fourteenth Century, in the renaissance which followed the restoration of the Byzantine Empire, after the Venetians and the residue of the crusading usurpers had been expelled.

Set into the floor, opposite the Deesis, is a fragment of tombstone, on which is inscribed the name 'Henricus Dandolo'. This, I believe, is the only memorial to the evil Doge of Venice, and very fitting it seems, that his name should be set into the floor, to be walked upon. More than any other single person, he was responsible for the havoc that the Fourth Crusade wreaked upon this city. He had been in Constantinople thirty years earlier, on a diplomatic mission. On that occasion he had partially lost his sight in a brawl. Subsequent difficulties in negotiating favourable trading terms had added to his sense of bitterness against the Byzantines. It seems, therefore, that there was a strong element of revenge and spite, as well as avarice and power-seeking, in his motivation for bringing ruin to this city.

The behaviour of the Crusaders is less easy to understand; they were attacking their allies, fellow Christians, not Jews, infidels, heretics, or other 'enemies of true religion'. They had already overcome any inhibitions about attacking fellow Christians when they sacked and pillaged Zara, on the way. Perhaps it was easier a second time. Or perhaps, because it did do violence to their conscience, to their vows and their principles of chivalry, it goes a little way to explaining why the sack of Constantinople was such a bloody and barbarous affair.

The Fourth Crusade entered Constantinople in 1204 with little difficulty since the city was in a state of confusion at the time. The Doge and the leading Crusaders settled themselves in the Imperial Palace and the soldiers were given leave to begin a three-day pillage.

For the nine preceding centuries Constantinople had been the centre of the Christian world. It was filled with great works of art, including the best of what remained from classical Greece and the ancient world. In those three days of mindless destruction much of this priceless heritage was lost for ever. Nothing was sacrosanct to the marauding crusaders; churches suffered the same fate as palaces, libraries, and monasteries. What was not carried away was hacked or slashed to pieces, or trampled underfoot. Haghia Sophia itself was entered and a scene enacted there to rival

Belshazzar's feast, with drunken soldiers desecrating the sacred altar-vessels and setting a prostitute on the Patriarch's throne, while their fellow looters smashed the great silver iconostasis and tore down the silken hangings. For three days the armies ran amok through the streets in an orgy of lust and killing. Nuns were raped; priests were dragged from their altars and put to the sword. Dead bodies lay in heaps everywhere; and in gutters running with blood, women and children lay dying of their wounds. The most glorious city in Christendom had been reduced to a shambles, by the defending armies of Christendom. As Nicetas, the historian, wrote: 'Even the Saracens would have been more merciful.'

Haghia Sophia, witness to all this mayhem, has somehow survived all the vicissitudes of fortune: substantially, it is the same building that the brilliant architects of Justinian's reign built in 532 AD. It is called a museum now, but apart from a Muslim pulpit and some huge and very obtrusive black plaques, inscribed with sacred Arabic calligraphy and suspended against the columns - whose lines they absolutely ruin - the building has reverted to being the empty shell of a very great Christian church. 'The most moving space in Christendom.'

I got to know it well since I went in every day. My hotel was practically in the grounds and called itself Biyuk Aya Sofia, which means Big Haghia Sophia. It was an interesting hotel that just missed being a disaster. Plumbing and electricity worked, but only just; I felt that the sword of Damocles was suspended over it by a particularly weak thread. The night it rained and all the people sleeping on the roof decamped to the landings, so that in the morning there were bodies everywhere and no one could get out of their rooms, was typical of the place.

Whenever a guest returned, he or she would have to run the gauntlet of an army of tough old women who made a faint show of cleaning the rooms. Someone at some time had introduced these old ladies to tips, and now they were determined to make their fortunes. Their ploy was to hide the room keys in plastic bags, so that guests had to go to them to get their door opened. This gave the ladies the opportunity to show (in mime) how they had laboured on the guest's behalf. Since they never did more than pull the bedding roughly together, and spent the rest of their time gossiping and waiting to pounce, it was really a blatant attempt at obtaining money under false pretences - and you gave in at your peril, for they then expected more and more. Towels were another problem; they were available, but only after a period of firm and constant pressure. Yet for all that, I wouldn't have moved elsewhere, for it was conveniently central, and, in any case, rooms were scarce in Istanbul in August. Every morning the vestibule was filled with would-be guests, waiting for vacancies.

I was lucky and had to spend only one night on the roof. The next two nights I shared a double room with Ita, an Irish girl from Clapham, who earned her living as a drummer, and whose striking blonde good looks caused half the male population of Istanbul to tag along after her. She managed to shake off most of them with an easy good humour; a trick which she said she'd picked up working with the band.

One day Ita and I took a boat trip up the Bosphorus, on an old-fashioned Turkish steamer which visited all the little seaside towns on either bank. It was a trip which lasted all day, and cost almost nothing. And although there were any number of castles, palaces, and famous places to be identified along the banks, there was no officious guide instructing one to look: so it was all wonderfully relaxed. We went ashore for lunch at a small seaside resort on the Asian shore that looked as though it was left over from a film set of the thirties. Restaurants with wooden balconies jutting out over the litter-strewn front catered for the tourists. The same delicious seafood as the restaurants served could be bought direct from the braziers in the street, or from fishermen's cafés, at a fraction of the cost. Mussels on skewers, coated in a garlic batter and grilled, or whitebait and chips - these were even served in newspaper, which brought waves of nostalgia. While we waited for the boat back, an old fisherman, attracted by Ita's striking looks, insisted on buying us beer and telling us his favourite joke about how all the Russian fish swim down from the Russian side of the Black Sea in autumn to be caught by the Turks and sent back to Russia again, in tins.

Coming back down the Bosphorus took a quarter of the time that going up had done, and we swept under the only bridge which joins Europe to Asia like a racehorse with the bit between its teeth, into the seething mass of shipping where the Golden Horn, the Sea of Marmara, and the Bosphorus meet. It is these three bodies of water which kept Constantinople inviolate for eleven centuries, and they still remain of the utmost importance to the life of Istanbul.

Around the Galata Bridge where most of the shipping is concentrated, the air is thick with the black smoke that pours from the funnels of the steamer fleet that carry Turks to and fro to ports in the Black Sea and around the sea of Marmara. There are ships and boats everywhere; big liners moored at the quays; cargo boats being unloaded with a great screeching of cranes and pulleys, and bustling tugs and ferries, hooting impatiently as they jockey for position in the crowded waters. Rowing boats weave in and out courting disaster as they indulge in the Turkish passion for fishing. Boys climb hand over hand along the hawsers of the liners, seeing who can reach the highest before they have to let go and fall into the water.

Any space left alongside the quays is at once occupied by boats selling fish from their foredecks; all manner of fish, from tiny whitebait to cuts of huge marlin whose dark red flesh looks faintly sinister and unfish-like. The indescribable noise of all this bustle is added to by the horn-happy traffic on both shores and on the Galata Bridge. I loved this part of Istanbul, and often came there, but I could take only small doses of it at a time.

Nearly all the other guests of the Biyuk Aya Sofia spoke English of some sort or another, and most were friendly, so the place had more of the atmosphere of a hostel than a hotel. Meals were nearly always eaten in company, even if they had been begun alone, as other guests from the Biyuk came to join one. There were cheap eating houses near by, which served good nourishing food and delicious Turkish lager. A typical meal of rice, stewed, spicy meat, a salad, and a lager would cost about a pound.

I spent my days sight-seeing, either on my own, or with some of the others from the hotel. One young student from Wigan, Stephen, was the only other cyclist. I was able to adjust his malfunctioning bicycle gears, and in return he agreed to take my tent back to England for me. He was studying town planning and was spending his summer vacation writing a thesis on how Istanbul was coping with being the fastest growing city in the world. I went walking with him around a part of the city which had been taken over by Turks who had recently arrived from the harsh eastern region. I gathered that a general exodus from country to town was taking place all over Turkey, as people sought a better standard of living; which was why Istanbul was growing at such a rate. This creates a terrible housing shortage, so people are encouraged to build for themselves. All spare land can be built on, and as long as a single-storeyed dwelling is erected and roofed in a single night, it then becomes the property of the builders, including the land on which it stands. Funds can then be made available to convert it into a five or six-floored structure, which will provide accommodation for further homeless families. It seems rather haphazard, but perhaps it is a better solution than the usual shanty towns which ring so many cities of developing nations.

Sunday is a holiday in Turkey, which is odd, because Friday is the Muslim Sabbath. But then Turkey is odd, and I suppose it must come of being half an Asiatic country and half a European one. It is said that this causes a kind of racial schizophrenia. There are certainly two distinct physical types among the men. One type has a round head, broad shoulders and a short neck, and tends to run to fat; the sort of man who goes in for heavy-weight wrestling. The other type is tall and melancholy looking, with a pale thin face and droopy moustaches; looks associated with playing the violin in a gypsy band. The women fall into different categories; they are either modern or traditional. The traditional ones, who are by far the majority, all look very much alike, being bundled up in heavy clothing, their heads wrapped in shawls. Their modern sisters are as varied in appearance as women anywhere, and are to be seen only in the cities, and not very often there. Most women seem to be hidden away, labouring to keep their menfolk free to spend their days in the cafés playing tric-trac.

The Sunday holiday was being taken very seriously as Stephen and I made our tour. Everywhere, where there was a little piece of open ground, families were having picnics. Kettles were bubbling merrily on stoves and kebabs were cooking on little braziers. Where no patch of grass or earth existed, rugs had been spread on the pavements and the picnics took place there. The tea houses were filled with men playing tric-trac and drinking tea or smoking hubble-bubble pipes. We walked into the main park, which had once been the gardens of the Topkapi Palace, and here too every inch of ground that wasn't being walked on was being sat upon by picnicking families.

I spent the best part of two days wandering around the great palace of the Ottoman sultans, Topkapi Sarayi, and even then I had seen only a fraction of the treasures it houses. It was built on a supremely beautiful site, which was originally the acropolis of Byzantium and overlooks the circlet of seas and the Asian and European shores. Terraces and gardens led down to the water's edge at Saray Point, and an Arab writer who saw it in its heyday wrote:

*'A more delightful residence hath never been erected by man's artifice: it seemeth not a mere palace, but a noble town, situated on the confluence of two seas.'*

The whole of the vast Ottoman Empire was once ruled from this spot, at times with brilliance; but intrigue and dark deeds also flourished in the claustrophobic atmosphere of the harem, among deposed favourites and superseded princes, and a moral decline soon set in.

The niches on either side of the entrance to the Saray frequently displayed the heads of those executed within; there was even a special fountain for the chief executioner (who was also the head gardener) to wash his hands after the beheadings. Janissaries in the outer court, white eunuchs in charge of the council chamber, black eunuchs in the harem, the whole place was a powder keg of potential insurrection. Sultans and favourites could come and go but, like our own Civil Service today, the eunuchs and janissaries were there to stay. There were many times when the Chief Black Eunuch wielded more power than the Sultan himself.

The buildings of the Topkapi are now used to display some of the treasures accumulated over the six centuries of Ottoman rule and a strange and varied collection it is; from priceless Chinese porcelain still in its original packing cases and unopened until this century, to a room filled with the costumes of sultans, spanning the whole period of the Empire; including the blood-stained robes of Osman II killed by his own janissaries in 1622. It is such a rich collection that I got mental indigestion after these two rooms, and had to go into the gardens for a while to recover. It was a relief just to sit and watch the ships rounding the point, while other visitors stumbled out of rooms and pavilions with that glazed, unfocused look that people wear when they have tried to see too much, or are worried about what they might have missed.

I find that I have to be very firm with myself when I visit a gallery or museum. The amount I can absorb at any one time is strictly limited - about an hour is right, after that I don't really take in what I'm seeing. So I've learnt to do my homework first, decide what I want to see, and try to stop myself being sidetracked once I'm there. The last part is by far the most difficult. On my final sortie into the Topkapi Palace I made sure I saw the room dedicated to relics of Mohammed; six hairs from his beard, his tooth, dirt from his coffin, his weapons, and so forth. Why I wanted to see these I can't think now, but I suppose they had the attraction of uniqueness. I also saw the gold-encased arm of John the Baptist, which had a small opening at the wrist to expose the brown bones inside. There were a couple of skulls too, which were precious, holy relics. I can't remember whose skulls they were supposed to be, but they were studded all over with gems which struck me as being rather repulsive.

A less pleasant aspect of the twentieth-century Istanbul scene was the heavy military presence. There were soldiers everywhere, and with their close-fitting caps and unattractive uniforms they tended to remind one of the brutal and licentious side of armies. The ones on guard duty were uncompromisingly menacing. They were to be seen outside most museums and public places, armed with powerful automatic guns. With their aggressive stance, feet wide apart, loaded weapon at the ready with finger permanently in place on the trigger, they made me very nervous. When one of my companions told me chattily that a burst from one of those guns could cut a man in half my nervousness increased. Their presence was a constant reminder that there is another side to life in Turkey of which the casual visitor is only dimly aware.

The time spent wandering through the streets, between visiting places of especial interest, is what gives the true flavour of a city. Most of the rest of Istanbul I was indifferent to, except for the area around the Galata Bridge. But I felt I could have spent a long time wandering around Stamboul without ever tiring of it. This was the area of the original Byzantine city, bounded by the sea on three sides and by the land wall of Theodosius on the fourth. It is an area full of tumbledown Turkish hovels, some of them built in old Byzantine cisterns, with chickens and peacocks scratching in the patches of garden in front of the doors. Old Turkish houses are full of a rackety sort of charm. They look as though they have been built out of bits and pieces and might fall down at any moment. They are usually festooned with greenery - any old paint tin or petrol can having been pressed into service to grow plants in. Byzantine churches are tucked in among the crooked streets, some of them in ruins, others changed into mosques or museums. Cats and kittens are everywhere, tumbling in and out of doorways and staring out from among the flower tins on window-sills, posing in threes and fours. The Turks like cats and don't drown the many and frequent litters of kittens; but they don't feed them either, so all the cats stay very small.

It was an area I was quite happy to wander in on my own. No one bothered me and, whenever I was trying to track down a particular church, people would take infinite pains to make sure I found it. Turks, I decided, were very kind; sometimes even too kind, as when carpet sellers dragged me into their shops and insisted that I take a glass of tea with them, while they showed me their range of carpets.

'Only just in from Edremit. No problem, we can send' — which dealt with my glib excuse of being unable to buy anything because of travelling by bicycle. I soon learnt to change my defence to a plea of poverty. Carpet sellers are the most importunate salesmen I have ever met; it must be a grossly over-subscribed market, something else the poor, overworked women are doubtless kept slaving away at, when they aren't busy doing anything else.

The place I visited most frequently after Haghia Sophia was the fourteenth-century Church of St Saviour in Chora - the Church of Christ in the Country - so called because it was outside the walled Byzantine city. Since the Ottoman conquest this church, like many others, had masqueraded as a mosque, but recently it had been restored by the American Byzantine Institute, and was now a museum called Kariye Camii. It contains the most important series of Byzantine mosaics in the city, and possibly in the world, and was originally planned as a pictorial statement of the theology of the times. Every surface had been utilized to depict the life of Christ, His ministry and genealogy, and the life and genealogy of the Blessed Virgin. The sophistication of Byzantine theology is apparent in all their art, but it is particularly shown in the play on words in the dedicatory panel: Christ Pantocrater becomes Christ the Country - not just the rural countryside outside the walls, but the country in which we have our true life; or as the TwentiethCentury theologian, Paul Tillich phrased it, 'the ground of our being'.

No one knows who the artist was, but it is thought that he was also responsible for the superb frescoes in the adjoining paraclesion. The central one of these, which fills the conch of the apse, is a depiction of the Harrowing of Hell, in which Christ with his right hand draws Adam and his descendants from the tomb, and with his left raises Eve. It was this fresco, especially, that drew me back there so often, though the whole place exerted a powerful influence. I could imagine endless generations of pilgrims leaving its portals with their faith renewed and strengthened and setting off, like Abraham, to seek that `other country'.

In the account of St Willibald's pilgrimage, there is only a pitifully-short piece about his two-year stay in Constantinople, 726 - 728. He makes no mention of my two favourite churches, seeming to have spent all his time in a cell in the Church of the Holy Apostles, now alas destroyed. It had been built to contain the relics of three saints brought from the Holy Land: St Andrew, St Timothy, and St Luke the Evangelist. Also buried there according to Willibald was St John Chrysostom, an early Church Father, so clearly it would have been a centre for pilgrims.

Bishop Arculf, who visited the city at much the same time, had his story subsequently written down by Adamnan, a Bishop of Iona, who, like the Venerable Bede, was keen on doing biographies. He had written up St Columba earlier, and as his subject had been dead for a couple of hundred years by then, he had been able to give plenty of rein to his imagination. His account of Arculf's pilgrimage is very sober in comparison. He certainly seems to have visited Haghia Sophia and been present at the ceremony of venerating the cross on Good Friday. This would have been the supposed True Cross on which Christ was crucified and which Constantine's mother, the Empress Helena, had found when she was establishing the sites of all the Holy Places in Palestine.

Arculf has lots to say about Constantinople. He was obviously as taken with it as I was, but most of his stories are about miraculous happenings - sinners being engulfed by marble columns, and holy portraits oozing oil. In the last of these he gives us an interesting picture of an Eighth-Century Byzantine public lavatory. It seems to have been a companionable sort of place 'in which people sat at holes in long benches'.

The longer I lingered in Istanbul, the harder it became to drag myself away. Normally, a week in a city is as much as I can cope with at any one time, but here I kept finding new delights, as well as becoming increasingly fond of the old ones. Having my hotel on the edge of so much open space also contributed to my feeling of contentment, as I never felt closed in. But wonderful and exciting though I found

Istanbul, I also realized that if I was to get to Jerusalem before the winter rains set in, it was high time I got started.

I booked a passage on a boat which was leaving in three days, and which would take me across the Sea of Marmara to the Asian shore, and then set about making the most of the remaining time in Byzantium.

I felt rather apprehensive about the journey ahead, not about anything in particular, just a vague feeling of uncertainty about the people whose lands I would be travelling through. So far, nearly all the Turks I had met in the streets of Istanbul had been friendly and considerate, sometimes even exceptionally so, as on one occasion when I had been queueing for a bus and had been pushed up to the front as soon as it was realized that I was a tourist. And yet there also seemed to be an underlying hint of callousness, cruelty even. There was nothing specific that I could put my finger on, it just seemed that they treated one another rather insensitively. Perhaps I felt this because of Turkey's record and its poor reputation with Amnesty International. I had no doubts that there was a cavalier disregard of people's basic human rights in this country, but how far that was a    reflection of the Turkish temperament I didn't know. The news that a young British cyclist had just been brutally stabbed to death, in a town along my route, added weight to my vague fears.

So it was with a mixture of regret and apprehension that I stood on the quay on my final morning in Istanbul with Evans loaded up and looking a lot sturdier and more dependable than I felt. The weather, which had been hot and sunny for the past weeks, had changed to a depressing, thin, grey drizzle, which didn't help my mood.

Before setting out, I had paid my last visit to Haghia Sophia to fortify myself by reading through my pilgrim's itinerary there. Standing on the quayside, waiting for the boat, I thought of a line from it, about being a 'well-wishing in our setting out and a solace on the way'. I did have the well-wishing, for some of the guests from The Biyuk Aya Sofia were there to wave me off.

# Chapter Six

*..... it was the Grekkes hors Synon,*
*That brochte Troye to destruccion,*
*As men may in thise olde gestes rede*

Chaucer

During the voyage across the Sea of Marmara, as we had sailed out of the grey drizzle, into bright sunshine, my spirits had risen considerably. But as I wheeled Evans onto the quay at Karabiga, they plummeted again like a stone. I was suddenly in an alien country. Faces looked surly and unfriendly, and the further I ventured into the interior of the small fishing port the less happy I felt. New impressions were flooding in, none of them favourable. Narrow, pot-holed roads, paved with buckled cobble stones and lined with hovels; snarling dogs and piles of rotting rubbish, horrid smells and more unfriendly faces. What had I let myself in for,. What if all of Turkey was like this? I had weeks, months of it ahead of me. How on earth would I cope? It was not just an alien country, but an alien continent, with a set of values that were entirely different to mine. It was Asia versus Europe: East versus West. A few hour's boat journey and I seemed to be in a totally different world; as different from Istanbul as Istanbul was from London.

It was the impact of Asia that I was experiencing, and I don't think there is any way one can prepare for it. Once it has struck, all one can do is to wait until the effect has worn off and a sense of proportion has returned. This was my second such experience of Asian culture shock, so perhaps the fact that I had survived the first occasion gave me the courage to get on Evans and set off into the unknown, rather than wheel him back onto the boat and abandon the journey. In these situations, the bicycle is a great comfort; I might not know where I shall find a resting place for the night, but at least I have the means to go off and look for one, and the effort of turning the pedals helps to keep my mind from dwelling on useless dark imaginings. When I am worried or a bit apprehensive, I cycle with far more energy.

The road I took was not easy, being half made up and half a dirt track, and for a while it was busy with taxis and minibuses taking my fellow passengers on to Canakkale. Many of them would board another boat there, to sail off to seaside holidays at the small resorts along the coast of the Dardanelles, or on islands in the straits and down the Aegean coast. One Turkish couple who were on their way to such a holiday had told me that there would probably be a hotel of sorts at Biga, which was about twenty miles away. I hoped they were right because I didn't have more than a couple of hours' daylight left, and I was anxious to be under cover before nightfall.

The countryside I was passing through was not unlike England at first sight: a rural landscape of fields with clumps of deciduous trees here and there. The fields looked bare and dried up, except for patches of tomatoes, glowing redly among the brown stubble of recent grain harvests. I passed patches of melons and red peppers too; some of these were in small piles by the side of the road, placed there to be picked up later by returning field workers. After a few miles, tractors carrying the homeward-bound workers began to trundle past in the opposite direction. Women, their heads wrapped around with scarves, were sitting on the mudguards, while their menfolk drove, staring stolidly ahead. The women averted their faces as they passed me but I could see in my wing mirror that they turned around to stare at my departing figure. The feeling that I was the only one of my kind in a hostile land steadily increased. Then a large van passed, going in my direction; it slowed down and stopped, and the driver put his head out of the window and indicated that he wished to give me a lift. Suspicion and alarm were my immediate reactions to this probably innocent and kindly gesture. I could think of a dozen reasons for the offer and all of them were unpleasant. Smiling placatingly and waving my hand, in what I hoped would be taken for a polite but firm refusal, I cycled past the van, giving it a wide berth.

At this point I decided that I was behaving stupidly. If I was going to regard everyone as a potential enemy, I might as well go home. Perpetually expecting a knife in the back, or robbers lurking behind every bush is no way to travel,. There might well be both these things, but looking out for them all the time meant that I would see nothing else. If someone was determined to attack and rob me, it would happen anyway; there was no question of me being able to prevent it by superior force, since the most lethal weapon I carried was my Swiss army penknife, and even that was not readily to hand. Nor did I believe that everybody could really be as unfriendly as they appeared. They were probably just struck dumb with amazement at seeing a lone female on a bicycle. Putting thoughts into action, I waved to the very next tractor that passed; the driver responded immediately, and after some hesitation the women also returned the greeting.

Looking back at those first few hours in Asia Minor, it strikes me as odd that my first impression of the people should have been like that, because in all the time I spent in Turkey, I never felt like that again. Whatever faults could be found in the Turkish character, it was not usually a lack of friendliness towards strangers.

Having taken the initiative in approaching the Turk, I had no difficulty in finding Biga's one and only hostelry. In fact I

Sea

PONTUS

POLEMONIS

GALATIA

■ Ankara

Sivas ●

CAPPADOCIA

Uchisar
Goreme ●
● Urgup
Kayseri ●

● Konya

Cilician
Gates

ANTIOCH

● Anazarbus

Adana ● Ceyhan

Tarsus

Plain of Issus ✕

Iskenderun ●

Alanya ●

Kanlidivane

Silifke ●

Anamurian

Antakya ●
(Antioch)

SYRIA

Sea

Legend:
— · — Bettina's route
— — — by sea
∴ Ancient sites
⌂ Crusader castles
✕ Battles

was escorted to it by a motorcyclist, after I had mimed 'I am looking for an hotel' - which I did by closing my eyes and resting my head sideways on folded hands. This, used with the one word 'otel', works well in Turkey. I think the Turks are particularly good at mime, as they have such an odd language and do not expect that strangers will be able to speak it. This is quite different from English speakers who tend to expect everyone else in the world to understand their language, as long as they speak it slowly and loudly enough.

The hotel was a very curious place, full of beds all along the corridors and landings as well as in the rooms - rather like a hospital under siege in a war zone. I could see that I was expected to haggle over the charges, because after I had agreed to the first price asked, about one pound, a man with greater authority came over and doubled it. I was given quite a clean room with just two beds in it. The top sheet was fastened to the blanket with several dozen safety pins and I thought that was a good idea as it meant that I would be protected from the rather tacky blanket. The mattress was a straw palliasse with a layer of newspapers beneath it to protect it from the rusty wire frame. From my window I had a fine view of Biga's roofs and chimneys; and on one of the chimney pots was a huge rough nest on which was perched a stork feeding two offspring as large as itself.

I went to sleep that night with a sense of great achievement, as though I'd conquered Everest or something similar. I'd survived my first day in Asian Turkey; I'd found a bed and a restaurant where I had ordered a meal and eaten well, and I had seen my first nesting storks; all by my own efforts. The journey was promising to turn out well. Even the knock at the door in the middle of the night, and a man's voice calling me 'mademoiselle' and inviting me to take *chay* with him, didn't spoil my contentment. There was a stout lock on the door and the second bed was wedged up against it too, just in case.

When I awoke in the morning it was to a cadenza of snores, very close by. Last night's would-be *chay* drinker was asleep in a bed just outside my door - why, I shall never know, as I didn't stay around long enough to find out. Other men, wearing voluminous, old-fashioned underwear, waited outside the hotel's two washrooms. I decided not to bother.

Before I left Biga, I went in search of breakfast, only to find that Turkish breakfast consisted of greasy lentil soup and bread. I was not yet seasoned enough for this and asked for tea instead, not realizing that soup and tea would not be available in the same establishment. The proprietor kindly sent out for some and refused to accept any payment for it. I was to stay in this sort of small town several times, when I was off the tourist routes, and what I found at Biga was typical of most of them in the way of accommodation; perfectly adequate and very cheap. The little courtesies and kindnesses were also a frequent feature of such places.

A few days later I was energetically essaying a hill on the way to Troy when a young Australian man leapt out of a taxi and asked if he could film me with his movie camera. I recognized him as one of the group who had been standing around in the cocktail bar of my hotel the previous night, admiring Evans. It was rather a grand hotel by my standards, having all the luxuries which I'm prepared to forgo when travelling, in the interests of economy. However, when I had arrived at Canakkale, after a long, hot, dusty ride, I had finished up on the shore of the Dardanelles just outside this hotel; the staff, who were not very busy at that moment, all came out to have a look at me and Evans. They wanted to know all about me and where I had ridden from; and the information was passed on to the ones who didn't speak English. They seemed to take it for granted that we were going to stay there, so I had to explain that I was in search of something more modest. How modest? they asked. I told them how much I had paid at Biga. They gulped rather at this and put their heads together to confer. The result was that I was offered, for a modest two pounds, the nicest double room in the hotel. It hadn't been possible to offer it to anyone else, as the previous occupant had left the shower tap on and flooded the whole floor. As long as I didn't mind doing without carpets - these were still being dried out - I was welcome to the room; breakfast would be included, naturally. I would have stayed anyway because they were so nice to Evans, wheeling him in through the main entrance and insisting that he spend the night in the bar, where someone would be on duty to keep an eye on him. There are many hotels which are quite insensitive to a bicycle's need for dry, secure shelter.

I didn't mind the young man filming me, in fact I was flattered; no one has ever asked to film me before. As long as he didn't want me to stop on the hill, that is, for if I did that, I'd probably not be able to get going again on so steep a slope. He said no, he could run alongside, which was true, since I was in my lowest gear, in which I trundle along at about five miles an hour, at most. 'Nobody is going to believe this back home,' he said with relish as he loped along, camera whirring and taxi following on behind. He said he had tried to cycle this coast with his girl friend last year, but that the traffic had frightened them and they had abandoned the attempt. I found this strange, because I hadn't been unduly bothered by traffic. In fact, I'd been thinking how restrained the other road users were in comparison with those of Italy. I was still considering this piece of information when the young man had finished filming and returned to the taxi: so why he wanted to film me pounding uphill I never discovered, and just had to add it to the growing list of unsolved mysteries of the journey.

Cycling over these wooded spurs of Mount Ida, I was following neither a Crusader route nor one of any recorded Christian pilgrim paths, for both went inland at this point. But in another sense it was very much pilgrim territory; for it was the country of the *Iliad* and the birth of Western literature. Soon, below me, I caught my first glimpse of the plains of the Troad, where Troy 'that strong city' had stood, and where the Greeks had ridden up to the walls in their chariots, after dragging their `sharp-prowed blackships' onto the shore and setting up the tented camp.

Most of the guide books try to warn people not to be disappointed on first seeing Troy because it is such a confusing excavation, with all the different levels from its 4000 years of chequered history. Not being an archaeologist, I didn't really care about which bits belonged to which level, but what did strike me most forcibly was how very small Priam's walled city was, apparently not as much as two hundred yards across. What remains of the walls and towers, however, is enough to show the massive strength it must have had in his day; and the remains of the largest dwelling place would be of palatial dimensions for ancient Greece. But it is the position of the site that is so dramatic. From the crest of the mound there is a clear uninterrupted view of the entire Trojan Plain - the stage of the Homeric drama.

It was difficult at first to imagine the Trojan princes sitting there, on the tower of Ilium, marvelling at Helen's beauty as she came up to the Scaean Gate, to watch her husband, Menelaus, engage in single combat with Paris. The pathos of the scene, with Helen's loyalties and longings in chaos, torn between her former home and Greek countrymen, and the Trojans with whom she has lived for the last nineteen years. It is made doubly poignant by King Priam's loving acceptance of her: 'Dear child,' Homer has him say 'come here and sit in front of me, so that you may see your former husband and your relatives and friends. I bear you no ill will at all: I blame the gods. It is they who brought this terrible Archaean war upon me.'

Far easier to imagine the battle scenes on those unchanged plains below, with the Scamander River, which nearly drowned Achilles, still glinting in the sun. Homer didn't go in much for descriptions of places; it is men and their actions that he portrayed so vividly - heroes wreaking havoc with their long spears: mighty Achilles; 'Hector of the shining helmet'; Diomedes; Agamemnon; 'Odysseus of the nimble wits'. Victors and vanquished all fighting, not for prizes, but for glory and honour for themselves and their kith and kin; so that they might live on in the songs of the poets, which was the only sort of immortality that had any importance for them. Life was for living to the full, now; the hereafter was a dreary, shadowy place: as Achilles says, 'I would rather be a slave on earth than a king in Hades'.

It felt very strange to be in an actual place which up to then had seemed as legendary as Homer's heroes. That there was a real, an actual Troy, even if it was now just broken walls, made Homer's characters more real too. I stayed there a long while thinking of all those vivid heroes and of their womenfolk: Andromache pleading with Hector not to return to the fight, while their little son cries, frightened by the swirling crest of his father's battle helmet. Cassandra knowing of the forthcoming ruin, and no one able to believe her warnings; and even poorer Helen, a mere pawn, for all her marvellous beauty. All of them to become the spoils of war after their menfolk have been slain. The women of Homer's world certainly had the worst of it, and it is difficult to think of a time when this was not the case. The Greek view of the world was very attractive, with its emphasis on the worth and quality of life, but it applied only to the minority, who were neither slaves nor women.

Homer's stories were the foundation of the education of all the succeeding generations of the Greeks. The battles of Marathon and Thermopylae were a living out of the codes of which he had sung, in the legends enacted on these Plains of Scamander. The same codes have also exerted no small influence on British education, particularly since the days of Dr Arnold, though I personally find it difficult to equate the playing fields of Eton and Rugby with the battle-fields of the Troad. Perhaps that is because the sports of cricket and rugby are not very important aspects of life at a girls' school.

By the time I had cycled back up to the road after the Troy visit, I had been out in the hot sun for about six hours and was feeling quite dehydrated. Along the roadside were farmers selling huge melons and water melons from the backs of carts and trailers. Much as I longed to buy some, I felt hesitant because of the language problem; I thought they might not be prepared to cut one up for me and I could hardly manage a four- or five-pound melon on my own. Cars stopped and the occupants got out and devoured the fruit there and then by the roadside. Several such groups waved to me as I passed by them, salivating pathetically. I formed the impression that some of them were inviting me to share the feast, and when one man actually held out a succulent slice towards me, I needed no further invitation. It was delicious, so was the second slice, and the third, and the fourth; in fact, I demolished half a dozen slices before shame intervened. Not that there was any need for embarassment, my benefactors were delighted with my appetite and so were other groups who had crowded round, ready to thrust another slice into my hand as soon as I had finished the last one. The farmers had also expressed their approval at my appreciation of their produce, and one of them bustled up with a whole melon weighing at least six pounds, which he stuffed into one of the panniers. Then they all shook hands with me, still beaming delightedly, and sent me on my way, wondering what I had done to deserve being treated so royally.

The melon was so fortifying that I rode on for hours without stopping; up and down great rolling forested hills, with sudden glimpses of the glorious Aegean coastline below. When I did come to a halt, in order to see how my melon was doing, I found that it not been improved by the heat and the bouncing about, so I ate what I could of it and fed the rest to some pretty-faced Turkish cows, who happened to be around, and who seemed to appreciate melon as much as I had done earlier. Then I cycled on to the next watering place to wash the spilt juices out of the pannier and to rest a while.

Some days seem to be imbued with a magical quality that transforms ordinary things into objects of wonder and pleasure - this had been just such a day. Perhaps it was something to do with the clear Aegean light, or with visiting fabled Troy. Whatever it was, I couldn't remember another day of such perfect enjoyment. I cycled on, over another succession of steep hills, where a lorry stopped to offer me a lift and I wasn't the least bit tempted to accept, because I was quite content to climb even those long hills with Evans.

I reached the top of the coastal ridge, at a dizzy height above the Gulf of Edremit, with the island of Lesbos below, its dark mountains rising from a turquoise sea, and the sun beginning to sink down behind it. Across the Gulf were the rolling hills of Aeolia and the next stage of the journey. I stayed for a long time, gazing at the marvellous panorama, and thinking about Sappho on her island, and of how it wasn't true what I had thought earlier, about women always having had such a poor time. Sappho, at least, had lived at an intensity to equal any of her male contemporaries, and the scraps of her poetry which have survived are of quality second to none. I stayed on my high place so long that the sun had almost set before I rode Evans down the steep, winding road, to seek shelter in the village of Kuccukuyu, beside the splashing waves.

# Chapter Seven

*The stars around the lovely moon*
*Veil again their shining beauty*
*When the moon grows full and blazes*
*Down on all the earth.*

Sappho

All along the curve of the bay were small, ramshackle holiday complexes, collections of wooden huts, looking as if they might tumble down about their occupants' ears at any moment. But as the evening darkened, defects disappeared, and it became a tremendously romantic setting, with the moon making a broad silver swathe across the sea towards Lesbos. The sky looked more blue than black, like a Van Gogh painting, with the stars smudging a little at their edges. The heat of the day had given way to a gentle warmth that didn't call for a sweater. It was the sort of night that was perfect for sleeping out, though I wouldn't choose to do so amongst all those huts. The most promising place looked to be the motel and so it proved. It was a two-tiered structure of twin-bedded rooms, each with a small shower, and spartanly furnished. All around were gardens full of roses and aromatic plants, with places amongst them for tents. There was a private patch of sandy beach, a restaurant-cum-dance-floor, and a bar. Judging by the parked cars, quite well-to-do Turkish people went there for their holidays.

I had to do some stiff bargaining for a room, because of that iniquitous practice of trying to make one person pay for both beds when no single rooms are available. Eventually the management relented, because at that late hour it was unlikely that anyone else would arrive - better a single in the hand, so to speak. One of the best meals I ate in Turkey was in this motel, and that was because I was invited to dine with some Dutch oil people who had passed me on the road, earlier in the day. They were touring around for a brief holiday and had pitched their tent amongst the roses. I had apparently won a bet for one of them, who, spotting me on Evans, had said that only a Dutch or an English woman would be riding a bicycle alone through Turkey. They had lived in Ankara for quite a while and could speak Turkish, and knew how to ask about what food was best, and if it was fresh and so forth. They ordered a great many dishes; kebabs, octopus, fish, vine leaves stuffed with rice and with spiced minced lamb, salads of aubergine, houmous, and things no one knew the English name for. Nothing came in any particular order, it just came when it was ready, and it was all quite delicious. The wine was delicious too, and, coming on top of the beer I had drunk in the bar, earlier, made the view of the bay, with Sappho's island bathed in the bright moonlight, seem even more romantic.

Changing a traveller's cheque in Turkey, other than in a bank in a reasonably large town, is impossible. Towns are far apart, and banks close on Saturday and Sunday: some of them also close on Friday. Travelling with large amounts of currency is not advised - this is why one takes traveller's cheques in the first place. Putting all these facts together, it was not unlikely that I would find myself without money at some point in the journey. I did, and it happened to be on my fiftieth birthday, which fell on a Saturday while I was riding down through Aeolia. There could be many worse places to find oneself destitute. Not that I was totally so, but I certainly didn't have enough to pay for hotels and meals until Monday. As food is to the bicyclist what petrol is to vehicles, I bought some nourishing things like cheese, olives, and bread, which I hoped would provide enough energy to carry me through the weekend. What was left would pay for entrance fees to historic sites, and maybe even stretch to one night's lodging.

My provisions would have gone stale in the panniers had I accepted all the hospitality I was offered that day and the next. Every time I stopped at that most lovely of all Turkish road signs - the blue dripping tap on a white ground, which denotes a safe watering place - people waiting to use the tap would press gifts of fruit upon me: a few figs, a melon, grapes, or a handful of nuts. Often they would turn away before I could even thank them. I wondered if it was because they had the same idea as the ancient Greeks and early Christians, that a traveller somehow carries a blessing. In the Hebrides, until quite recent times, an extra place was set at mealtimes in case a stranger should chance by. At every café I passed, and there was one every few miles, men would call out for me to join them in a glass of *chay*. In Turkey tea comes in small, tulip-shaped glasses, with no milk and lots of sugar. The proper form, I discovered when I took up these invitations, was to accept two of these glasses, which gave the men time to put their three most usual questions:

1) How old are you?
2) Are you married?
3) How do you like Turkey?

They were then quite happy for me to pedal away and leave them to their television, which is the main attraction of café life today in Turkey, even more so than tric-trac. The men and boys sit in decorous rows, under a shady vine, watching an endless succession of sad and sentimental love stories. Women never frequent these village cafés, as they are too busy slaving away in the fields or in the home. The men take the women out to the scenes of their outdoor labours in the morning and bring them back at night; in between they appear to spend most of the day in the tea houses. There are other cafés where buses stop for their passengers to refresh themselves; and their forecourts were normally filled with ancient German cars driven by Turks working in Germany and home with their families for a holiday. I hardly ever saw a car in Turkey which did not have a 'D' plate on it. I had many conversations, subsequently, with these expatriate Turks: all of whom professed to being very happy with their lives in Germany, and who said that they wouldn't dream of coming back to Turkey, except for holidays. The women were particularly adamant about this; and seeing the greater freedom and equality they enjoyed, compared with their sisters at home, this was not really surprising.

The pines of Mount Ida had given way to groves of olive trees along the Aeolian coast, and all day I rode through endless forests of them, with glimpses of the sea away to the right. It is a rich, well-cultivated land which never produced as much in the way of creative brilliance as the other civilizations of the Aegean. Herodotus said it had much better soil than Ionia, but that the weather was not so good, so perhaps that had something to do with it.

There was nothing wrong with the Aeolian weather when I rode through, and my only complaints were about the rather dashing driving of the buses, though fortunately there were not too many of them. A more constant irritation was the road surface which was of large chippings set in a very thin layer of tar so that they protruded sharply, causing a bicycle rider acute discomfort from the perpetual juddering. Sometimes the gravel had been piled on extremely lavishly and, not being able to adhere to the miserly quantity of tar, it had collected in great drifts on either side of the road. If I had allowed the buses to edge me into these gravel drifts, there would have been no way that I could have kept Evans upright, and I would have probably suffered an injury a lot more serious than a sore posterior.

Evans was also adding one or two unaccustomed noises to the various rattles and rustles of the luggage in the panniers. A cyclist is always subconsciously listening for any unusual sounds from the moving parts of the machinery, for these can alert the rider to the beginning of trouble. It is extremely important to investigate any noises straight away, for nuts and bolts can work loose on rough roads, and if ignored they fall off and are lost for ever. It takes little time to get off and tighten them, but trying to find replacements can take days. In a foreign country, it will probably prove impossible and another 'foolish virgin' will have to tie things together with bits of string. Actually, none of Evans's nuts and bolts was loose; the noises seemed to be coming from the front wheel hub and the left pedal: it sounded as though there was something wrong in the bearings. I spun both wheel and pedal and both turned beautifully as they should, without any noise at all. I checked everything I could think of; headset bearings, bottom bracket, gear mechanism, the other pedal; but there was nothing that appeared to be functioning less perfectly than such finely-engineered parts should. I rode on and back came the noises. I got off, repeated the inspection as before, with the same result.

Throughout the journey these same noises occurred, but not continuously; some days they were not there, and some days they were there all the time. I never discovered what caused them, nor did the mechanics who built Evans. To this day it remains a mystery. Someone did suggest that perhaps the name of the bicycle being Welsh might have something to do with it, and that Evans felt as I did at times, and was breaking into song. In other ways he was outstandingly trouble-free, and the only bicycle I've owned which has done more than four thousand miles without a single puncture.

I had hoped to reach Pergamon that day, but with all the stops to look for the causes of Evans's noises, and with all the friendly tea drinking, I was still many miles away when it became time to think of a resting place for the night. A camping site would be best in my present financial circumstances, and I kept an eye out for one. None appeared however and soon I came to a small coastal town, called Dikili. After trying several holiday hotels, none of whom was interested in my traveller's cheques, credit cards, or my emergency hoard of dollars, I was directed by a helpful Turkish bystander to an hotel away from the tourist areas on the front. It was a substantial-looking building, overlooking a tree-lined square; just a block away from the sea and amazingly cheap. For a little over a pound I was given a room with a wash-basin, a balcony, and a choice of three beds. The only problem was that I had to haul Evans up the long precipitous flight of stairs to share my room, as the proprietor said it wouldn't be safe for him below. On the ground floor was one of the best restaurants in town and the proprietor was quite happy to accept two of my dollars in exchange for a satisfying meal of kebab, salad, bread, and beer.

Later when I had finished all my evening chores, walked around the town, and was ready to make my choice of the beds, I discovered why my hotel was so cheap. Three cafés were housed in the square below; chairs and tables stood in every space between the trees and the flowering plants in their ornamental oil drums. Each café had, as its main attraction, a very large television set with additional speakers, their volume set to be clearly audible above all other noises, such as roaring traffic, shouting men playing tric-trac, and boys playing nothing in particular but just adding their voices to the clamour. Asia is much noisier than Europe, and Turkey is totally Asian in this respect, no matter how much it strives to be Western in other ways.

It was an exclusively male world in this small-town square; women did pass by occasionally with their menfolk, but these were almost certainly visiting holiday-makers. Young men carried around the trays of tea and boys prepared the special Turkish hubble bubble pipes, the narghilahs, for the old men. As the evening wore on, the television sets, which were showing the usual succession of very old Italian films, dubbed into Turkish, became increasingly the focus of everyone's attention. The volume, which would already have exceeded the legal level, had such a thing existed in Turkey, was turned up even higher. I had neglected to pack my wax earplugs, a lifesaver on occasions like these, so there was nothing I could do to alleviate the situation. It was difficult even to read in the dreadful din. The last film featured a very young Gina Lollobrigida and had a soundtrack full of fury and passion, although the action looked innocent enough. Heavy mood music kept rising to crescendos, raising false hopes that it was about to end.

I was later than usual setting out the next morning because of not having got to sleep until two a.m., which was when the television had finished, and the men had wandered home, calling out their last greetings to one another as they went. Consequently I reached Bergama in the heat of the day, with four kilometres of very steep hillside to ascend to the top of the acropolis and the site of ancient Pergamon. I was just looking for somewhere safe to leave Evans, so that I could walk up more easily, when I became aware of a camel breathing down my neck. He was a particularly large, fine-looking camel, decked out in colourful trappings, and his driver wanted me to hire him to transport myself and Evans to the summit. When I tried to explain that I had no money for camel hire (or for anything else by that time) he became rather cross and made what I took to be derogatory remarks about Evans. My pride stung, I rashly decided that I would cycle up to show him that bicycles were in no way inferior to camels. The road wove to and fro in snake-like coils, but even so it was a gradient which I found almost impossible. Had the camel driver not been standing below, closely watching my progress, I would have abandoned the attempt almost at once. Pride is a great spur, however, and on this occasion it was not followed by a fall. I probably established a record as being the only bicyclist to have made the ascent of Pergamon but I wouldn't do it again, and I would advise other visitors to take either the camel or the more conventional taxi.

One good effect of this showing off, however, was that I was received with tremendous enthusiasm by the custodians of the site, who had a greater regard for bicycles than had the camel driver. After they had fed me lots of bottled water, which was expensive at this height, and made me tea, I was given a free conducted tour.

Pergamon is the most spectacularly placed city I saw in Turkey; it crowns the summit of a hill which rises abruptly from the plains to a height of a thousand feet, with a wide river sweeping around its base on either side. It dominates the countryside in every direction; a fitting site for the capital of a kingdom that at one time included all of Western Asia Minor. It dates back to at least 2000 BC. and is known to have sent men to fight in the Trojan Wars, though it had no real significance until the Fourth Century BC, when an extremely clever eunuch named Philetairos took advantage of the confusion following Alexander the Great's death, which was all about which of the ex-generals should have which territories. Philetairos did a lot of double dealing with someone else's money, buying friendship and alliances with the right people, including the up-and-coming Romans. As a result of all this chicanery, Pergamon became very rich and powerful and a great patron of the arts. It built up a library which rivalled the one at Alexandria and even discovered how to use animal skins for parchment, after Ptolemy, jealous for the reputation of his library, had placed an embargo on the exportation of Egyptian papyrus. This was ironic because later on, when the Romans took over Pergamon (so much for friendship), Anthony gave Cleopatra the famous library to add to the one at Alexandria.

Medicine had flourished here too under the famous Galen. I had visited the Asklepieion on the way up, to view the remains of the hospitals, sacred spring, baths, and so forth. Galen's reputation seems to have lasted a lot longer than the buildings. His writings, which included a treatise on psychotherapy, were being read far into the Middle Ages, when he was still known as the Prince of Physicians.

Temples, palaces, and other monumental buildings cover the top of the acropolis of Pergamon, and perch on terraces built into the hillside - acres and acres of marble fragments. The most famous building was an immense altar to Zeus, once covered with carvings which are now in the Pergamon Museum in Berlin. A great deal of ancient marble found its way from Turkey to Europe during excavations in the Nineteenth and early part of the Twentieth centuries. Probably it was a very good thing that they were rescued in time, as it is only in the last few decades that Turkey has become aware of the worth and importance of antiquities. Before that, priceless treasures were used for target practice, road construction, and repairing cottage walls. Now there are strict laws forbidding the export of anything remotely antique, and archaeology has become a very popular subject at the Turkish universities. Most authorities believe that there are far more buried cities awaiting excavation than have so far been uncovered; thrust a spade in the ground almost anywhere in Turkey and it seems it will strike against marble. The only problem is money. Turkey is not a wealthy country, and has to rely largely on foreign universities to undertake the expensive restoration work. A German team were working on the site during my visit, restoring the temple of Trajan. It looked very odd to see their black crane jutting out from among the colossal columns, in that setting of white marble.

I could happily have spent more time in Pergamon. I'd seen only a half of what was there, but apart from the spur of the thousands of miles I still had before me, I hadn't enough money left to pay for an hotel, no matter how cheap. So, in the late afternoon I cycled back towards the coast to look for somewhere safe and rural to sleep. I wasn't prepared to lay my sleeping bag down in just any patch of empty sand; there are few places in the world where I believe it's safe to do that, and Turkey is not one of them. Had it been so, I think I might have slept for an hour or two by the side of the road, as I felt totally exhausted with all the touring around the ruins in the hot sun coming after my rash, if heroic, climb to the top of the acropolis. Eventually I came to a turning which led towards the sea and advertised camping facilities. When I reached it I found it to be a rather grand place, on the lines of a country club, with expensive chalet accommodation. Even here they expressed no great interest in my traveller's cheques but for my very last few Turkish lire I could place my sleeping bag anywhere I liked on the grass.

The best feature of the place was the access it afforded to the sea. In spite of having cycled down the coast road, I hadn't yet had a swim in the Aegean. Now I made up for the omission and swam about and floated for a long time, watching the sky fill with feathery, pink-and-orange clouds, as the sun set between the islands of Chios and Lesbos. The salty Aegean washed away all the aches and tiredness, and I thought how sensible the Greeks had been to place so much emphasis on the healing properties of water. I still had some bread left, rather stale after two days in the heat; the remains of the cheese and olives were a little sweaty too, but it all tasted wonderful after the swim and I wished there had been more of it.

There were two young German men also camping without a tent and they suggested that we should sleep fairly close together, there being safety in numbers. It was not as cloudless and magical a night as the one in the Gulf of Edremit had been, but there were stars; and not one single television set could be heard. Tomorrow, with luck, I should reach Izmir, and be able to change some money and have an enormous meal to make up for today's short commons.

As though to prove Herodotus right in his assessment of Aeolia's weather, just before I arrived at the hideous northern environs of Izmir, it rained heavily, and I was forced to stop on the edge of the stinking, polluted waterfront to don my cape. After days of riding beside the clear Aegean, in brilliant sunshine, it came as an awful shock to hit rain and such appalling industrial pollution, both together. Izmir, Greek Smyrna, was once a famous city, celebrated for its beautiful setting along the curve of a deep indented bay with the flat-topped Mount Kadifekale forming a backdrop behind it. What attractions it once had, however, were lost in the Greek-Turkish wars of the 1920s, when the fleeing Greeks burnt down half the town and the attacking Turks burnt the other half. Now it is just a busy modern port and tourist centre, with miles of luxury hotels and, of course, banks.

I was determined not to be caught without Turkish lire again so I changed more than I thought I needed, 120 dollars in all, in two fifty-dollar cheques and one twenty-dollar cheque - I am writing these details to explain the curious and rather chilling incident which followed. The girl who dealt with my business at the bank was offhand, chatting with her colleagues while she wrote out the forms. No one spoke English so the whole transaction was conducted silently on my part. Eventually, after the lengthy process had been completed, and the forms had been checked by several other clerks, I was given my lire and I left.

The following morning, the British Vice-Consul received a visit from the manager of this particular bank. He claimed that a British subject had perpetrated a fraud upon his establishment. Producing my three cheques he told the Vice-Consul that 'the person had claimed that all three were for fifty dollars, and she had been given lire to that amount. The fraud had been discovered after she had left. She must be found and made to return the thirty dollars or the matter would be taken to the police.

It so happened that I was also visiting the consulate and, having discovered the mistake that the bank had made, had already discussed the matter with the Vice-Consul. The bank manager was seen in an adjacent room where I could hear what was said. The Vice-Consul did not at first reveal that he knew me. He asked the bank manager how it could possibly be fraud, when the amounts were clearly written in large numerals on the cheques? The manager replied that I had told the girl that they were all fifties, and as the bank had been busy at the time, the girl had taken my word and hadn't really looked. What about all the other clerks who have to check the amounts? asked the consul. They too had been busy, claimed the manager, and anyway the English woman had claimed the cheques were all fifties, and that was the point. At this the Consul revealed the fact that he had met me and knew that I didn't speak a word of Turkish.

I would have thought that this would provoke some sort of apology, but not a bit of it, the manager replied to the effect that everyone in the bank would swear that I had spoken in Turkish and the police would believe them.

It seemed curious that the manager of a bank would admit so openly to a willingness to commit perjury, when he was accusing me of fraud, especially over such a small sum. I also wondered why he could not just have admitted that his bank clerk had made a mistake, apologized, and taken his money back without all this nonsense. But it seems that is not the Turkish way. The loss of face was the most important aspect of the whole affair, and he could not possibly admit to being in the wrong. He wasn't even prepared to meet me and conclude the matter there and then, but hurried off  muttering threats about what would happen if the money was not brought back to the bank that day.

Later a settlement was reached over the telephone: the Vice-Consul had said firmly that we would come, with the excess lire, but that we must have a written apology concerning the accusation of fraud. This was agreed, but when we arrived at the bank, at the appointed time, the manager had gone home, indisposed, and an assistant was left to do the honours. As a final flourish they tried first to extract more dollars instead of  accepting the excess liras, and when that failed, they tried to claw back a little more than was due, by working it out at a different rate. Still, I was only too relieved not to have been flung into a Turkish gaol.

# Chapter Eight

*All with one voice for the space of about
two hours cried out,
Great is Diana of the Ephesians.*
Acts 19

I left Izmir with no regrets, my first impression of it remaining unchanged. In spite of its claim to having been the birthplace of Homer, I wouldn't rate it worth a detour. Perhaps as ancient Smyrna it had been a better place; and in St Paul's time, when it was one of the Seven Churches of Asia, it got a very good write-up in the Book of Revelation; better even than Ephesus, to which I was now heading. My visit had been, perhaps somewhat coloured by the incident with the bank and by the stories of police callousness and general corruption, which I had been hearing from some of the British community there. The Vice-Consul's account of the murder of the young British cyclist, which I had been first told of in Istanbul, had happened a few miles from Izmir, and was particularly unnerving. The police hadn't even bothered to inform the British Consulate of the incident, and the Vice-Consul had learnt about it only by accident the following day, when he saw it reported in a newspaper. When he had arrived on the scene, he discovered that the boy had been very brutally killed, while putting up what looked like a spirited defence, for there was a tuft of his assailant's hair clutched in one hand. After the killing, the boy's throat had been cut from ear to ear and his possessions rifled. All this had happened in broad daylight, in a busy holiday village, and yet no one had apparently intervened, nor had there were any witnesses. The impression I gained was that the case was being pursued with no great energy because the boy was a foreigner, a non-Muslim.

Pondering this incident rather than concentrating on route finding, I became totally lost in the backwaters of Izmir, going up and down many quite unnecessary hills until I lost all sense of direction and had to be rescued by a taxi driver, who kindly led me back to the correct road. After that, I was out of Aeolia and into neighbouring Ionia, and all my gloomy thoughts just evaporated in the clear air.

The further I travelled from Izmir the happier I became. A good road led me inland, to cut across the neck of a promontory towards Ephesus, passing through the prettiest countryside I had yet seen in Turkey. Stands of pine trees, cypresses, and silver birch were dotted about the rich fields, with ruins of castles on the flanking hills.

On the way I was invited to another melon feast by people travelling in a lorry convoy - the modern equivalent of a camel train. Like many Asian vehicles, Turkish lorries have a high incidence of mechanical failure, so they travel in convoy for mutual support. One of the drivers was keen to know what I thought of Turkish men in relation to Greek men. As I had spent only a few hours in Greece I was able to get neatly out of that potential minefield. I was all too aware of the fierce hatred of Turk for Greek, which is why it is not as easy as it should be to visit the Greek islands which lie so temptingly close to the Aegean coast. Another driver informed me that his brother was at Sheffield University and did I think it was as good as Oxford? I found it altogether a much more challenging exchange than my usual café conversations.

Lunch, which I had at one of the cafés built to serve the coach trade, was served by a young lad, bursting with pride because he could speak enough English to take my order. I think the café was a family business, as the older men there appeared equally proud of the boy's linguistic ability. Many Turkish boys work at an age which would be illegal in Britain, but watching the skill and enjoyment with which they carry out their tasks, it is hard to think of them as deprived, especially in relation to so many of our unemployed and aimless young. The boy suggested that I should have meat stew, with aubergines, and potatoes fried in thin, crisp slices as a side dish. It was perfectly delicious and with beer and bread it came to less than a pound. I wasn't permitted to tip; instead they knocked about 2p off the bill with a flourish of the biro, and I was invited to a complimentary cup of Turkish coffee, which I drank while the waiters stood around nodding their approval of Evans.

I had done only a few more miles when again I was beckoned to come and exchange the compliments of the day, this time it was in a spot where two men and a women were resting under the shade of a tree. They had small piles of tomatoes, peppers, and melons beside them, for selling to passing motorists. It was pleasant to sit for a while out of the hot noonday sun, sharing tea from a thermos flask, with these hospitable people. It was also my first face-to-face encounter with a Turkish country woman; back-views, bent over the crops, were all I normally glimpsed, though occasionally one of the younger women would take a swift, sideways glance at me. This woman looked as though she had lived a hard life, and it was difficult to guess her age from her lined face and gnarled hands. But there was humour in her twinkling, brown eyes, and I think she must have been very attractive when she was young. We took it in turns to drink tea from the single tulip-shaped glass, while we tried to learn something about one another.

We had to converse in mime, because apart from the Turkish words for 'I am English', I still wasn't making much headway with my Turkish phrase book. This was not just on account of my natural lack of talent at foreign languages; the phrases in the book were also not much help, especially in my particular circumstances. Such commands as 'Tell the maid to bring my bags here', 'The mechanic is to inspect - the carburettor, the magneto, the gasket, etc.', or 'Take me to - the nightclub, the casino, a better hotel', expressed nothing for which I had a need, except perhaps the last; but then, I went everywhere on Evans and I didn't need to give a taxi-driver orders in Turkish or English. There was nothing in the book like, 'This is my wife.' 'We live in that house over there'. 'Are you married?' 'Do you have children?' Which was the sort of exchange I was normally involved in. Fortunately most of these ideas can be put over without words, as we did on this occasion, with lots of laughter and enjoyment, as is always the case when inventive gesture takes the place of words. They were delightful people and the wife didn't act at all in a downtrodden way. I would have liked to have bought a melon before I left, but I knew that they would have refused my money and made me a gift of whatever I wanted. It can get very hard, being always on the receiving end of generosity.

Because of all this kindness I arrived at Ephesus hours later than I thought I would, and found that all the rooms in the little village *pansyon* had been taken, and only roof space remained. Sleeping under the stars in hot dry weather, however, was no hardship, especially with the use of a reasonable washroom and pleasant people with whom to share the space.

A very tall young Texan, Jed, who had been one of my roof companions came with me next day to visit the nearby ruins of ancient Ephesus, where we found his six foot six height to be of great advantage in picking ripe figs from the trees which grow among the ruins, wonderfully refreshing in all the miles and miles of hot marble fragments.

Like many Americans, Jed was almost totally ignorant of European history, and was glad to 'string along' with someone who could explain a little of what it was all about. I was very glad of his company, not least because he was one of the few people who didn't make me feel over-dressed. The many hundreds of tourists flocking off the coaches seemed to be mainly intent on seeing how much flesh they could expose at any one time; age or shape making little difference to this urge. Turkish men flocked there too in droves, to stare at the more attractive bottoms peeping provocatively from beneath the briefest of shorts. The whole site was a curious mixture of frivolity and fretfulness. In earlier times the town had been full of fountains and shade to refresh the inhabitants. Now there is just the unrelenting sun beating down on unprotected, sweating bodies and reflecting off dazzling marble.

Children whined as they were dragged unwillingly along, protesting that they wanted to go back to the beach. Women tottereing precariously along the worn marble roads of the ancient Roman city in their stiletto-heeled, open-backed shoes; resentful of the stares of the Turks, were complaining loudly about having come there. Only the men, vast, reddening stomachs shaking with indignation at their families' moans and ingratitude, preserved an offended silence.

Ephesus is the showpiece of all the ruins of the Aegean and, not unnaturally, is on the itinerary of every package tour. In August it is difficult to see the place for the tourists. Nearly all European languages can be heard in the streets, as they would have been in Roman times; this being the capital of the Roman province of Asia. It was also a great pilgrimage centre, long before the Romans took it over from the Greeks, for it contained one of the seven wonders of the ancient world, the Temple of Artemis.

With all the restoration work going on there, among temples, baths, theatres, and houses, the ruins of Ephesus are beginning to rival those of Pompei. An Austrian team were busy rebuilding one of the monumental entrances to the agora while I was there. The work was obviously costing the Austrian authorities no small amount, but the notice telling visitors all about it, had prominently displayed in very large letters the information that the Turkish authorities were kindly allowing the Austrians to do this work. One of the archaeologists who saw me puzzling over this sentiment, told me that they themselves hardly saw it that way, but were forced by the Turkish authorities to put up the notice with that precise wording.

What I liked best at Ephesus was the theatre, which was a little way off the beaten track, and so not as beset by visitors. I sat there trying to imagine what it was like in St Paul's day. There is an account in Acts 19 of his visit here in about 60 AD. It is all about how the craftsmen and tradespeople of Ephesus got fed up with St Paul preaching Christianity, and attacking the making of graven images. The craftsmen of Ephesus had been making their living for centuries out of the statuettes and cult objects of Artemis - the Roman Diana - which they sold to the pilgrims, and here was this man Paul threatening the livelihood of every temple craftsman in Asia, as well as decrying the magnificence of their great Temple of Diana-Artemis. They got very worked up about it all and rushed off to the theatre to have a protest meeting. From there on, the account reads very like some sittings of Parliament today: 'Some cried one thing and some another, for the assembly was confused and for the most part did not know why they were come together.' A man named Alexander had tried to restore order, but because he was a Jew, no one would listen, and the whole assembly had, apparently, sat there for two hours, shouting, 'Great is Diana of the Ephesians.' I could certainly feel sympathy for their case. After all, it can't have been pleasant for them, having their skills despised and their security threatened; not to mention being told that every-thing they had believed in up to then was all rubbish. St Paul was not always the most tactful of men, which was probably why his followers hadn't allowed him to go to the theatre to address the protesters in person.

St Paul won in the end, of course, and by the time Christianity was the official religion of Rome, the great

Temple of Artemis had almost vanished beneath the silt of the River Cayster. It was entirely lost for centuries until an Englishman, J T Woods, rediscovered it in 1869. Now one short column stands in a sea of dried mud, with a few scattered drums from other columns lying forlornly around it, and Turkish children drive cattle across what was once the sacred inner sanctuary. In its heyday it must have presented a magnificent and awe-inspiring spectacle, being four times larger than the Parthenon, and having 127 columns, sixty-five feet tall, the whole building constructed in marble. No wonder it was rated equal with the Pyramids. Like them it had many centuries to reach perfection for worship at this site goes back to the eighth century BC. and was originally in honour of the Anatolian Cybele, the great earth mother. The more male-orientated Greek religion gradually replaced Cybele with Artemis. Some interesting early statues of the Anatolian Artemis are in the museum; they have triple rows of breasts to  emphasize her fertility aspect.

Jed was particular intrigued with details like the ruts in the marble streets of Ephesus, caused by the passage of Roman carts, and by the dice games scratched into marble surfaces. 'Gosh, how about that?' he kept intoning with suitable reverence. And such things can indeed be more thrilling than great, impersonal buildings, because they touch the quick of simple, everyday life, so that suddenly, for a moment, the people who made the marks seem quite real, and history is now and a part of our world. I enjoyed being accompanied by so responsive a young man; his enthusiasm reminded me of my own son, flown from the nest for some years now. Jed was also very useful at keeping away pests, for sad to say the tourist influx had made many local men rather pushy, and it was not unusual to see them trying to put an arm around the waists of unaccompanied female visitors. All this, coupled with the endless supply of fresh figs from the branches, which lesser men could not reach, made me quite sad when I saw him off on the afternoon bus, *en route* for Cyprus.

In the late afternoon, I rode Evans up the side of a very steep mountain to visit the shrine of what local legend claims is the final resting place of the Virgin Mary. There is quite a lot to support the idea that Christ's mother was brought here by the Apostle John, after the persecutions in Jerusalem following Christ's death made prime figures of the movement especially vulnerable. St John is also believed to have died at Ephesus. The Byzantines certainly thought so, and built an enormous basilica over his tomb, a church which, alas, is now in ruins.

'The House of the Virgin' is on a spot which had, for centuries before Christ, been associated with the fertility cult of a virgin goddess, known variously throughout the ancient world as Marion, Merriane, Mary the Egyptian, and other similar variations. Her symbol was the moon or a scallop shell. The confusion in people's mind over the Virgin Mary and the Mary of the older cult worried the Byzantine Church so much that in the interests of orthodoxy, they banned the reverence of Mary from the liturgy for a while. I don't know what the Church's official position is on this particular shrine, but it attracts a great deal of devotion from Muslims and Christians of all shades of belief, though I do not fully understand how the former manage to fit the idea into the Islamic notion of women.

It was eight kilometres to the top of the mountain where the House of the Virgin stands, and if Mary did spend the last years of her life there she must have been a strong old lady, for it was all I could do to ride the unladen Evans up to it. In one sense, at least, Mary must have been a woman of extraordinary strength, for how else could she have borne all that terrible, crushing pain and suffering? The superb Greek concept of Mary as 'the container of the uncontainable' had, I realized, another dimension that included the sorrow with the Godhead. Western art seldom portrays that strength, Mary seems always to be depicted as very young, rather timid, naïve even. Byzantine painting on the other hand, more often concentrates on the maturity and the awe-inspiring quality of the Mother of God, as she is described in the Mary Litany, which uses words from the

Song of Songs - 'Terrible as an army with banners' - to express something of this awe and wonder and mystery.

Thinking about Mary took my mind off the climb and I was almost surprised when I reached the summit and discovered how high it was. The views of ancient, broken battlements marching for miles over shaggy hills, with the turquoise sea beyond, were beautiful but remote. It was very peaceful and quiet up there, even in the shrine, which was just a simple, small and rather dark two-roomed house with a plain altar in one corner and a nun sitting quietly in another. Outside were terraced gardens and delicious water from sacred springs, and I was surprised how much I liked it there, for such places often set me on edge.

After the bustle of tourist-besieged Ephesus, the remaining Ionian cities were a pure delight. They were not on most coach party routes, and so could be explored in peace. The first one, Priene, remains my favourite Greek site in all of Turkey. It has a lovely setting, high on a hillside above the Meander Valley, and when it was founded it was even lovelier, for then the sparkling Aegean lapped about its walls. Now nine kilometres of rich soil lie between it and the coast, for over the centuries great quantities of silt have been brought down by all the rivers that drain into the sea along this coast, and the sea has moved ever further westwards. Cut off from its vital sea trade early on, Priene's importance dwindled, and no succeeding cultures have been built on top of the fifth-century Greek city, which makes it unique. It was an orderly site, constructed on a grid pattern, with straight roads running east and west, crossed at right-angles by smaller, stepped roads going up and down the hillside.

What I most wanted to do was to climb up to the top of the acropolis and look at the plan of the city from there, but unfortunately one of the guides who had been sitting at the entrance where I had left Evans had followed me up. I suppose, with so few visitors about, guides had to take what opportunities came their way, even solitary cyclists. But I was not at all happy about hiking up a rough, lonely mountain-side with this man on my heels, so I hung about the city, dutifully following the guide through all the notable places, until some other visitors showed up, and I could get away. He did not go off happily with his tip so perhaps it wasn't enough, but then I had not asked for his services and no one really needs a guide at Priene anyway, as it is quite easy to find one's own way about.

After he had gone, I enjoyed it much more, which is often the way; very seldom does anyone else want to spend as much time at the things which interest you, whereas they'll spend ages looking at other things which you find not at all interesting. Apart from the companionship and having someone to fend off importunate guides, it is really more satisfactory to look at ruins and similar things alone; whereas eating, swimming, going to the theatre, and similar pursuits are often the better for the presence of a friend or two.

One of the special things at Priene was the very lovely small theatre, or rather odeon, which had, incidentally, the base of a water clock that used to stand where the orators could see it, so as to be reminded not to go on for too long. It had the usual rows of curved seating and one or two throne-like chairs for the most important people. Although mainly used for civic matters, I could imagine intimate plays being staged there to small select audiences. Certainly the riotous assembly at Ephesus could not have occurred in such a place, it was far too civilized. My most abiding memory of Priene, however, is of five slender columns against the peerless blue sky, with lizards sunning themselves at their base. This was all that was left of the Temple of Athena, the archetype of all Ionic temples, and the most outstanding building that Priene had ever possessed. Alexander the Great had paid for its completion when he had passed that way with his armies in 334 BC, on condition that his name went on the dedication stone.

I didn't make the climb to the top of the acropolis, as the sun was by this time hot enough to make me content to sit in the shade of the trees which were growing out of the wall of a small church - the only Byzantine building there. Had the cicadas not been making such a din I might even have fallen asleep. As it was, I decided to retire to the restaurant which I had noticed near the entrance.

Water is what makes the difference between pleasure and purgatory in these southern latitudes. The Greeks and Romans built elaborate fountains and nymphaeums of marble; with aqueducts to carry ice-cold water to them, from the high mountains. The modern Turks make do with scraps of piping and lumps of old rubble, to contrive similar amenities on a less elaborate scale. This restaurant was typical of their ingenuity in low-cost comfort. It was called the Waterfall Restaurant and the waterfall had been achieved by utilizing a twelve-foot-high section of brick - probably the remaining side of a defunct house. The water ran down this wall from perforations bored in a length of galvanized piping balanced precariously along the top. It ran into a shallow concrete tank (painted blue) which had a rail of the same piping all around it. The rail had also been perforated so that jets of water arched over the tank; and around its edge were plants and greenery growing out of the usual oil cans and old paint tins. It possessed a certain rustic charm, helped considerably by the riot of greenery which had spread over many of the surfaces, including a beautiful, inch-thick algae on the wall itself. Anyone visiting Priene should eat there, for delicious kebabs are served, and the soothing splashing water provides a tenuous link with the Priene of antiquity.

It is only about fifteen kilometres across the flat alluvial plain to the next city of the Ionian league, Miletus. I made heavy weather of it in the heat and once again regretted my folly in drinking beer when I still had work to do. The trouble is that the Turkish lager - they call it *Efes*, their version of Ephesus - is so refreshing and thirst quenching that I often had a mental image of it as I rode. I could see the cool drops of moisture running down the outside of the bottle in my mind's eye, and the thought acted as a spur to my flagging energies. So whenever the chance arose I ordered an *Efes* almost automatically.

The heat was so intense that even the women picking cotton in the fields along the way were taking a rest. It was nice to see them the right way up for a change rather than bent over like hairpins. They were having a tea break and laughing and larking about. When they saw me several of them jumped up and waved for me to come and join them, but I didn't dare stop, because of still having a lot of ground to cover.

I could see Miletus a long way before I came to it, because like all ancient Greek cities it had originally been built on top of a small steep-sided hill, an acropolis, which was easy to defend. As I was wheeling Evans along the badly broken entrance road a man came towards me carrying a large basket of figs. Without a word he filled my handlebar bag with them, nodded and walked on.

Miletus was the main city of Ionia, far greater than Ephesus, in fact it was once the most influential of all Greek cities; philosophy, mathematics, astronomy, and architecture flourished, and students flocked there from all over the Greek world. It is reckoned to have established at least a hundred colonies around the coasts of Asia Minor, which accounts for the very wide influence of Ionian culture. The Miletans were a people who asked impractical questions, like, 'What is the earth made of?' but were not content with mythological answers, making them, in one sense at least, the first modern men.

The theatre at Miletus is simply enormous, with seating for 15,000, but it is all that is left in any reasonable state; the rest just mouldered away for centuries in the marsh left by the silting up of the harbours. It is being drained at last, and I was able to ride Evans down the street of the inner port, but I didn't choose to explore further afield because of the quantities of vicious thorns that were growing in profusion.

My final objective in Ionia was the great Temple of Apollo at Didyma and to get there I had to call on reserves of energy to ride Evans up from the plains and onto the skirts of Mount Labadadagi. There used to be foot races from Miletus to Didyma during their festivals. Twenty-two kilometres of tough hilly ground; no easy course, as I could testify. Homer sang of these athletes and of the whole delightful festival and of the grace of the 'long-robed Ionians with their swift ships and great wealth'.

I was helped on my way by the workers returning from the fields. The women rode in trailers pulled by tractors, as many as thirty to a trailer. Most of them looked as tired as I felt, and had little energy left for waving. By trying to keep in front of the tractors, or overtaking the ones ahead, I managed to get up a little more speed. At one point the road came down to a pretty bay of clear, inviting water, but I thought I had better not stop to swim in case I used up the last of my remaining strength. Instead I cycled on and came at last to the small Turkish village of Yenihisar. With no warning at all I turned a corner and facing me was a colossal, classical structure with the sun going down behind it in a sky of pink and primrose - an extraordinary and splendid finale to a day spent amongst so many ancient splendours.

I sat at a café across the way drinking a beer with some Germans and Americans who had also been touring the ruins of Ionia; our-paths had been crossing and recrossing all day, and we had exchanged a few words here and there. Even though they had travelled by car they professed themselves totally exhausted, and couldn't think how I managed to keep going in the heat. I didn't attempt to convince them that it is really less exhausting by bicycle than by car, as few people are prepared to believe this. Didyma was a strangely happy place, and everyone there said they felt an unusual contentment, which couldn't be just the beer. No one talked much, we just sat drinking and watching the people passing in the square, while the sun cast ever longer purple shadows across the ruins.

That night I slept in a simple, whitewashed room overlooking the temple from the other side; in a pretty pink *pansyon,* built on the outer wall of the temple and having lots of bits of masonry from it in the tiny garden. Most of the village houses had, in fact, been built from temple masonry, which gave the place a unified appearance, rare in Turkish villages. In case anyone feels censorious about this, I might add that many of the statues from the Sacred Way at Didyma are in the British Museum.

The temple had a mysteriousness about it in the moonlight which had not been there by day, and the two remaining fluted columns looked unbelievably tall, their tops almost invisible against the star-studded sky. The oracle here had rivalled the one at Delphi, but before the cult of Apollo had been brought here by the People of the Sea, the older mysteries of Anatolian Cybele were celebrated on the spot, and her sanctuary had been displaced by his - just as his was displaced by Christianity. By the middle of the Fifteenth Century Christianity had been driven out by Islam, in an intensity of religious intolerance that had no parallel in the pluralistic ancient world. Nothing seems to have advanced either religion's ideal of unity since then, and both their positions seem to me as unbridgeable as they ever were.

# Chapter Nine

*Phebus the sonne ful joly was and cleer;*
*FuL lusty was the weder and benigne.*
Chaucer

In spite of an early start I found the heat quite burdensome as I retraced my tracks over the western skirts of Mount Labadadagi, only to have to toil up its other side, in order to make for Lake Bafa and the beginning of the long eastward stage of the journey. The small squiggles on the map, so easily overlooked, meant hours of hard climbing; I didn't relish the prospect. Looking back at this particular morning I realize that I was over-tired and in need of a rest day. I'd been going hard at it since Istanbul, and had made no allowance for the steadily rising temperatures as I had come south. But as so often happens when the body gets tired, the mind also works less efficiently, finding spurious reasons for the discomfort and totally missing the real cause. I made very heavy weather of the climb, wondering the while whether cycling was such a pleasant means of travel after all. Evans certainly didn't seem to be helping; he felt more like a dead weight than a responsive and lively companion.

In this thoroughly disgruntled mood, I hauled myself up the last of the slopes, dripping with perspiration and ready to drop. No sight other than the one that met my eyes, as I wiped them clear of the salty sweat, could have been more welcome. Before me lay an enormous lake, its clear and placid water mirroring the jagged peaks of Mount Latmos, which rose abruptly from its farther shores in austere splendour. Although the first sight of all this water was quite breathtaking, it was its immediate practical use, rather than its beauty, that lifted my heart. In no time I had found somewhere to don my swimming costume and was in the water and fast recovering my enjoyment of life. Further on I came to a restaurant at the water's edge and had a belated breakfast of cheese, olives, and tomatoes, followed by bread and the delicious honey for which the region is famous.

From the restaurant a boat goes across the lake to the romantic site of ancient Heracleia-under-Latmos, which some people consider to be the most fascinating ruins in all of Turkey. I think perhaps I do too, although I did see them under perfect conditions, which always colours one's view of places. Slowly approaching across the still water, we passed small islands on which the remains of Byzantine churches and monasteries stood. More of them lay drowned on the lake-bed, but were still visible beneath the water. The ruins themselves were not particularly special, it was just the lovely setting that made them such a unique experience.

When the city of Heracleia was first established, it was a coastal city built on the shores of the Gulf of Latmia. The silting up of the city by the same River Meander which had ruined both Priene and Miletus had completely cut off the inner end of the Gulf, forming a freshwater lake over twelve kilometres in length. Legend has it that Endymion, the shepherd boy with whom the moon fell in love, lay here in the perpetual youthful sleep imposed upon him by Zeus.

The early Christian anchorites who settled here in the Eighth Century decided that Endymion was really a mystic saint, and one of the many tombs which litter the hillside was thought to contain his remains. Each year, on his special day, monks would open the coffin, whereupon the skeleton was said to sit up and sing the sacred name of God, which the moon had revealed to him during their love-making.

I spent most of the day at Heracleia, just lazing in the shade of the trees near the lake, and swimming from a beach littered with marble columns and sarcophagi. Before it was dark I returned to the restaurant having decided that I would spend the night in the nearby camping place, which was charmingly sited in an olive grove. I didn't find any other tentless campers to gang up with for security, so I waited in the restaurant until there was no one around, before laying out my mat and sleeping bag in an inconspicuous place. Evans was under cover, where he had been all day, as a guest of the kind managers of the lakeside restaurant, so I didn't have him to worry about. I thought I probably would not sleep, having had such an inactive day, but in spite of that, and of feeling a little guilty about breaking my resolve (for the second time) to be under cover before dark, I had hardly had time to admire the beauty of the stars before I was waking up to a fresh dawn.

It was a significant point in the journey, for I had now made my ninety-degree swing and had turned my back upon the Aegean Sea. I would still have the sea somewhere close on my right, but from now on it would be the Mediterranean Sea. It felt strange to be riding straight into the path of the rising sun, when for so long I had started the day with it on my left. It also helped to emphasize the fact that I had passed into another region. Asia Minor has always been split up differently, depending upon who was in power. I was now in Caria of antiquity, but still in the Roman province of Asia. At the time of the First Crusade I would have just passed out from the coastal strip, recently conquered by the Seljuk Turks, and be back in the Byzantine territory. But of course if I had been a Christian pilgrim at that period, I wouldn't have been able to come down the Aegean coast at all, for the barbarous Seljuk Turks had conquered a strip ten miles wide, right around the coast from the Bosphorus almost to Syria. All the wonders of antiquity that I had seen over the last weeks, the areas of St Paul's labours and the growth of the early Church would have been denied me. No wonder there had been a lot of support for the First Crusade; I felt rather differently about it myself after seeing what I would have missed.

Caria comprised the south-west corner of Anatolia, an area which rivals Ionia in beauty, or at least Herodotus thought so, but then he was born in the province, at Bodrum. All through the morning, as I rode towards the principal city - once the seat of the Persian satraps when they were in power - I kept passing bits of Carian ruins; once a Temple of Zeus in an olive grove, and here and there a fallen column.

At Milas I had to make the decision of whether or not to visit Bodrum to see the famous Crusader castle of St Peter. It was more than a hundred miles out of my way, there and back; too much I thought, but then, later, I would be sure to regret the lost opportunity. If I could leave Evans in an hotel and take a bus . . . I was just considering the various possibilities when a smallish lorry, loaded high with straw bales, pulled up and the driver asked me in German if I would like a lift. I don't speak German, but I have enough Dutch, from having lived in Holland for a year or two to cope with basic exchanges in German, Dutch being somewhat similar. I discovered that the driver was going to Bodrum, and that there was a good place to tie Evans on behind the straw bales. It seemed to solve the problem satisfactorily, so I accepted. I didn't exactly regret my decision, though in my haste to get away from my benefactor at Bodrum I left both my water bottle and the frame of my handlebar bag in the cab.

It certainly would have been quicker to cycle, as we stopped at every café between Milas and Bodrum in order, it seemed, for me to be shown to his friends. It was a lesson in patience and also an excellent opportunity for observing Turkish fathers playing with their children, for there were

120

quantities of both at every stop, although no mothers were to be seen. I formed the impression that Turks were very loving and indulgent fathers. They always seemed to be stuffing food into their offspring, when not cuddling them; and even when the children were behaving quite outrageously, they were never chastised or admonished in any way. At one stop there was a café where the fish pond was used for dish washing, and also had dirty ashtrays soaking in it. As I watched, a sturdy young infant tottered towards the pond, dropped to all fours and drank from it; the father kept a watchful eye on the child, presumably to see that he didn't drown, but did nothing to stop him drinking the polluted water.

Between stops we proceeded at a sedate pace which suited me, for I get nervous at speeds in excess of twenty miles an hour. The strain of trying to converse in German was made no easier by having constantly to express admiration for Irfan's lorry - his joy and delight - newly acquired, though at least twenty years old: *'Ein Ford aus England, sehr gut'*. It didn't look English, but that was because the inside of the cab was hung about with an amazing collection of Eastern-style plastic decorations which swung and dangled and cut down the area of vision considerably. He confessed that the many stops were not only for showing me off to his friends, but also for avoiding the police, as his lorry was grossly overloaded and Turkish police were very quick on handing out fines . This was not at all encouraging, I had visions of the whole load collapsing on top of Evans and crushing him beyond repair. Trying to concentrate on Irfan's German, however, kept me from dwelling too exclusively on this possible disaster. Irfan had spent several years in Germany as a *Gastarbeiter,* and while he was there, his Turkish wife had left him for another man. He hadn't minded much, he said, as he had another woman in Germany. When he had come home he had gone to get his son back from his wife and now the boy lived with Irfan's parents. He would return to Germany if he could, as life was better there, and he much preferred German women.

Tantalizing glimpses of marvellous coastal scenery, and of some strange little structures which looked like miniature mosques, kept reminding me that I had relinquished my freedom and could no longer stop when I chose. I also grew tired of Irfan's resolutely chauvinist approach to life, and of trying to persuade him that I was not going to spend *'ein fröhliche abend'* with him. Lifts were not for me, I decided. In future I would accept one only in an emergency, and if I made other lengthy sidetracks, it would be by bus.

Bodrum appeared before I finally lost my temper in trying to persuade Irfan that I really did mean *'nein'* and not 'maybe'.

The tedium of the journey was at once dispelled by the first sight of the charming little port. Bodrum stands on the south-western corner of Turkey, where the Aegean and the Mediterranean meet, a significant point for defence . The alleyways of small, flower-bedecked and whitewashed cottages around the water front have an air of prosperity which comes from the booming tourist trade. The sponge-fishing boats in the harbour are heavily outnumbered by sleek yachts and the atmosphere on the bustling quays is all very cosmopolitan; more reminiscent of Antibes or St Tropez than of the places I had seen on the Aegean coast. At the end of the peninsula, the Greek island of Kos is just a stone's throw away. Sweeping round from Marmaris at right-angles to the coast is another slender peninsula, over seventy kilometres long, which comes to within twenty kilometres of Kos. Beyond is Rhodes and other, smaller Greek islands, all forming a natural shelter for Bodrum as well as creating a superb panorama: a fitting setting for the *Odyssey*.

The Crusader castle towers above the little town and, having recently been restored, is very much as it was in 1402 when it was built by the Knights Hospitallers of St John of Rhodes. It never saw much action, for the Crusades were virtually finished by then and it was more than a hundred years since the last of the Christian armies had been expelled from the Holy Land. This marvellous castle was to fall to the Ottoman Empire a hundred and twenty years later, when they had also captured Rhodes, forcing the Knights of St John to their last stand on Malta, while the Ottoman armies swept on through Europe and all of Christendom trembled.

What is particularly fascinating about St Peter's Castle is that it has a strong flavour of the Greek about it, which softens the grim quality of a building constructed primarily for strength. This is because the quarry which supplied the building materials was, originally, another of the seven wonders of the ancient world: the Mausoleum of Halicarnassus. It was the Persian satrap Mausolas, whose name became synonymous with grand tomb-building, who made Halicarnassus the principal city of Caria. Work started on the grandiose scheme during his lifetime, along with other schemes for an enlarged and glorious empire. He died, however, before most of his ideas could be realized, and his sister, Artemisia, who was also his wife, employed the four greatest sculptors of the Fourth Century BC to finish the Mausoleum. The result was the most enormous and, reputedly, the most beautiful tomb ever built.

Alexander the Great spared the Mausoleum when he expelled the Persians from Halicarnassus, although he destroyed most of the city. For the next seventeen centuries, it stood there slowly falling into disrepair, in a city which never regained its importance. It didn't suffer the fate of many great buildings of antiquity until a temporary, local victory over the Turk had allowed the Knights Hospitallers to seize a footing on the mainland. They then demolished the Mausoleum and used the worked stones to build St Peter's Castle. Some of the discarded bits were later excavated by Sir Charles Newton and the British Museum gained the two colossal statues of Mausolas and Artemisia and many of the fine friezes.

What wasn't built into the castle or shipped to Britain has been incorporated into the houses and gardens of the town. This gives the place tremendous charm, but it also brings home something else - the vexed question of nations owning archaeological treasures acquired in countries which would now like to have them returned.

It is, of course, doubtful that many of these treasures would even exist now, had they not been bought or collected by people like Lord Elgin and Sir Charles Newton: the Parthenon, after all, was used by the Turks for storing gunpowder. Vandalism is as old as mankind, and what is not protected quickly becomes broken or covered in graffiti. European collectors have, at the very least, preserved some of the treasures of antiquity for everyone's enjoyment. Those in London can be seen without payment, and perhaps one day they might even be the focus of some unity between the Greeks and the Turks, when the latter join in the passionate Greek pleas for the return of their marbles.

When I was returning from this little deviation I realized what I had missed by coming down this peninsula on a lorry. I think it must have some of the loveliest coastal scenery anywhere. Unfortunately for me, the best views strike one from the other direction, so I had to keep stopping to look behind me, like Lot's wife. Unlike her, I was not changed into a pillar of salt, even though I felt like it at times, as my face ran continuously with perspiration and I had to keep taking dips in the adjacent sea to keep my temperature down.

I discovered that the curious little mosque-shaped buildings were really cunning water-storage tanks, with half their depth below the ground. Close to, I could see that they were designed to catch the rainwater which flowed over the domes onto the projecting walls. These sloped inwards and directed the water through narrow slits into the tank. Presumably the dome also helped the cooling process as well as preventing evaporation. There was a small, low entrance and steps down to the water, which was as cold as that in a deep well. They were wonderful examples of simple technology, seemingly quite ancient, but although they were still in use, I suppose piped water was gradually replacing them. They were dotted about everywhere, sometimes miles from the nearest habitation, and I found them good places to sit and cool off, when no other shade was available.

Of the next stage of the journey, I retain a strong sense of tremendous and almost overwhelming forces of nature. I found it was in some ways the hardest region of the Turkish coast, a very rugged and sparsely-inhabited land. The temperatures created the biggest problem as they were higher than I had expected for this time of year, which was now well past the peak of summer. Progress was often a matter of riding through the barrier when the body claimed it had had enough. There was no alternative: I couldn't stop for a rest where there was no shade, and as long as I kept bicycling there was air flowing past, which helped a little. I kept reminding myself that no matter how high the temperature rose, it could never reach the terrible levels I had struggled through on the Northern Indian Plains; and as I had survived there, I could survive anything. Apart from counting blessings, when the need arose, I also worked on a system of rewards, looking forward to the next drink of warm water or a piece of fruit, at predetermined intervals.

After a couple of days, however, I became almost impervious to the discomfort because the surroundings were so splendid. Even in the heat of the day I was conscious of how happy I was to be there. My only real feeling of dissatisfaction was that the heat created a haze, which cut off the distant prospects of sea and mountains, leaving me yearning to know what lay beyond the nearer ranges and the fringes of the turquoise sea.

Evans gave little cause for complaint; after two thousand miles I had still not had a single puncture - I added this to the list of blessings, together with the fact that not a nut or a bolt had worked loose, that the wheels were still perfectly true and all the moving parts were functioning as they should. Nevertheless, I did worry about him because the strange creaking and clicking noises kept on occurring from time to time, and I couldn't quite accept the theory that this was his way of singing. One easily diagnosable fault which he did have, however, was of keeping my hands permanently black, so that I was in a serious dilemma about shaking hands with the people I met. This was not exactly his fault, being due to the foam rubber padding on the handlebars which perpetually leaked black dye which no amount of scrubbing could stop.

During this stage of the journey I met no Europeans at all, and spoke only to the occasional Turk who knew a few words of English. My most frequent human contact was with shepherd boys who would spot me approaching and run down from the fields to beg cigarettes or bonbons from me as I passed. They looked a rough lot, and I was always a little apprehensive in case they inadvertently caught hold of the bicycle and had me off. In fact they were perfectly harmless, and once I had been instructed in how to answer them they returned to their goats with no fuss. *'Yok'* was the one word I needed to learn; it is used for 'no' but means literally 'it does not exist'. Turkish being a complicated language, however, the word must be preceded by a slight upward toss of the head and a click of the tongue, and all that needed a good deal of practice before I got it quite right. Toss, click, *'Yok* bonbons.' Toss, click, *'Yok* cigarettes.'

Before leaving Izmir I had consulted the tourist office about my route and about any difficulties I might be likely to encounter. The consensus of opinion had been that I should have great difficulty in finding accommodation on this stretch of the journey and they had advised me to go by bus. They were a little touchy about cyclists anyway, because of the recent murder. The lady who was handling my enquiry said that such things did the Turkish tourist trade no good at all, adding darkly, that lying films like *Midnight Express* did even more harm. I told her that I had not seen this film and had absolutely no intention of being murdered, if it could possibly be avoided. Both these pieces of information seemed to present me in a much better light and she and her colleagues became more helpful.

After looking at all other alternatives, they agreed that the coast route was the best all-round choice. There was now, they thought, a surfaced road for most of the way; but their lists of accommodation were pathetically devoid of entries between Milas and Fethiye, about two hundred miles of mountainous terrain. One person decided that the best thing they could do to help me was to have a letter written in Turkish asking villagers along the way to find me somewhere to sleep, in the event of being totally stuck. This letter was duly written and I had it carefully stowed away for emergencies. It was addressed to the headman of the village, the *muhktar,* and told how I was a bona-fide traveller, with own sleeping bag, and asked if I could be taken to the schoolmaster, or to someone else who knew English, and would he arrange somewhere safe for me to sleep.

I didn't need to use this letter, however, at least not on this particular section of the journey, as 'otels' of sorts were to be found at suitable intervals. It transpired that the sort of places where I was prepared to stay did not appear on the tourist office lists. As long as there was a door to close I think I would have slept anywhere; probably I would have slept even without a door. After twelve hours out in the sun - eight of them pounding up and down mountains and four of them swimming or looking for shade - I felt I could happily have slept for the other twelve. It was all I could do to get through the evening chores of washing my clothes, and myself, and dusting down Evans, while I checked him for any loose or malfunctioning parts, or for flints stuck in tyres. Writing my journal and reading were daytime pursuits, as there was never enough light from the low-wattage electric light bulbs to do these things after sunset.

The biggest hardship I found was starting off without breakfast. Few of the hotels I stayed at served meals at all, and even had they done so I doubt they would have been keen on giving it to me at five a m, which was about the time I usually set out. Sometimes it would still be dark and I'd have the dynamo on, riding along in my own cocoon of yellow light. These were magical beginnings to the day, as the skies ahead gradually lightened and colour built up in bands of pinks, greys and orange. The cut-out shapes of shaggy mountains would begin to separate from the general blackness and grow ever sharper. From behind one of them, a thin sliver of intense light would appear and grow slowly into an enormous red sphere. No matter how carefully I watched this drama, there came the moment I always missed, when the sphere separated itself from the mountain and leapt free into the sky, flooding the earth with colour. Although I know intellectually that there is no sudden movement, that the whole thing is a gradual process, I also know that many times in Turkey I almost saw the sun leap free of the mountains, as though Apollo's horses had lengthened their stride.

I carried supplies of food with me in the form of dried fruit, which I could munch in lieu of breakfast, as I rode. I also carried lots of water, as the sign of the blue tap was scarce on this coast. Mineral water in plastic bottles was available in the towns and I found I could squeeze one of these into the cage which had held the water bottle I'd left on Irfan's lorry, and have another tied on to the luggage rack behind. But the sweet, milkless Turkish *chay* was a lot more refreshing than this warm mineral water, and I never passed up the opportunity to stop and have a glass whenever it was available. Once I was invited to *chay* at six a.m. with four young Turkish holiday-makers - *Gastarbeiters,* who had stopped to brew up by the side of the road.

There were hardly any antiquities between Milas and Fethiye, as the road is a recent form of communication in these parts and does not pass through the centres of ancient civilization, which were nearly all on the coast. Until recent times, ships supplied the only method of reaching these coastal towns and villages. The account of St Paul's journeys in Acts shows how very efficient sea transport was in Roman times, with frequent interconnecting ferry services enabling him to pass up and down the coast at an average speed of about four knots; much faster than I could travel on my infinitely more circuitous route. Now alas, the buses and motorcars reign supreme, and all the local coastal ferry services have vanished. Until a few years ago it was still possible to go from port to port, all the way around Turkey from Istanbul to Iskenderun. The map I was using showed these routes, and I had thought I might travel this way for a few stages, where there were interesting antiquities at the sea's edge. But the tourist office informed me that the routes had been  discontinued for lack of use.

St Willibald had also been compelled to travel this stretch by road. This seems to have been because he ran out of money after arriving by ship at Ephesus. He was very taken with the great Basilica of St John the Evangelist, which must still have been standing then, and a most marvellous building. Characteristically, he gives us no details of it. He even came upon two anchorites at Miletus, living on pillars like St Simon Stylites, but he merely records the fact with no further comment. A man of few words he might have been, but he was certainly a hardy one, walking this rugged terrain, with no money left for food and shelter.

I was eventually very glad that I had chosen the coastal route, and had ridden through the wild land of Caria, which had yielded such different delights from the archaeological feasts of Ionia. For the best part of a week it had been the land itself, and the sea around it, which had supplied the main focus of attention, and I had experienced not a moment's boredom. The continuous riding with few stops had done me good, and I felt fit and strong.

Then came the moment when, after spending an entire day riding over the peninsula at the end of the great mountain range of Golgeli Daglari, I climbed the final slope and saw an immense, island-studded bay below, fully fifteen miles across, with natural breakwaters and shelter for a thousand ships. It was the Bay of Glaucus, the principal port of ancient Lycia, and named for one of Homer's heroes who had led the men of Lycia to fight for Troy in the Trojan Wars.

# Chapter Ten

*Sarpedon and the peerless Glaucus led the Lycians,*
*from distant Lycia and the swirling streams of Xanthus*
Homer

To have reached 'distant Lycia' made me feel that I had come half-way around the world, even though the arrival itself was something of an anti-climax. Fethiye, built on the ruins of ancient Telemessus and rebuilt again after a strong earthquake in 1958, is rather a grubby little town. It is nonetheless very popular with Turkish holiday-makers and with the flotillas of smart sailing boats which are hired out to British tourists, who sail about in these waters from Bodrum to Antalya, drinking large quantities of gin and tonic in order to stay cool. This does not work; you stay just as hot, but no longer care so much about it, as I discovered when the crew of one of these modern, fibre-glass homes-from-home invited me aboard for drinks. They kept the gin in five-litre demi-johns, and told me stories of the riotous times they had ashore, in expensive restaurants, falling into swimming pools, or pushing headwaiters in, instead. Among all these jolly G and T types, I found it hard to picture the 'black hollow ships' of the Lycians assembling here to sail off to the Trojan Wars. On the other hand Homer often mentions the tossing back of a bowl or two of the dark red wine of the country; so on second thoughts, perhaps they would have had lots in common with the yachties and have got on splendidly.

I had the utmost difficulty in finding somewhere to stay for the night in Fethiye, as the four-day Muslim feast celebrating Abraham not sacrificing Isaac was about to happen. It is the most important Islamic festival in this part of the world and, like Christmas in Australia, Turks apparently are keen to celebrate it on the beach. I traipsed all over the town, but everyone who had a room to let was not interested in hiring it to a single person; most squashed as many beds as they could into every corner. Eventually I found a *pansyon*-restaurant which had a vacancy, a sort of cupboard behind a kitchen, where there was hardly space enough even for one bed. This was let to me as a great favour, though it cost far more than I had yet paid anywhere in Turkey.

I took advantage of the hosepipe in the courtyard to wash down Evans and all the panniers, as everything was very dusty after the ride through Caria. Perhaps there is something erotic about a woman washing down a bicycle, because when I had finished, the manager of the *pansyon* made a formal proposal, in French, of spending the night with me. I turned him down, equally politely I hope; but must admit to being intrigued by the practical difficulties which would have arisen from trying to squeeze two people into the minute space of my bedroom, especially when one of them was of generous proportions.

There was nothing to keep me in Fethiye beyond a single night. The only antiquity left there is the necropolis - the city of the dead - and that was on my road out of the town. Lycia has always been known as 'the Land of Tombs'. Like many ancient races, the greatest architectural creations of the

Lycians were monuments and dwelling places for their dead. Where the Greeks achieved immortality through the songs of praise singers like Homer, the Lycians' memorials were the elaborate tombs in which they buried their heroes and chiefs. Some of these were chambers carved into cliff faces with elaborate façades. Others were sarcophagi with cottage-roof-shaped lids, often covered in pictorial relief and mounted on high pillars.

I was just making my way towards some of these cliff tombs, which could be reached by a series of steps, when my attention was caught by a small boy who was lying down in the middle of the road, having a temper tantrum. A young woman came out of a nearby house and scooped the child up just as I drew level. She called out to me in English asking if I would like a cup of tea. It was one of the few times when I did not want a drink, having just had breakfast with a group of people on one of the holiday yachts. I needed moreover to get on the road as soon as possible as it was a very long way to the next small town. There was something strained in this young woman's face, however, and a note of desperation in her voice, which made me accept her invitation and go with her into her dark and gloomy two-roomed cottage.

Her name was Ayesha and she did indeed seem rather desperate. She was an Armenian, married to a Turk, and her neighbours wanted nothing to do with her, she told me, so she lived in a state of dreadful isolation. All her family were now in America, where she had spent some years before returning to marry the Turkish boy whom she had known since childhood. He worked throughout the summer as a waiter in Kas, a town two hundred miles away. So, for months at a time, she talked to no one but the child. I asked her why she didn't go out for walks along the seafront. She said it was clear I didn't understand life in Turkey; women went out only to shop or hang out the washing; if they were out just walking, then they must be prostitutes. Her neighbours already disliked her because she was Armenian; they hated Armenians worse than the Greeks, she said, and were always finding ways of hurting her or letting her know that they despised her. Her loneliness poured out in a great spate of words, while her sullen little boy wheedled and whined for attention. He would receive first a hug and then a reprimand, there seemed to be no consistency in her treatment of him, though it was obvious that she loved him deeply, passionately even. She said the children in the street would not play with him because their parents forbade it. At the time I suspected that it was more probably a case of him proving an unpleasant little bully. He was kicking and pinching me whenever his mother's back was turned and, while I felt very sorry for him, it didn't exactly endear him to me.

I thought the isolation and the sense of rejection which they were both suffering were probably exaggerated, and as much Ayesha's fault as her neighbours'. I didn't know then about the continuous persecutions and massacres which the Turks had perpetrated against the Armenians since the Fourteenth Century, or how deep seated was the antipathy between the races. So many Armenians had been wiped out between 1894 and 1896 that Europe had been moved to protest. Yet in spite of this, in 1915 when Europe was busy with the First World War, Turkey took the opportunity to launch the most devastating pogrom against the remaining two million Armenians, reducing them through mass murder and death marches to a mere handful. It is a very nasty page of Turkish history, and one that shows the ruthless streak in the national character. In the light of this knowledge, I feel even sorrier for Ayesha than I did when she was pouring out her unhappiness. I have thought of her often since and wondered what became of her: it is almost impossible to think of a more unworkable combination of mixed marriage, except perhaps between Greek and Turk.

I stayed as long as I could, but simply couldn't accept Ayesha's plea to sleep the night there. After four hours of being used as a sponge to absorb her loneliness and frustrations, coupled with the child's resentment of my presence, I was desperate to get out of the claustrophobic little house. Even with most of the day gone, I felt I must get on my way. The little boy was outside when I was unlocking Evans. He was in a garden where there was a coop of young chickens; he had the door open and was throwing stones in at them, slamming the door to after each throw to prevent them escaping. I felt as though I was running away from a situation I couldn't handle.

It soon became clear that there was unlikely to be anywhere to stay before Kas, which was still a hundred kilometres off, so it was on this day that the letter from the tourist office found a use. I tried it out in a busy village called Essen.

When I stopped there in the main square, by the bus stop, I feared I would be squashed by the inquisitive crowd that gathered around. But order was soon restored and someone who spoke English was thrust forward to talk to me. Chairs were brought and drinks were ordered and another, younger man, who also spoke English joined us. I showed them my letter and competition ensued as to where I should spend the night. The first man to read the letter said I should go to the house of his uncle who lived in the next village and who had a son studying English in the university; this was obviously the right place for me. The young man thought I should go to his house in another village, for his sister also spoke English, and I would feel at home there. I would have preferred to go with the young man, who seemed a nice, quiet type. But the older man, who was rather bossy, appeared to be deeply offended by the idea, so in the interests of peace and good village relations I thought I'd better accept his offer. He wrote a short note to his uncle on the back of my letter and off I went with all the men in the village square waving a friendly farewell.

I found the uncle's house about five miles further on. He was the village storekeeper and he welcomed me with a formal handshake after reading both sides of the letter. His house looked as though it was in the process of being built or demolished, I couldn't tell which. Two women were labouring away in a sort of outside kitchen, vaguely roofed over. They smiled shyly as I was brought up and then carried on with their work. An early model of washing machine was pumping out dirty water directly onto the dirt floor, which had already been churned into mud by people and animals walking through it. Flies attracted to the damp ground and to the animals buzzed busily around everywhere. A cow, a couple of calves, a sheep or two, and a goat were tethered in close proximity. One woman busied herself cooking something on a primitive open fireplace against a wall, the other woman squatted on a rug picking through a pile of tobacco leaves. No one spoke English, but there was a boy of about eleven there who, I discovered later, was called Birol and was the schoolmaster's son. He was quick to guess what I might be needing; like a lavatory and somewhere to lean Evans out of the sun and the mud. I was led me off to a rather noisome midden in the garden but was called back by the younger of the women, whom I now saw to be a pretty girl of about sixteen, bundled up in layers of shawls, petticoats, and long skirts. She led me to an Asian lavatory inside the house.

The house looked a lot better inside, not that I could see very much. The front opened into a wide tiled corridor, with two wooden doors leading off on both sides. The glimpses I got as I passed were of simple, rather bare rooms so perhaps the family were in the process of moving in. At the end of the corridor were two small rooms, one the hole-in-the-floor-type Asian lavatory, and the other a simple washroom. I was really desperate to have a wash, being sticky with dried perspiration, but I was hurried outside again so as the girl could return to her work.

Birol, and my host's son, Demit, a youth of great conceit but a frightful dunce walked me up and down the village street. It was Demit who was supposed to be studying English at university, but whatever he had been doing with his time there, he certainly hadn't spent it learning English. We walked up and down for some time, and I formed the impression that the village men stayed out until the womenfolk had completed the day's labours, and had prepared the evening meal. I think the men were glad to have a little diversion while they waited. I must have shaken hands with every adult male in the village and with some of the younger ones too, and still we walked up and down the village street.

One by one the men drifted home, but not until nightfall was Demit or I allowed into the house. Then it was shoes off, a ceremonious pouring of water over my dye-blackened hands, and into supper. What I really wanted was a wash. Somewhere private with a bucket of water would have done quite adequately; I'd learnt to bath this way in India and it would have been as welcome as a Hilton luxury bath suite in my hot, sticky condition. I'd expressed this wish to Birol several times in mime and, clever boy that he was, I knew he'd understood the message and had passed it on, but nothing in the washing line had materialized.

A cloth was spread for the evening meal on the carpeted floor of a pleasant, whitewashed room in which were two modern divan beds, a sideboard, and a television set. On the cloth a low, round table was placed, with various dishes upon it. Everyone sat round the table, cross-legged on the floor, with the 'tablecloth' over their knees. Each person had a spoon and a pile of flat round cakes of unleavened bread, with which to dip into whichever dishes took his fancy. There was soup, yoghurt, olives, green beans with tomatoes and macaroni cheese. It all tasted good, but people ate with a speed and concentration I was unused to, and they were all finished long before my appetite was satisfied.

No sooner was the supper table taken out than village men began to troop in and take their places cross-legged on the two beds. Television was switched on and the room began to fill with smoke from home-cured, locally-grown tobacco. It was an interesting but also a very trying evening. The blaring television would have been bad enough, but in addition everyone wanted to ask me questions, via the dunce. With the help of my phrase book and Birol who, thank goodness, returned half-way through supper, I think we managed somehow to answer most of the questions. They were all variations on the 'How do you like Turkey?' theme, with a few references to the fact that the English had 'made the mistake of going to war with them once' - 'no hard feelings, of course'. The pretty daughter was a help too and seemed possessed of an intelligence far in excess of her brother's. She got out her old school books to assist in the translations, and it was plain to see that she could have made a better use of further education than her brother was doing.

I was reminded of a conversation I had had with a young man in a café earlier in the day. He had been to university, and now had a good job in a bank. I had asked him if he was married. He'd said no, none of the women in his village was suitable, as they were all field workers. He agreed that none of the girls got the opportunity for other than basic schooling, but was unable to connect the two facts in his mind. He couldn't see that education for girls would have provided him with a suitable wife, and was convinced that women worked in the fields because they chose to. In other words it was the natural inferiority of the female, inherent in all Islamic teaching, the doctrine of 'and treat your women well for they are with you as captives and prisoners; they have not power over anything as regards themselves.'

Rounds of tea came and went, but the evening didn't end until television did. The last half-hour was all military display and patriotic fervour, reminiscent of pre-war fascist propaganda films. I was relieved to see the villagers sending it up, even the Imam, who was somewhat simple-witted, I thought, and a butt for the heavy humour of the other village men. I hadn't known he was the Imam at first, as no priest in Turkey is allowed to wear religious apparel outside his place of worship.

When the party broke up, only the mother (who seemed to have the lowliest position in the whole house and was treated with what I can only describe as contempt), the daughter, and myself were left in the smoke-filled room. The mother immediately lay down on the floor and the daughter threw a heavy cotton quilt over her. She put another quilt on one of the beds for me and took the second bed herself. Neither mother nor daughter had removed a single item of their many- layered garments, so I didn't either, but lay down fully-clothed and unwashed. It was not the best preparation for a comfortable night's sleep, but I doubt that

I would have had that anyway, because the farm animals seemed to have no idea that it was night-time. The calves bleated, the sheep baa'd all night, and the penitential goat, doomed for the knife in the morning to celebrate the Feast of Abraham, kept up a wild keening from where he was staked just outside the window, about a foot from my right ear.

I was up and away as soon as anyone was stirring in the morning and made my thank-yous and farewells practically in the dark. With the aid of my map I set off to find the first available body of water in which belatedly to wash. I was early enough to risk a bathe in the 'swirling streams of Xanthus', without shocking any locals. The relief of washing my skin free of the layer of dried salt reminded me once more of the importance that water had in the Greek world. It made me feel a lot closer to their culture than to the one I had just shared for a night. Which was no bad way to begin a visit to the city of Xanthus itself, which was, according to Homer, the oldest and most important of all the Lycian cities.

I saw it under ideal conditions, early in the morning, before the heat made it unbearable, and without anyone at all around to frighten off whatever ghosts might be there. I sat in the middle of the theatre, facing the empty stage and the agora beyond, and ate a breakfast of cheese and olives and small green grapes. It was so quiet that the large black lizards which are seen only among ruins ran freely around the seats. The place had a familiar air about it: for some pieces from here, including the very finest pillar tomb in Lycia (a replica of which is now restored to its place in the agora), I had often seen, together with sketches of the ruins, in the Lycian Room of the British Museum. It was like being inside a well-known picture which hearing, scent and touch had expanded into a wider experience. It didn't need ghosts.

The Xanthians were a fiercely independent people; twice they destroyed themselves and their town rather than be captured by invading armies. The first time was in the Sixth Century, when the Persian armies of Cyrus the Great conquered all of Western Anatolia. Herodotus recorded the event:

*They fought with much bravery though they were greatly outnumbered. At length they were defeated and forced to withdraw within their walls; at which they collected their women, children, slaves and property and shut them up in the citadel of the city and set fire to it, so that it burned to the ground. Then they marched forth to confront the enemy and were slain to the last man.*

When Brutus was besieging the city for the Romans in 42 BC, the Lycians repeated their ancestors' action and again the city and everyone in it was destroyed. Plutarch claimed that Brutus wept whenever Xanthus was mentioned after that. But Brutus seemed to be more heart-broken by the bravery of the men and the destruction of property, whereas I would have thought that it was harder for the women, slaves, and children, who seem to have had no say at all as to whether they wished to be burned rather than captured.

Just as I was about to leave the theatre, two young men arrived to set up a mobile refreshment bar under a rustic structure of poles and leaves. One of them, who was about sixteen, came and spoke to me in French, asking if I had seen the nearby necropolis and the Byzantine church. I hadn't, because my guide book had said the place wasn't very good and was covered all over with thorns. Neither of these things was true, however, as I discovered when I agreed to let the boy guide me, while his older brother kept an eye on Evans - we put him under the rustic shelter to protect the tyres from the heat.

It was well worth the slog over the neighbouring mountain-side to see the tombs and the cunning way that any rock there had been adapted and carved into one or more burial chambers, just where it stood. What made it all doubly enjoyable was the knowledge and enthusiasm of the courteous young guide. The French had been responsible for excavations in this area in the last few years, and he, apparently, had made himself useful around their camp. In the process he had learnt their language and had developed a passion for history. Needless to say he was hoping one day to join the growing army of Turkish archaeologists.

In the ruins of the Byzantine church he scraped the protecting gravel from various places to expose fragments of mosaic floor - rabbits playing, a tortoise, a woman's face - all superb little pictures. He was careful to cover them over again, for the sun would bleach the colour out of them if they were left exposed. At the end of our tour he told me with some dignity that he accepted tips only from groups; individuals he escorted for pleasure and interest, because he might learn something new. I didn't think I'd had anything to add to his knowledge, so I treated him to one of his own soft drinks instead.

The heat had been increasing relentlessly with each mile east I made, just as it had done on the leg south. Every slope was a gruelling effort and, no matter how much of the warm mineral water I drank, I felt   permanently thirsty and dehydrated. There were not many villages on this barren stretch of land, for which I was grateful, because for the first time in Turkey I encountered hostility from small boys throwing stones at me as I passed. This was probably to do with all the slaughtering of goats which had been taking place that morning. Every family which can afford it buys a sheep or a goat for the Feast of Abraham; these are ritually killed and the headless bodies are suspended in trees to drain. I think that all the excitement had stirred up the boys to an unwonted display of aggression. Fortunately I wasn't hit, but I didn't dare stop anywhere for a rest, even to see the ruins of Patara which had been the port for Xanthus. I had meant to make the detour to see this ancient site because Willibald had spent the winter there after his long walk from Ephesus. St Paul had changed ships there too on his final visit to Jerusalem, but I was somewhat comforted for missing it on being told that the ruins were very overgrown and unimpressive.

After struggling up an enormous promontory ridge, on which I was convinced I should finally expire, I was suddenly overlooking an island-studded sea again; and for the last thirty kilometres to Kas, I rode among some of the most magnificent coastal scenery in Turkey. It was so lovely that I even forgot the heat and thirst for a while.

Nonetheless, when I reached Kas, it took several beers and bottles of cold mineral water before I felt remotely human again. I drank them, sitting at a waterside restaurant, overlooking the crescent-shaped  harbour of the prettiest seaside town I had yet seen in Turkey. A Lycian sarcophagus was perched on the sea wall, a few more were scattered among the streets and the squares of pretty Greek houses strung in ascending layers about the steep mountainside. Many of the houses were *pansyons* and I had no trouble finding a room to hire near the sea front.

Kas was an excellent place to rest up for a day or two; there was fine swimming from rock platforms, lots of company, and trips to some of the ruins which can be reached only by boat. Actually, I didn't manage to get to these ruins because, although I had booked for the trip, on the morning in question the skipper failed to make an appearance, due to an over indulgence of the local spirit the previous evening. Whilst waiting, I met two Irish girls who had booked for the same abortive trip. I had been escorted to the boat by a young, importunate Turk who promptly transferred his  attentions to one of the Irish girls. They, poor things, had no hope at all of evading his company, and he became quite a problem, following them about everywhere and trying to pay for any refreshments they were having. Sometimes he'd turn up in the middle of a meal, assume he was welcome, and then try to pick up the bill at the end of it. The girl he had attached himself to was soft-hearted and couldn't bear to have him hurt by an outright rejection. So they carried on, getting more and more exhausted from the struggle of coping with his English and with resisting his attempts to take them over. In the end they decided to pack up and go before it wrecked their friendship and their holiday.

The atmosphere amongst the European tourists was as casually friendly as it had been in Istanbul. Turkish men found this difficult to cope with. Whether they were local men or visitors, they quickly became proprietorial, thinking that after drinking a coke with someone they had become life-long friends. The presence of European girls they found particularly difficult, because none of their own women would ever be seen alone on the streets, and they could not hope for any sort of relationship with girls before marriage. I stayed in Kas for only three days, but during that time many young Turks enquired if I knew where one or other of the Western visitors had got to. They were very hurt when they discovered that their `friends' had left town without a goodbye. There are times when being older is a blessing; and as far as I know, I did not become the object of anyone's undying friendship in Kas.

Continuing the journey meant clawing my way up the mountainside against which the town shelters, and dragging and pushing Evans for about fifteen kilometres along a steeply ascending road in the first stages of construction - all loose boulders and sand. I couldn't ride any of it, and I think it was one of the hardest sections of the journey, especially considering the heat and the choking clouds of dust thrown up by any passing vehicles. If the motor traffic had been more than just occasional, I doubt I would have made it. Once the tarmac started again I was too grateful even to make my usual inward complaint about the paucity of the tar coupled with the generosity of the chippings, which causes a bicycle rider such danger and discomfort. At about lunchtime the road started a downward trend back towards the sea, passing along the top of spectacular gorges and the edges of plunging depths. For almost an hour, I just sat on Evans while the wind rushed wonderfully and refreshingly past my face, and I had nothing more energetic to do than apply a little pressure to the brakes now and then, and to lean into the sharper corners. This was the reward for all the earlier effort.

At the end of the descent was Myra, which had also been an important Lycian town and had very good rock tombs, a Roman theatre and much else of that nature. But for the moment I had seen enough Lycian ruins and was more interested in finding lunch in the nearby modern village of Demre. One place I had to visit first, though, was the shrine of St Nicholas - Father Christmas - who had been a bishop here in the Seventh Century. After he had been martyred by Arab raiders, and subsequently sainted, his bones became an object of pilgrimage. In 1087 some Italian sailors from Bari came and stole the bones, just beating the Venetians to it. By the end of the Crusades there was hardly a holy relic left anywhere along these Mediterranean coasts, for they were a most marketable commodity. I found no record of Willibald coming here, but I cannot think that he would have missed the opportunity to worship at such a special shrine when he spent the winter so close to it. Moreover, this was the only other place in Lycia where St Paul is known to have set foot; once again it was only to change ship. This was during his last journey of all, when he was under escort and on the way to his trial in Rome.

Today's ruins are well restored; Eleventh-Century Byzantine, and built over the original sixth-century structure. It wasn't anything special except for the associations, but I was intrigued by the insistence of the guide that the bones of St Nicholas are still there in a Byzantine sarcophagus.

Lunch proved to be at least as memorable as the ruins, partly because it was so unexpected. After riding right through Demre, which took about three minutes, I despaired of finding anywhere suitable. Having cycled for six hours on no more than a handful of walnuts and a few grapes, the body must have something, so I chose the least repulsive looking of the eating places and started to lock up Evans. I don't always do this, but here I was suspicious of the local boys, who swarmed around him like bees around a honey pot. Before I could complete the job, however, out of the chosen restaurant came another boy, who, after shooing away the crowd, took Evans and wheeled him inside. I was then taken into the kitchen to select what I would eat, before being led out through the back door into a sort of meadow. Here every one of the town's three restaurants had their main eating areas, the tables set out under vine-shaded pergolas. There were cloths on the tables and it was cool and quite clean and a greater contrast to the grubby fronts than could be imagined. During the meal the young waiter brought me a notebook and pencil with the request that I should write down some English words for him to add to his collection; he already had separate lists of French and German words.

The last day of the Feast of Abraham was also my last day in 'distant Lycia'. I spent it on a beach of fine shell sand which was too hot even to step on without shoes. I had been invited to share the barbecue of some English-speaking Turkish people. So I stayed there all day, swimming in the totally clear water and feasting on huge quantities of beef, mutton, and goat's meat, baked aubergines, salad, and pitta bread. At times I felt energetic enough to explore the ruins scattered about in the woods, which came down almost to the sea's edge, providing shade from the burning sun and fuel for the barbecues. It was more like finding seventeenth-century follies scattered in a sylvan setting than exploring an ancient city. Fragments of aqueducts, the portico of a classical temple, tombs and columns seem to have been planted there already in ruins and mere enhancements to the natural beauty of the scene.

# Chapter Eleven

*Ware the sonne in his ascencioun*
*Ne fynde yow nat repleet of humours hote;*
*And if it do, I dar wel leye a grote,*
*That ye shul have a fevere terciane,*
*Or an agu, that may be youre bane.*

Chaucer

Contrast is a great thing in a journey. The thought of something different to look forward to can keep flagging energies from giving out entirely. Wonderful though the mountain scenery of Wild Lycia was, there were times when the thought that ahead lay the flat 'piratical plains' of Pamphylia, was all that kept me going. There had been places on the remote Lycian peninsula where the existence of any sort of path had seemed nothing short of miraculous. For mile after mile the road had clung crazily to precipitous mountain-sides, at times ascending almost vertically, to cross great peaks, like Olympus, where I could push Evans for only a few yards at a time, before I needed to rest. After such herculean endeavours flat plains, with a civilized city at the start of them, were something to anticipate with pleasure. In the meantime I struggled on, as Alexander and his army had done before me. There is no record of any other army having covered this ground before or since, which is just one more example of the brilliance of that young Macedonian at getting his men to achieve the impossible.

Within sight of the 'civilized city' of Antalya, however, I knew I was going to wish myself back in beautiful Lycia. The contrast was too great. Continuous beaches, many with unattractive, shanty town camping sites on them, together with all the modern amenities of brash cafés, churning out 'Cha wawa wawa, I love yew, Cha wawawawa, really I dew' music in dreadful polyphonic distortion, were painful to both ear and eye. The city itself presented a depressingly Western appearance of high-rise, rectangular concrete structures; though the setting was magnificent, at the head of an enormous bay of great natural beauty, fringed with white sands and with the Taurus Mountains towering theatrically behind it.

It is not a particularly ancient city for these parts, having existed since only the Second Century BC, when the need for the Kingdom of Pergamon to have a port on the Mediterranean brought it into existence. The Romans used it later as a base for Pompey to deal with the pirate menace, which flourished all along these Eastern Mediterranean shores. Having been in continuous occupation since it was built, there is very little of the Hellenic or of the Roman town left, except for some ancient walls and a rather grand, triple-arched gate which was put up to impress Hadrian, when he visited these parts in 130 AD. I liked it best around the harbour, where the steep twisting streets of old Turkish houses are gradually giving way to smart restaurants and hotels, built to accommodate the increasing tourist trade. With direct flights from Europe and Britain, Antalya is fast becoming the tourist centre of Turkey's Mediterranean coast.

The French section of the contentious and ill-managed Second Crusade arrived at this port in 1148 with what was left of their forces, after being seriously harried by Turks in the hills along the way. In many respects the Second Crusade was the least attractive of tall the Holy Land Crusades, and it achieved absolutely nothing. It was called because the new Kingdom of Jerusalem, established by the First Crusade, soon found itself in difficulties and needed a constant flow of military aid from the West to maintain its position. Unless the whole coast of the Eastern Mediterranean and a good deal of the territory to the east and north of it could be controlled, the new kingdom had little hope of becoming a permanent self-supporting nation. All the Crusades after the first one were really just rather desperate attempts to shore up a crumbling edifice.

Conrad III had led the Germans, and Louis VII the French, accompanied by his wife Queen Eleanor of Aquitaine (later to be divorced and married to Henry II of England). Rivalry between the French and the English kings was reflected in the hostility and bitterness between their two armies. Much of the German strength was dissipated in separate sorties, and the remnant of their forces retired to Constantinople to await ships to the Holy Land. Louis decided that he would take ship from Antalya, and avoid the long march around the coast. Unfortunately, not enough ships could be found, so first the King with his entourage, and then the rest of the mounted nobles, sailed away, leaving the foot soldiers and the pilgrim band they were escorting to make their long march to Antioch without protection. It would be the route of this leaderless force of the Second Crusade that I would be following from here.

The museum of Antalya was well worth a visit, I found, even though it was not yet completed. Only the outside gardens were open, but the wealth of exhibits on display was more than enough to show the culture of the five cities of the plains of ancient Pamphylia, very different from that of Lycia, for Pamphylia had always been a rich area, yielding heavy crops, as was clear from the elaborate carvings on the many excavated sarcophagi and the abundant statuary and decorative friezes - no one can afford to pay artists and craftsmen unless their lands produce a surplus. Three of these ancient city sites lay along my route and I looked forward to exploring them. They were so close together that I should be able to see them all in one day.

While I was wandering around Antalya, looking at the empty mosques and crumbling fragments of Byzantine masonry, I had a sudden shock, coming without warning upon two bicycles, unmistakably British, locked companionably together against a railing. I think I now have some insight into what Robinson Crusoe thought, when he saw the footsteps of another human being in the sand of his island. I had not seen another bicyclist since Istanbul, and not at any time on the journey had I come upon one of the touring variety. I almost rushed back to my *pansyon,* to get Evans, so that he could share in the excitement, only then the other cyclists might have got away in the meanwhile. One of the bicycles was the sort of hybrid I described earlier with its crossbar dropped down; the other was a heavy town bicycle with flat handlebars; but both were undoubtedly on a tour, as they were all hung about with pannier bags and baskets and gadgets for recording mileages and so forth. They also had flight baggage labels stuck on the saddles, so I gathered they had flown in and not come overland as I had done.

As I was taking in all these details, the owners of the bicycles arrived and I had hurriedly to explain my avid interest in their machines, before they could begin to suspect that I had dishonest designs upon them. We immediately began one of those delightful conversations, dear to the heart of all enthusiasts, full of technical matters and 'shop talk', meaning nothing at all to those not in the know.

Once the first flush of excitement and enthusiasm had moderated, and we had adjourned to a tea house to continue the conversation, it soon transpired that we were not in fact three enthusiasts, but only two. The male of the party, Phil, whose bicycle was the heavy one with flat handlebars, was about twenty-six and new to the pursuit. He was not yet a bicycling devotee, and was, in fact, suffering from many difficulties and ailments due to the inadequate preparation of body, mind and machine. The flat handlebars, which meant that his hands remained always in the same position, had given him a stiff neck and a bad case of backache. His lack of gears (he had a total of only three) meant that most hills had to be walked up, and he had thereby acquired painful blisters - a very rare ailment for bicyclists, at least on the feet. Most serious of all (and incidentally the reason for his wearing a tee shirt draped around his head, desert-patrol style), was that he had sun-stroke from riding in the sizzling temperatures of Southern Anatolia without a sun hat.

His companion, Maggie, was a little older. She made her living from bow ties, which she constructed at home and sold in venues such as the Edinburgh Festival, where I gather there is a ready market for them. She was riding the hybrid bicycle because it was all she could get at the last moment when she discovered, just hours before the flight out, that someone had removed her bicycle from the London lamp-post to which it had been chained. She had cycled in Turkey previously, as well as in other parts of the world, and was in a good position to advise Phil on how to equip himself for the 'holiday'. Clearly, he had not listened to good advice, and even then, faced with the combined expertise of two female cyclists, not to mention his painful physical condition, he was still not convinced that he had 'got it all wrong'. While admiring his courage and tenacity, sadly I rather doubted that he would last long enough to become a true enthusiast.

Later, after they had come back to my place to admire Evans and to borrow one of my guide books which, incidentally, they never did return, we spent a convivial evening having dinner and drinking the local, dark, fruity wine, carefully avoiding the by now contentious subject of bicycle design. Instead we talked about Turkey, and of how easy it was to travel there because of the kindness of the people, and they knew more about this than I did. They cycled only as long as they felt they were positively enjoying it (this would not take Phil far, I thought); after that they sat at the side of the road until someone gave them a lift. I didn't think that this method would do for me. I have no objection to taking a lift in an emergency, but if I did so the moment cycling became less than a conscious pleasure - like when yet another steep hill loomed up, or when the wind was against me - I am sure I would soon grow soft and give up travelling altogether. I am not a masochist, and I do my share of grumbling when the going is tough, but I have also found that if I want the rewards of cycling, I have to put up with some of the pains as well. It is all a question of proportion really, and of knowing my own limits; but it is extraordinary how it is possible to ride through barriers of pain and tiredness, and feel very much the better for it, both in body and spirit.

I saw Phil and Maggie several times over the next few days when our routes coincided. My last glimpse was of them sitting, squashed in the back of a jeep, with their bicycles tied on behind. I quite envied them at that moment, for the plains of Pamphylia had not lived up to my expectations of pleasant easy progress. They were hot and humid; the dust-laden wind was in totally the wrong direction, and the endless fields of the two main cash crops of Turkey, cotton and tobacco, were monotonous. Still, there was less than a hundred miles of them and the compensations were the splendid ruins.

Perge was particularly good. There were enough walls, gates, and buildings still standing to imagine what life there might have been like under the Romans. Again it was the use that was made of water, more than two thousand years ago, which impressed me most; the aqueduct, cisterns, pools and fountains, even a substantial channel down the centre of the wide main thoroughfare, all for bringing cold refreshing mountain water to every part of the city. What a difference this must have made to the citizens was obvious as one toured the now dry marble streets, wilting in the heat. Cold water becomes an obsession in this sort of climate and terrain. The presence of scores of tour parties added to the feeling of oppressive heat, as their guides rushed around, like football referees, blowing whistles to get their parties back to the coaches.

One ruin is really enough for the day, but Asphendos was only fifteen miles further on and was supposed to have the finest Roman theatre still standing. I knew I would regret it if I passed it by, so I turned off the highway and rode up the hill towards the site. All of these cities which were first settled by the Greeks are built on an acropolis - a high place. Later, when times were more settled, and particularly during the period of the Pax Romana, the cities spread onto the plains around the defended hill, but a visit to any ancient site in Turkey inevitably means ascending steep slopes.

The reward for my perseverance was finding a delightful restaurant. It was tucked away in a primitive Turkish village with a vine-hung terrace, overlooking the historic Eurymedon River on which, in 486 BC the Greeks won a famous double victory over the Persian armies. The meal I had here was interesting in that it was served by a young girl, and I had been waited on only by boys and men up till then. She didn't speak any English but was quick to understand what I asked for. She seemed an affectionate child and very inquisitive about everything I did.

I had already met some Pamphylian children in the theatre at Perge. They had come running down the tiers of seats with their goats, who were feeding on the scant foilage among the stones. All the children had ancient coins and marble fragments for sale, and my immediate thought had been that piracy was still very much alive in Pamphylia. Nowhere else had I been offered illegal merchandise. The penalties for taking any antique things out of Turkey are dire and, although these coins were probably fakes, the children assumed a suitable air of secrecy about their trade. On the way up to Asphendos I had been waylaid by some older boys who had tried very hard to direct me in the wrong direction, over a graceful Seljuk bridge, for who knows what nefarious purpose. They were definitely a roguish lot, but possessed of tremendous charm, and I wished I could have had some conversation with them.

The little girl at the restaurant gave me a bunch of flowers, carefully chosen with no two alike, and walked beside me, holding my hand, to where I had left Evans. I gave her a biro pen, at which she jumped up and down in great delight and yet still managed to convey the impression that she was sad to see me go.

There were more young pirates in the stunning Roman theatre of Asphendos, a suitably imposing building with a two-storeyed façade which served as the backdrop to the stage, as well as providing the sort of amenities that are found backstage in a modern theatre. Greek theatres had no such façade but were open to the countryside and more a part of the landscape. The Asphendos children were quite knowledgeable about their coins, at least to the point of being able to say which ones were Byzantine, and which Greek; and they were not too pushy. I was able to inspect the coins, and hand them back and say they were fine (my Turkish was increasing at the rate of about one new word a day). As long as I offered a low enough price for their goods they didn't persist, but moved off to rest in the arcaded gallery at the top of the theatre, until more amenable tourists appeared.

My final encounter with Pamphylian children was with another small girl. She was quite alone, and followed me around the overgrown ruins of the acropolis where I had gone to trace the line of the aqueduct on its way from the hills. I wanted to inspect the two towers which had been erected along its length to reduce the pressure and I could see these quite clearly. I rather hoped the child would know of some good paths to follow among the thorn bushes and wild thyme, but she was new to the game of anticipating what tourists want to see and, apart from thrusting another bouquet into my hand, she hung back shyly. I gave her a small coin for her services, for she seemed a nice child and there was no question of making beggars of these children, as is the case in more primitive parts of the world. The Pamphylian children have been used to tourists for years and are well able to cope with them.

According to a praise singer called Stratonicus, the city to which I was now heading had once been filled with the most rascally men in the whole world. The historian Strabo also wrote about how this port, called Side, thrived from the pirate trade. He claimed to have seen Cilician pirates tying up at the quays and selling off their merchandise there. But no sooner had Pompey got rid of the corsairs in 67 AD, than the citizens of Side hurriedly erected a statue in his honour and so escaped retribution. Like the rest of Pamphylia, Side was never really in the main stream of history. It had a peaceful time under the Romans and the Byzantines, and was strong enough to withstand the seventh-century Arab raids, so perhaps Willibald might have put in here on the next stage of his journey to Cyprus.

I certainly had no desire to see yet another ancient site that day, but Side was the nearest place I could hope to get a bed. Covering the twenty miles there meant riding through one of the tiredness barriers I had been talking about with Phil and Maggie. There were no rewards for effort either, or at least not immediately, for finding any sort of bed proved to be very difficult, and I wandered around the extraordinary little fishing village, now expanded into a booming holiday resort, for hours before I found a kind hotel proprietor who had no free rooms, but who was prepared to make me up a bed on a balcony. An Austrian couple, whose room led off that particular balcony, also took pity upon me and gave me the spare bed in their room. By the time all this had been organized, it was quite dark and there was no question of seeing ancient Side until morning. Obsessed with water as I had been all day, however, I felt that I must swim, and accordingly made my way through the ruins to the sea with the aid of a borrowed torch. No sooner was I in the water than the skies were suddenly riven with great, jagged streaks of lightning and rain crashed down in solid sheets all around me. I hurried back into my sodden shirt and trousers, teeth chattering, cold for the first time in months.

The storm cleared the air and brought a sparkling morning in which to view the site, but even so I didn't take to it. Side is an extraordinary place, a rather vulgar holiday village, full of electronic amusement places, with a ribbon development of *pansyons* and hotels stretching three miles back to the main road, all cheek by jowl with the most extensive and systematically restored ruins on Turkey's south coast. I found the mixture of styles painful and the noise and pollution even more so, for like the British, the Turks are frightful tossers away of wrappings and other effluvia, and their preferred noise level is even higher. So although I caught tantalizing glimpses of superb bits and pieces, I rode away without exploring Side properly, promising myself to return in a quieter season.

The end of the Pamphylian plains and the start of Rough Cilicia are at the dramatically sited town of Alanya, a citadel perched over sheer drops, on top of a soaring promontory rock. It is a fairy-tale castle, with an ancient town hanging on to the steep slopes below it, enclosed by great sweeps of crenellated walls. The modern town, which is not too modern to lack charm, is at sea level and I could have happily spent a good while here, exploring it all, and strolling around the streets of the old quarter. But a sense of urgency was upon me now, for I was not as free as Willibald and the other pilgrims of those leisured times had been. I did not have years, as they had, in which to complete my journey. I had only a few months, and half of those were already gone. If I was to arrive in Jerusalem before the winter rains, I felt I must press on, especially as the excessive heat on this coast was cutting down my daily mileage.

So I spent only one night at Alanya and did my sight-seeing by taxi, to give myself and Evans a rest. Even by taxi it takes twenty minutes to reach the citadel, and that is with the driver sweeping around the blind corners with a total disregard for what might be coming down the other way. It was bakingly hot at the top and I felt quite giddy, especially looking out from the platform called 'the place from which men are thrown', which, as the name suggests, was the spot from which condemned prisoners had once been hurled onto the rocks a thousand feet below.

In spite of its impressive appearance, Alanya - ancient Coracesium - had not been of much importance in classical and Roman times. After the murder of Julius Caesar, Mark Anthony gave the city and quite a lot of the surrounding territory to Cleopatra, who found the timber from the mountains extremely useful for building her navies; timber was always the main product of these southern shores, as it still is today.

In Byzantine times, when Armenians began to establish separate dynasties, which they maintained with cunning judicious marriages into the new Crusader Kingdoms, Alanya was one of the places they took over. I would be seeing many more such Armenian stongholds as I rode on through Rough Cilicia and I looked forward to this, for the Armenians were a fascinating people with a long history.

The Armenian ancestral lands were extensive and lay south of the Caucasus, between the Black Sea and the Caspian Sea. Throughout the ages, they had been harried and conquered, successively, by Assyrians, Medes, Persians, and Romans. Many of them were displaced from Northern Anatolia by waves of early Turkish invaders, and at the invitation of the Byzantines, some of them moved south to the mountainous areas of Cilicia, which soon became known as Little Armenia. They were the very first nation to adopt Christianity. This was early in the Third Century, and for a long time Armenians were the leaders of the Asiatic Christian Church, and at the forefront of theology and biblical scholarship. After the Crusaders pulled out of the East, at the beginning of the Fourteenth Century, poor Armenia suffered continuous persecutions and annexations by Persia and Turkey, until her peoples were scattered all through the Middle East and beyond. A tiny homeland in the Caucasus, within the USSR's borders, is now all that remains to them of their once vast lands.

The first of the really fine Armenian sites that I saw was that of Anamurium, which was like a great ghost town, spread out on a hillside, looking as though it had been sacked and abandoned only yesterday. I could find out nothing about it from my guide book, or from any local sources; it is as though a great wall of silence has lain over all things Armenian until the present day. There had been some attempts to preserve certain things, like gravel laid over mosaic pavements and a roof restored over a painted tomb chamber, but the purpose of most of the structures had to be guessed at. The architectural style was very like Byzantine, but who had lived in the fine palaces or worshipped in the basilicas remained a blank. No wonder so many young Turks want to be archaeologists, there is enough work to keep an army of them busy for years. I spent a day scrambling over these ruins with two history undergraduates, Mark and Katie, who were as puzzled by their details as I was.

We were staying at the same pleasant, cheap *pansyon* near by, in a town which had nothing of note and which was not by the sea, and so had hardly any tourists. We took our meals together in the local workman's café, and it was good to have a man in the party because beer had to be obtained from a sort of male preserve on the roof of the café, given over to the serious business of tric-trac and raki drinking. I think I might have been too intimidated to run the gauntlet of the male stares had I been alone. Katie would not, though; she was more shocked than I by the total absence of women in cafés and by the down-trodden female state in general. She would not have hesitated to invade male preserves, but then the young usually have more courage in these matters. We had a really good lunch at the café, at a nominal cost; it was a sort of aubergine stew with chunks of lamb in it. When we returned in the evening, however, we found that Turks don't seem to go in for two elaborate meals in one day, and the only food available was leftovers from lunch, warmed through, which was not really so good. I made do with beer and conversation, for exploring ruins doesn't work up an appetite in the same way that cycling does. These meetings along the way added tremendously to the pleasure of the journey, indeed they were an important element of it. Travelling alone by day, taking in the sights, and mulling over experiences are fine, but at the end of the day, the ideal is congenial company, a shared meal and an exchanging of experiences. My pilgrim predecessors probably found this too; whether travelling in bands or more rarely alone, they would meet other fellow pilgrims travelling their route, or lose touch with others who stayed awhile in one place, or sidetracked somewhere else. Quite a different experience from travelling in an organized group where you are sure of company but less open to surprises.

As cycling terrain, Rough Cilicia was almost as challenging as Lycia had been. The Taurus Mountains throw out great spurs of rock, which end in beetling cliffs, high above the sea. Up and up them I toiled to quite dizzy heights, only to sweep gloriously around the corniches with, far below, a turquoise sea rushing up to meet me. Back down at sea level, by some delightful, and often, deserted cove, I could enjoy a swim and a rest before beginning on the next huge ascent. It was not surprising that over such terrain and in such temperatures all I could manage on the heavily-laden Evans was around fifty such miles a day.

I had only one real problem all the time I was in Turkey and it really came to a head on this stretch. Noise. I could no longer even sleep because of the noise. All the accommodation I found tended to be beside the road, and traffic in Turkey never ceases, day or night. The animals equally have no idea about knocking-off time. So there was an unending cacophony of night-time chatter, as dogs, donkeys, horses, cows, goats, cocks, and the occasional camel held animated conversations with one another.

The daytimes could be equally trying because of the radios and tape recorders. I'd stop for breakfast at some beach café having had an hour or two of wonderful riding as the sun rose. The moment I sat down and ordered my meal on would go the sound, full volume, blasting the birds from the beach. And always the same mindless-sounding modern popular music. The owners of these cafés and their staff were invariably kind and co-operative. I had only to ask and the machine would be switched off or turned down immediately; only to be switched on again full volume the next minute, by somebody else, or even by the same person who had forgotten what he'd been asked. All the foreign visitors complained about it, even the young ones who liked pop music, though they said they wouldn't really object so much if only some less ancient numbers were played.

If I could find accommodation situated on dirt roads with no passing traffic, that helped with the sleeping problem, but the daytime noise just had to be endured.

From time to time it occurred to me to wonder about all the unpleasant stories I had heard concerning travel in Turkey, from which it would seem that rape, robbery, and murder were commonplace happenings. Certainly many of my friends had thought this, and had expressed horror at the idea of my making the journey alone. But although I realized that there was a strong element of ruthlessness in the Turkish temperament, as evidenced by their treatment of Greeks and Armenians and other minority groups, I had received such kindness all the way that I really began to be puzzled as to how such dark stories about the Turks could ever have arisen. Apart from the one particular bank manager in Izmir, I had decided that all Turks were gentlemen. But along one of the glorious stretches of cliffs in Cilicia, I was confronted by one who was not.

I had stopped at the top of a long pull up, in order to wipe the sweat from my sunglasses, before beginning the descent, and I didn't notice the youngish-looking man who was standing by a car across the road, until he came over to me. He seemed perfectly normal and was trying to tell me something in Turkish, which I could not understand. Then he made a mime with which I was familiar and which up to then I had taken to mean 'Are you married?' This young man, however, was using it to mean that I should accompany him into the bushes immediately, and his meaning was quite unequivocal, as he then made a grab for me.

Fortunately I was still on Evans, with my right foot in the toe strap, and I didn't freeze, because I wasn't in the least frightened. I was just surprised, and then very angry. I beat off his hand and pushed hard on the pedal at the same time. He hesitated and made another grab, just too late; I was off. I heard him start the car but then the wind was in my ears and I was concentrating on the road. I don't know how long he followed me, I wasn't really that worried anyway; there are few ordinary drivers who can beat a determined cyclist on a really steep, winding descent, because a bicycle can corner much faster than a car. I had by, now, every confidence in Evans, and we practically flew. I thought there might be a café at the bottom and there was. So I sat there drinking tea and waiting for the reaction to set in, but it never did. I just felt angry that I hadn't thought to hit him with the pump. When I was quite sure that he wouldn't show up again I continued on towards the plains of Smooth Cilicia.

Because I had been pressing on so resolutely, I had reached this point in my journey somewhat earlier than I had anticipated, and as a result I felt I could afford to make a detour and spend a week visiting Cappadocia, an area which had long held a fascination for me. Accordingly, when I reached St Paul's 'no mean city' of Tarsus, I stayed there just long enough to find transport to take Evans and me up into the mountains, through the historical pass of the Cilician Gates.

# Chapter Twelve

*But Paul said I am a man*
*which am a Jew of Tarsus,*
*a city in Cilicia, a citizen*
*of no mean city.*

Acts 21:39

When I climbed down, stiffly, from the last of a succession of buses which had carried Evans and me the several hundred miles up into Cappadocia, I could not at first decide whether I had arrived in a landscape that was the origin of all fairy tales, or of all science fiction. Since the two are much the same, the distinction hardly matters. It was a wholly delightful, and at the same time, a wildly improbable landscape - a creamy-pink extravaganza of cliffs, towers, and pillars, all fantastically shaped, and interspersed with small patches of cultivation of a rich and vivid green. When I got closer to some of the cones and pillars, saw the windows and the doors in them, and realized that they were dwellings, the illusion of having arrived in a land of childhood fantasy was further heightened.

Cappadocia is the result of the abundant activity of some of the surrounding mountains when they were active volcanoes, aeons ago. The thick layer of soft lava, known as tufa, which spread all over the region, was then carved and hollowed out by wind and water into great canyons and valleys. Where there were larger harder stones in with the tufa, the softer material beneath was protected from erosion and the cones, pillars, pyramids, and towers were left, often with their protecting capstones precariously balanced on top - like elongated toadstools.

The tufa is very fertile, and abundant fruit is grown in the little pockets of ground - gardens, they are called appropriately. Often a small village of the elongated tufa toadstools is clustered around each such little plot. Hardly a soul lives in these hollowed-out rocks any longer. Most have moved into more conventional houses, and Turkish policy is to remove the few remaining traditionalists, so as to preserve the unique dwellings. I think this is a pity, as the few that are still in use as homes add immeasurably to the attraction of the place.

I stayed the first night in the small town of Urgüp, in a good *pansyon,* to which a young German trio had directed me. They were camping in a tent in the garden and I got to know them quite well. I was intrigued that one young man and two girls could get on so well on holiday; it seemed an odd combination. They were all trainee social workers, so perhaps that had something to do with it. Actually, more than half the Germans I met in Turkey were in social welfare work. I began to think that Germany must have terrible problems to need so many, but my friends told me that it was just that Germany had sufficient funds to pay for them.

With the two girls of the trio, Heidi and Helga, I spent an interesting hour or two one evening, when we visited the local *haman* - turkish baths. Thomas, their companion, might just as well have come too, in fact we wished he had, because when we arrived, on what was supposed to be the women's night, the place was full of Turkish men. We didn't know this when we paid our money and draped ourselves in the cotton sheets provided by the one-eyed man in charge. We followed him down some slippery marble steps, already feeling a trifle exposed, as one does wrapped in only a skimpy sheet in the presence of someone of the opposite sex who is fully clothed. In the dim light we found ourselves in a steamy hall, with marble benches all around the tiled walls and a low octagonal marble slab in the centre. Every one of these surfaces had a male figure reclining upon it, draped in their little sheets: Turks do not go in for nudity.

We were ushered by our guide into a small and unattractive side chamber, which had no light at all, except what could filter in through the holes in a tatty piece of curtaining which was all that separated us from the main chamber. When our eyes became used to the darkness we found that there was a marble basin full of water, with a scoop for throwing it over ourselves; we could hear the men doing this in the next room, so we understood the drill. There wasn't anywhere for us to recline, except the floor, and we did not choose to use that, even had we felt relaxed enough to do so. Instead we sat around telling stories and getting rather giggly because it seemed such a silly situation. I didn't try another turkish bath; I decided they were overrated, though possibly not for men.

I also took a conducted tour of the area with these three Germans. The tourist office organized day trips to the major sites in a minibus and, since my time in Cappadocia was strictly limited, it seemed like a good idea to join it. Apart from the extraordinary landscape, the area is of tremendous historical and archaeological interest and it would take a lifetime to see it all. The tour was organized rather well I thought; any number of persons could go as long as they could squeeze into the bus. The bus cost a fixed sum and this was shared equally among the passengers. There were perhaps too many on our trip and we were not really comfortable on the longer stretches, which led to a certain amount of friction.

Our tour was designed to give us some idea of all the different uses to which this extraordinary landscape has been put. Man has added to all the carving work which nature has affected, since earliest times. There are troglodyte cities which are built inside the gigantic cones, the whole thing hollowed out into passages and chambers, which wind through every part of it. Many later villages cluster around these primitive citadels, and these are tremendously interesting with their different layers of successive building styles. We visited one of these citadels, and a young American in our party, who was keen on rock climbing, went up the outside way and was told off by our guide, which made it a little reminiscent of a school outing. The views of the surrounding countryside were very extensive from the top and most of us would have been happy to sit there far longer than we were allowed.

We visited an underground city too. This descended by sloping tunnels to twelve layers, but I gather there are many others which go down to as many as twenty-four levels. All have air shafts, wells, and other technical innovations, and some of them have been in use up to the present century, though whether this was only when danger threatened, and the inhabitants lived in the cones when times were peaceful, is not really known. It was hard work going up and down the levels, bent double in the low corridors. There were no steps, just steeply ramped slopes, like an inside-out helter-skelter. I couldn't have lived down there, as I am not at all happy in narrow, dark places. Our young American, however, was very enthusiastic about it and succeeded in getting away from the guide and into other parts of the cave, off the beaten tourist route. It was cool below ground but out in the sun, waiting for our errant companion, it was very hot, and several of the party became a little fractious, including the guide, who blamed another, quite innocent American for the non-appearance of the adventurer. Fortunately the culprit showed up, suitably contrite, before the guide ran out of patience entirely.

It was time for lunch at this juncture, and the guide had somewhere in mind for that, a perfectly ordinary sort of place and very cheap to boot. Two German members of the expedition were highly suspicious about this; they were very pushy, not at all like my three friends from the *pansyon,* and had already caused some bad feeling by always taking the only two comfortable seats in the minibus, which were those in the front beside the driver. They refused to accept the choice of café, on the grounds that the guide probably got some perk from the management. The rest of us also thought this likely, but couldn't see that it mattered. Obviously it was a moral issue with the Germans, so we were driven to a small town instead and were suitably punished by being taken to an exhibition of extremely unattractive pottery, where we were expected to sit around in rows, watching a demonstration of another repulsive pot being constructed.

The afternoon was devoted to exploring some of the churches and monasteries for which the area is famous. Like the dwellings, these were carved out of rock faces and free-standing cones, and are quite unique and extraordinary. There are estimated to be about 150 of these churches in the area of Goreme alone, which contains only a quarter of the total number. This part of Cappadocia was the centre of Byzantine monasticism from the Fourth Century onwards; two of the early Church Fathers came from here, St Basil and St Gregory, both very influential in the theology of their day and in setting out the Monastic Rule. From the Seventh Century onwards, the hidden valleys and caves of Cappadocia provided bolt holes for escape from the Saracen pirate raids, Turkish incursions, and other hazards. Monasticism flourished here, and Christianity continued to be practised by Greeks and Armenians until the mass population exchanges in 1924, after Ataturk's victories.

Most of the churches I looked at were quite small and most were modelled on a conventional Byzantine church interior, with a barrel vaulted roof and a horseshoe-shaped apse. Some were more elaborate, with multiple domes, but simplicity was the keynote, which made the glowing frescoes, for which they are famous, all the more dramatic.

These span the periods from about 550 AD to 1200 AD, and are reckoned to be the most comprehensive collection of Byzantine painting anywhere.

Most of the paintings are scenes from the Gospels and, after one or two of them, I couldn't look at any more as they made me feel rather sick. This was because each painting had been defaced, in the true meaning of that word. The eyes or the whole face had been hacked out, and the effect was peculiarly horrific, particularly when the rest of the pictures appeared so very fine, and in such a good state of preservation. The mutilations was the work of Muslims, and although it was hard to forgive such destruction, in some ways it was easier to understand than other depredations, where visitors had scratched their names into the painted surfaces, since to Muslims such depictions are deeply offensive.

It is easy to forget what a scandal Christianity was to both Judaism and Islam. All three are Middle Eastern religions and have a common root in the Old Testament. Muslims were particularly aware of this common heritage and called the adherents of all three faiths 'the People of the Book'. For Jews and Muslims, God is totally 'other'; so far removed from man that it is unthinkable, a sin, to attempt any representation of Him. He speaks to man through a handful of chosen people; from a 'burning bush' or 'as a still small voice'. In Islam, he communicated only with Mohammed, and then only through the intermediary of an angel. To Jews and Muslims therefore God is altogether unimaginable. But Christianity has an incarnate God. In the person of Jesus Christ, God lived, suffered, died, and was resurrected on earth, in the sight of all men. So central is this to the faith, that it not only became possible to imagine God, but under this new revelation, it was almost obligatory to make images of Him, to celebrate and proclaim such an incredible and gracious act.

This gave birth very early on to all sorts of legends about 'icons not made by human hands' like the 'Holy Face of Odessa'. Such images were thought to have great power. The Crusaders' banners often carried such devices and, under them, the knights were able to fight with conviction and courage, no matter how at variance their behaviour and motivation were to the teaching those devices represented. This, coupled with the growing cult of collecting and venerating the relics of saints, convinced Muslims that Christians were heathen idol worshippers. In defacing Christian art they were performing their religious duty. Thank goodness that they so often found that whitewash did the job more tidily and easily, or we would be many glorious works the poorer.

The Jews of course found Christianity even more abhorrent than did the Muslims, as is always the case with a schism. In the eyes of Judaism, Christians were, after all, just heretical Jews. The hatred between the two found its outward expression in the terrible massacres of Jews by the Crusaders, in both Europe and the Holy Land; and in the East by the constant betrayals by Jews of the Christians. Christians never forgave the Jews for the occasion when they had treacherously opened the gates of Jerusalem to the invading Persian army of Sharhbaraz in 637 A D, when it was claimed that the Jews joined the Persians in the massacre of 60,000 Christians, and assiduously participated in the burning of the churches and the rounding up of the remaining 35,000 Christians, who were sold into slavery. Nor did the Christians forgive the way the Jews had actively helped the Arab armies overrun Palestine, later on in the Seventh Century. However, under the Arabic Caliphate, the Middle East enjoyed 300 years of peace. It seems strange now, when there is such terrible strife between Israel and the Arab world, to remember that Jews and Muslims lived in harmony for centuries.

Our tour also finished with some dissension, when one of the Australians decided that he would sit in the front seat for a change. The German couple were outraged and refused to get in, and the rest of us took sides. Not for the first time, I decided that independent travel had a lot to commend it.

The following day I explored the countryside on Evans, riding along some of the hilly, dirt roads which go on for miles, turning and twisting back on themselves, so that they often finish up in an entirely different direction from the way they started out. Whenever I stopped where people were working in the fields, a child would be sent running with a present of grapes. I went far from the main tourist area where the landscape was less spectacular, though still very strange and wonderful, passing through villages more primitive than any I had yet seen. In one of them I stopped to ask directions and was immediately taken over by some local women who had a good line in mime.

I was invited into one of the houses and most of the women of the village crowded in to have a look at me. We all sat on the floor on grubby mattresses and tea was made and drunk in turn, as one or other of the two glasses became available. The only males present were under two years of age, and crawling about on the dirt floor. The women did not appear down-trodden in this setting; they went in for what seemed like a lot of heavy banter, and were quite bawdy in their gestures when it came to miming. I thought they were great fun, except that one old lady had that annoying habit, which I had thought was the prerogative of the British: she spoke at me loudly and slowly in Turkish, convinced that if she persisted I must understand. It's amazing how stupid this makes one feel.

After a couple of days in my comfortable *pansyon* in Urgüp I thought I would take a look at the village of Uchisar and maybe stay the night there, at a *pansyon* I had heard about called Maison du Réve. I was intrigued by the description of the views it enjoyed and the 'ambience unique'. I wasn't too well at the time, being afflicted by a stomach bug, which seemed to be attacking most of the visitors. This was not really surprising as there were so many flies about and hygiene was not up to the standard it had been on the coast. I had plenty of medicine with me, so I took some and gave up eating for a while. This was a very good thing, as it happened, because I did not arrive at Maison du Rêve until it was too late to find anywhere else and, 'ambience unique notwithstanding, it was no place for anyone with an unreliable stomach. In fact it was  downright primitive, but with a lot of charm and I'm glad I spent a night there.

The Maison itself had in former times been hollowed out of the tufa hill against which, and into which, the whole village was built, in ascending layers,  culminating in an impressive troglodyte citadel. There was now a more modern façade on most of the houses, including the *pansyon,* together with courtyards, and balconies overflowing with old tins filled with flowers. It was the prettiest village I saw in Turkey.

The owner of Maison du Rêve was not from the village; he was a foreigner from ten miles away and out to make a killing. I was given all this information, the following morning, by an old man who spoke English and sold the tickets for visiting the citadel. Being so isolated, visitors were rather dependent for food, tours, and so forth on the *pansyon, and* having lured people there with cheap-priced rooms, every-thing else was double the price charged elsewhere. But as long as you only slept there it was a marvellous place, with views over one of the most fantastic gorges in Cappadocia.

There was a large cave-like room where everyone ate the evening meal around two huge, round, low tables. But I sat by the fire, continuing my abstinence and drinking *raki,* which can work either way with upset stomachs. After supper, the cooks, two slender youths, entertained us with very erotic, traditional dancing, one boy playing the female part, while the patron provided the rhythm with a pair of long narrow drums and another man played the long-necked, guitar-like instrument called a *saz.*

The normal sleeping rooms of the *pansyon* were all full and I was given a small cave, deep in the tufa hill and closed off with a wall of breeze-blocks which I found curiously horrid. The lavatories and washing facilities were also rather vile, and I took more medicine so as not to have to use the former.

Whatever minor inconveniences I suffered at Maison du Rêve, the pleasure of wandering around the village of Uchisar more than compensated for them. It was hard to believe that I had not strayed in another century. There were no roads as such, only roughly-cobbled paths, and the transport was pack horses and waggons with bowed and slatted sides. I could have used up my entire stock of film there. The people themselves are not as easy to photograph as other Asian people, particularly the women. There is a stiffness about them, and their layers and layers of clothes give them a bulky, rather graceless appearance; moreover they are particularly suspicious of cameras. The unconventional houses and little lanes are quite another matter, as are the Turkish cats, small and undernourished but tremendous characters, with indomitable curiosity and playfulness.

As I passed one old man sunning himself in the open space before his house, he called out to me, 'Allemande?' — Turks assume all Westerners are German. This can get annoying after a while, for national pride is a curious thing, and sometimes I found myself positively snapping, 'Angrezi!' ('English!') in reply. This usually happened only in towns, or in places where the carpet sellers were getting particularly heavy. This old man just wanted to be friendly and he showed he had understood my reply by singing Big Ben's tune - Ding dong, ding dong, ding dong, ding dong - and roaring with laughter at his own wit. Rather a delightful exchange, I thought, in the middle of an age-old village. He called to the women of the house to bring a chair and tea, and we sat overlooking that extraordinary landscape, raising our glasses to each other and humming a few notes of Ding dong, Ding dong, while tears of helpless laughter coursed down his cheeks. This was clearly one place where the B.B.C. World Service would be sorely missed.

From the moment I'd seen the small, hollowed-out rock cones and towers, with their windows and doors, I'd longed to go inside one, to see what the interior was like. That I should actually be able to sleep in such a place seemed too good to be true, but the opportunity came when I found a *pansyon* near Uchisar which was one such small tower, and in which a room was available. The tower had three floors and each floor was reached by an outside staircase, and consisted of one proper room, with a low window with a windowless and doorless space alongside. I had the room on the first floor, and found it everything such a place should be. To begin with, it was round, not like a cylinder, but like a roofed-over bowl, for it was hollowed out of the rock with nothing added, not even the floor or ceiling. The walls were so immensely thick that there was room to spread a mattress on the window-sill and sleep there, should one so wish. It was wonderfully cool in the heat of the day and gave good protection in the cold nights, which was the pattern of Cappadocia's weather.

Two simple beds, electric light, bright, locally woven carpets called *killims* hanging on the whitewashed walls, and a few pegs for clothes completed the furnishings. A shorter tower on the other side of the garden contained the bar, which in the evening was filled with people who were camping near by, and who came to hear the drum and *saz* music. The lavatories and washing facilities had been carved out of some low outcrops of tufa and, although not exactly nice, they were just about adequate.

The *pansyon* was run by two young Turkish men, though most of the work was being done by a British girl, Alison, who was about to be married to one of the Turks. I had quite a few conversations with Alison and came to understand something of what drew her to the life she would live in Turkey. She came from a conventional British middle-class background, and had received a reasonably-good education. Nothing had really interested her after leaving university, however, and although she had had quite good jobs, these had not led anywhere. She had come to Turkey and fallen in love, not only with her Mehmet, but also with the simplicity and the peacefulness of life in Cappadocia. The absence of obsessive material values suited her, and she found she missed none of the comforts of her old life in Britain.

I hoped the marriage would work out; clearly they were both very much in love, and Alison had a good deal of common sense; but they would need all of that, I thought, to bridge the cultural gap between them. Already pressure was being brought to bear, to bring Alison a little more in line with local culture. I thought the question of clothing and of spending most of her time with the other women would prove to be her most difficult problems.

All too soon my Cappadocian idyll drew to an end. The week had flown, and my plan to ride Evans back down through the Cilician Gates had to be given up for lack of time. Instead, I had a frightful hassle getting him put on the bus, and had to bribe countless young men, whose sole income seems derived from hiring out the space in the compartment that runs the length of the bus, under the seats. This I gather is not legal, but it goes on just the same. It was a fraught journey as I had to keep leaping out at halts to stop people from loading heavy objects on top of Evans. Once it almost came to fisticuffs, when some brute tried to force a hundredweight sack of potatoes on to the front wheel. Bicycles are very vulnerable to damage, particularly the wheels, when in a prone position. I think my moral indignation won, rather than physical force - after all I had paid more for Evans's place than for my own and these other people weren't even travelling on the bus, but just getting their produce illegally transported to Tarsus. .

I suppose it was not inappropriate to be in a fighting mood, as I was now crossing the route that the First Crusade had taken. They had stayed for a while on the edge of Cappadocia in 1097, before continuing along the upper way to Antioch, while Baldwin had made a detour down to the coast, by the route the bus was now taking. Even at that stage, Baldwin had shown his ability to lead men, which would later make him the most able of the Jerusalem Kings. He had hardly any knights of his own, and yet he was able to take more then two thousand mounted men down through the Cilician Gates to capture Tarsus. Land hungry as he was, he seems to have been considering the possibility of a kingdom on the rich Cilician Plains.

Some lesser Crusaders were also eager to get their hands on Tarsus, and one such band of about three hundred knights were forced to camp outside the walls, because Baldwin, having got there first, would not let them in. During the night, the former Turkish garrison fell upon this small Christian band and massacred every single one. This not unnaturally caused a great deal of ill feeling and in no way helped the unity of the Crusade. Finally Baldwin decided against a kingdom for himself in Cilicia, and hurried on to rejoin the main army.

While he had been gone, his wife and children had sickened of some unspecified illness, and died. There was now nothing to stop Baldwin from making an advantageous marriage and gaining himself a kingdom by diplomacy.

His opportunity came from the principalities on the middle Euphrates. The Armenians there were eager to have a strong Christian army around to protect them from the marauding Turks and from their hated Byzantine overlords. They welcomed the Crusaders with open arms as great liberators - and lived to regret it. Thoros, the ruler of Edessa, was old and had no children. With Turks pressing hard on his borders he adopted Baldwin as his heir and co-ruler. Within a month Thoros was deposed and killed by his own people. Opinion is divided about the part Baldwin played in this, but it seems certain that he did nothing to aid his adoptive father.

Baldwin had achieved his ambition, a principality, if not exactly in the Holy Land, at least in a good position to protect the northern approaches to it. He had no real title to the land, and had broken several oaths to obtain it, but none of that bothered Baldwin, now Count Baldwin of Edessa. While the rest of the Crusaders set about besieging Antioch, Baldwin consolidated his territories. He did it so well that many historians claim he incidentally saved the Crusade. For when the mighty Turkish army of Kerbogha came to raise the siege of Antioch, in 1098, it had first to deal with Baldwin. The walls of Edessa were attacked for three weeks, but to no avail, and the time lost in the siege kept Kerbogha from bringing his army to the field.

Baldwin's success did much to foster the ambitions of generations of Europe's younger sons. Penniless and landless, a third son, with nothing to his name, he had carved out a rich and powerful state for himself and shown his qualities as the ablest of all the knights of the First Crusade. He had also shown, as would the other leaders, that where personal ambition was concerned the interests of the Crusade came a poor second.

173

In spite of all the battles I had been called upon to fight, in the protection of Evans on the way down, I was glad I had not tried to cycle. In the stifling heat, with a continuous stream of traffic in both directions winding through the long, narrow gorge of the Cilician Gates, and pouring out clouds of exhaust gases, there was no room for a bicycle or its rider.

Not that my battles had ended, even when we at last reached the Cilician Plains: in the scramble to get Evans out of the bus at Tarsus, I found that the pump had been left aboard. This was one of those occasions when, without some powerful external help, I was not going to cope. A bicyclist cannot travel without a pump, as a puncture cannot be mended without it, and a pump to fit Evans's high-pressure valves was not available east of Italy.

There was no prayer in the Pilgrim's Itinerary especially appropriate for succouring bicyclists who have lost their pump. The closest was the one that began, 'Oh God who didst bring Abraham Thy servant out of Ur of the Chaldeans' and went on to speak of 'a fortress in adversity'. My fortress turned out to be the gentlest, most unassuming man I had yet met in Turkey. He succeeded, after innumerable telephone calls, in tracing the bus, and in getting the pump returned to Tarsus. During the hours which this took, he plied me with endless cups of tea, showed me stacks of photographs of his fiancée, and conducted me to the local museum, which wasn't worth a visit except that the walk there was nice and took my mind off the fraught drama of the wandering pump.

Such disinterested kindness is a memorable event on any journey. It was particularly welcome on this day and especially in this place - St Paul's Tarsus. St Paul's 'no mean city' is now buried under a rather squalid Turkish town, but the message of charity he preached was certainly shown to me there, and by a Muslim.

# Chapter Thirteen

*The barge she sat in,*
*like a burnished throne,*
*Burned on the water:*

*Shakespeare's Anthnony and Cleopatra,*

Tarsus lies in a strategic position at the foot of the Cilician Gates, on the western end of the flat, rich plains of Cilicia. It has seen many conquerors pass in its long history, from Sennacherib onwards. One very remarkable woman also came here in 41 B.C. to meet her lover, Mark Anthony.

I doubt that Cleopatra would recognize modern Tarsus any more than St Paul would, although the gate which was built for her triumphal entry into the city still stands - though not for much longer, unless some restoration work is undertaken soon. The Turks call it the Gate of the Bitch, perhaps because they have little appreciation for remarkable women.

She came here by boat, sailing up the River Cydnus, which was navigable then, right up to the walls of Tarsus. The city emptied to watch her arrival. She had to captivate Mark Anthony as she had Julius Caesar: it was the only hope she had of keeping Egypt free of Roman domination. The marvellous spectacle she produced to that end is described in fine detail in Plutarch's *Lives:*

*She came sailing up the Cydnus on a galley whose stern was golden; the sails were purple, and the oars were silver. These in their motion, kept tune to the music of flutes and pipes and harps. The Queen, in the dress and character of Aphrodite, lay on a couch of gold brocade, as though in a picture, while about her were pretty boys, bedight like cupids, who fanned her, and maidens habited as nereids and graces, and some made as though they were rowing, while others busied them about the sails. All manner of sweet perfumes were wafted ashore from the ship, and on the shore thousands were gathered to behold her.*

Alas for Cleopatra and Mark Anthony; just ten years ahead lay the battle of Actium and the snuffing out of all that style and imagination in two lonely suicides.

I spent some good days in Tarsus, largely because of the friends I made at the American College where I stayed while I was there. The college had been built at the turn of the Twentieth Century by a religious organization, which felt that in the birthplace of St Paul, the greatest of all the Christian teachers, there had to be a school. There was no question of there being any religious teaching now of course; that is strictly forbidden by Turkish law.

The school catered for the brightest Turkish children, and there was a lot of competition for a place there. The administration suffered frightful problems with interference from the authorities, rather as the foreign archaeologists did. When I was there, which was just days before a new academic year was due to start, the Head had been informed that he must increase his intake by another class immediately. This apparently was because some local dignitary's child hadn't made the grade in the selection examination. There tended to be a good deal of interference in other areas of the school's administration too, which seemed rather hard - strange too, when it was something Turkey was getting for nothing.

Amongst all the Americans, there was one British teacher, Frances, appropriately Head of English, with whom I felt an immediate rapport. It was her apartment, filled with books - a luxury that I miss very much on a long journey - that became my home while I was there. It was a welcome interlude, a holiday within a holiday. With school not yet begun, people had time to talk and relax. This was mostly around the swimming pool, which the teachers had dug out and built themselves in their spare time. It was only the size of an average Roman pool, four strokes and you were at the other end, but the water in it was always so cold that it acted like a tonic.

I was glad to rest there for a day or two as I was still a little groggy from my Cappadocian stomach bug, and everyone was most kind and welcoming. One night there was a celebration of teachers who had had birthdays in the last month. Ruth, the principal's wife, baked them all a cake and I got one too, as I'd had my birthday *en route.* Another night, Frances took several of us to a local restaurant - the Turkish equivalent of the railway tavern, where all the tables were arranged so as not to miss the great event of the bi-weekly train. The usual sort of Turkish food was served: kebabs, and various salads, but it felt very festive, lit by star- and candle-light, and with good conversation and lots of laughter.

The day before I was to leave and school was to begin, I went with Frances and some of the other teachers to visit an Armenian city in the hills. We travelled in the school minibus and had first to retrace my route through the industrial nightmare which begins the moment Rough Cilicia's last great promontory descends to the Cilician plains.

The pollution in emergent nations has to be seen to be believed. Western firms who have been responsible for the installation of factory plants, petrochemical works, cement works and the like, tell me that they plead hard with their customers to let them build in filtering devices to reduce harmful emissions. What the firms themselves want, however, is thick smoke (preferably black) pouring copiously from tall chimneys as visible signs of their new industrial status. Turkey certainly isn't lacking symbols of its 'progress' right across the Cilician Plains from Mersin to Ceyhan. Once one of the richest farming areas of the world, it is fast becoming a poisoned wasteland.

Beyond all this nastiness is a stretch of road, lined on each side with almost continuous ancient ruins. The extent of them is quite extraordinary: cities, aqueducts, necropolises; they continue for mile after mile, interspersed with marvellous castles, still largely intact, on the shore and on islands in the sea.

This was the centre of the kingdom of Lesser Armenia. Seeing the extent of the ruins, Greek, Roman, Byzantine, and Armenian, each built on the ruins of the previous culture, gave me some idea of the  magnificence of the Armenian flowering here. Two hundred years was all they had, between establishing a foothold in these Byzantine territories and being forced from them again, by a combination of powerful enemies - Turks, Mongols, Marmelukes, and Saracen pirates, to mention just a few. Once the Crusaders had pulled out of the East at the beginning of the Fourteenth Century, there was no ally to help the Armenians, and they gradually retreated to their mountain fastnesses, to suffer the long centuries of persecution. Their cities have been flattened as though to erase the memory of them, but the castles were preserved and used by the Ottomans up to the present day.

The ruined city of Kanlidivane was where we were heading, a strange place built on the edge of a huge chasm, where wild animals are said to have once been kept in order to have criminals fed to them. This is a typical example of Roman efficiency - combining entertaining the populace with discouraging wrong- doers. There were the substantial remains of several churches on the very edge of the abyss, indeed the wall of one had fallen the several hundred feet into it. I thought it must have been a chancy business raising children there.

Away from the chasm's edge the city was a lovely ruin of yellowy-pink stone, grown over by asphodel, capers, mandrake, and the less lovely crown of thorns. Graceful carob trees, fig, sweet bay, and turkey oaks provided shade, and in every tomb and sarcophagus, broken open long ago by tomb robbers, goats sheltered from the sun, their strange eyes steady and unblinking in the gloom. Nomads have their winter quarters among the broken fragments, and these were their goats; we could see that we were being stalked by a young girl, watchful that we did no harm to her charges. The nomads get their water from small cisterns with marble coverings which were constructed in Byzantine times, at least nine centuries ago.

From the hot dusty ruins we drove down to the sea and swam. Because I was with others and not alone, I found I could swim on and on to one of the romantic offshore castle. I lay floating in the very salty Mediterranean water, looking up at the castle walls. Close to it looked massive and formidable, a fitting memorial to the vanquished Armenians. When I had gazed enough and felt rested, I swam back to the shore with the others. It had been the most enjoyable swim of the journey, and a good ending to one of my best days in Turkey.

I always find it hard to leave people I've grown fond of and it was particularly hard leaving Frances, because we had so much in common, and I would have liked to get to know her better. It is one of the features of travelling that can be very frustrating, that so few new relationships have time to mature.

I cycled away early, across the ugly, polluted land, on a road filled with big, noisy, bullying trucks; and I felt my aggression level rising in response to the constant honking horns and the 'carving up' techniques of many of the drivers. There wasn't any alternative to this road; I had to use it. There was a strip alongside, but it was all boulders and quite unrideable. The truck drivers behaved as though

I was threatening their safety, although they had two lanes in each direction, and there was really ample room for all of us.

They kept up their harassment all the time, and even signalled to passing police cars, pointing me out to them. One policeman did stop me and tried to usher me on to the side strip, but when I shook my head and tried to convey the total impossibility of riding over a boulder field, he just shrugged and drove off. So I continued on the road with every man's hand, or rather his horn, against me, and I felt very miserable and ill-used.

The ride continued to be a running battle all the way to Iskenderun; but after the first day I stuffed my ears with cotton wool to protect them from the blaring horns, and tried to rise above the irritations.

I broke my journey at Ceyhan after having at last found a detour which took me off the horrid road for a few miles. This ran beside one of the few important rivers of Southern Turkey, the River Ceyhan. High on a dramatic crag above the river, the Snake Castle kept watch on the route, as it had since it was built by the joint efforts of Armenians and Crusaders. Only the Second Crusade followed this route; subsequent Crusaders preferred to travel by sea, which, by that time, was both faster and safer, but a line of defensive castles stretched from Cilicia right down into Oultrejourdain - modern Jordan.

Ceyhan was rather a dump, but I had no choice as there was nowhere else. Besides, there was the ancient site of Anazarbus near by which I wanted to visit.

I did not find much to choose between the two or three run-down hotels, but probably the Ensor Palais Oteli was the wrong choice, for I had a small contretemps with a young lad who carried up Evans, and afterwards tried to get me in a clinch, while he was showing me the bathroom. I dealt with him quite easily by pushing him through the doorway, and shooting the bolt on my door: but it did seem rather bizarre to be assaulted by what in Britain would have been a schoolboy.

Getting to Anazarbus wasn't simple; it was a fair distance away, so I took a bus. The other passengers were mostly peasants, going home to their villages after doing their marketing in Ceyhan. They all seemed concerned for my welfare, and kept tapping me on the shoulder, and pointing out that the ruins were a long way from the road. Actually I could see that for myself, for the enormously high acropolis was visible from afar. They seemed to be unconvinced by what were meant to be my smiles of reassurance, and continued to try to put over some message or other.

After much animated discussion amongst themselves, a young man, who spoke English, was pushed forward to sit beside me and explain the general concern.. He said everyone was worried, because I could not get to the ruins and back before nightfall, which would be dangerous. Several people, he said, wanted me to spend the night with them, so that I could make my visit the following morning. I was very warmed by their solicitude, though I did think they were exaggerating the distance, and I explained that I really had to get back to Ceyhan that night, as all my possessions were with Evans in the ropey hotel.

More animated discussion followed, and the young man announced that he was going to organize a taxi to get me to the foot of the acropolis, and would afterwards escort me back to Ceyhan. This seemed to satisfy everyone, so there was obviously no point in protesting. Whenever I think of less favourable aspects of life in Turkey, it is always balanced by the remembrance of a bus full of people concerned about the well-being of a total stranger.

My escort was a vet who had come to look at some chickens for a friend who lived in the village nearest to Anazarbus. It was a poor but, to me, fascinating place, with the houses built all higgledy-piggledy, and faintly reminiscent of a medieval Norman village. Fragments of superb cornices and capitals stuck out from walls and dykes like sore thumbs; making it obvious that an extensive ancient city was somewhere in the vicinity.

After the chickens had been inspected and  pronounced fit by the vet, Bulek, his two friends, Ibraihim and Ishmael, arrived with the taxi to take us all to the ruins. I was amazed that a car could survive to the age of this one, on the rough Turkish roads. The track we took was worse than most, just dirt and boulders, and full of pot-holes, where we grounded every few yards. Ibraihim said only Mercedes survived, and this was one of them, so not to worry.

Once we had arrived at the foot of the hill, the car could go no further, and it was a long, hard scramble to the top, which included climbing over 400 original marble steps, set into the hillside, on the most precipitous places. The boys set a punishing pace which I thought I'd never maintain, and certainly would not have done so had I been on my own. Fortunately, the heat of the day had passed. The final stage, getting through the wall, was quite a tricky climb, and the boys said that some visiting American airmen had come a cropper there the previous year, falling the sheer thousand-foot drop to their deaths. Although they were most impressed with my climbing ability (not being used to women in such situations), they took great care that I should not meet the same fate as the Americans. I think that there was an easier way up, but the people on the bus were right, and there was barely time to get there and back by nightfall, so we had come by a short cut.

It was a very good site, the last capital of Cilician Armenia, built originally by Greek colonists and occupied by Romans, Byzantines, and Arabs before the Armenians took it over. It finally fell to the Ottomans in 1375, when they thought it worth while to keep the extensive buildings and fortifications on the acropolis intact, and destroy the lower city. The palace, churches and store houses were all in a very good state of preservation and most interesting to explore, but it was the view onto the plains below that made the visit memorable.

The city had occupied a perfectly flat site, below the western side of the acropolis. Walls still enclose this space, interrupted by a massive ornamental gateway. It is a large area, and except for the remains of some low aqueducts, which once brought in water from four different sources, there is nothing at all in it. This levelled and walled nothingness is strangely eerie, an effect heightened by the broken sarcophagi scattered about over the hillside.

On the road which once wound around the back of the acropolis was a rock on which was inscribed a cross within a circle: according to local legend it commemorated Richard Coeur de Lion coming here. He went on the Third Crusade via Cyprus; which he captured and used as a valuable link in his line of communications. He could have reached these parts in a matter of days from there: I was pleased to think of him in this place. In spite of how little he actually achieved in the Holy Land, or of the brutal things he did there, he was a brilliant strategist and, perhaps more importantly, he personifies for many people the romance and chivalry of a vanished age.

The three young men were also rather chivalrous and I enjoyed their company, especially Ibraihim, who was studying engineering at university, and spoke fluent English. His family could afford to educate only one boy, so his brother had to stay home and look after the smallholding, which Ibraihim said put tremendous pressure on him to do well. He was the first Turk I met who could cope with cause and effect. While the other two were amazed at my physical competence at the advanced age of fifty, he pointed out that I had only three children, not ten like most of their village women. He didn't add that I hadn't had to put up with back-breaking labour since I was a young girl either.

After I'd been returned to my hotel and been allowed to pay some small sum for the petrol, I felt a little diffident at venturing out again into the ill-lit streets in search of an evening meal. I couldn't reckon on having breakfast, however, and I needed some fuel to make Iskenderun in a single day: so I plucked up my courage and went out into the dark streets. I'm glad I did so, because I found such a zany restaurant, that the memory of it kept me amused the whole of the following day, when I might have been snarling at the bullying trucks.

It was a large restaurant, dimly lit, and crowded with empty tables. The eye-catching central decoration was fifteen large galvanized pails, suspended from the ceiling and containing greenery resembling Jack's Beanstalk, except that, unlike Jack's soaring bean, the habit of this exuberant plant was downwards. As I groped my way through the burgeoning, sub-tropical jungle, a voice hailed me in English. 'Hallo, Miss. Coming in Miss. Thank you very much. Don't mention - YET!' - all in one breath except for the last word, which was shouted in triumph, after a dramatic pause. I looked round for a parrot, but it was the patron who came forward, a small round man who had once been to Brixton or Brixham, I couldn't gather which. He probably had lots of other jokes, but when I was there his one delight was to get me to say, 'Thank you very much', so that he could reply, 'Don't mention...YET!' and roar with helpless laughter at his own brilliance. He kept bringing me small gifts to provoke my thanks, a glass of wine, pieces of special kebab, a sugared almond, and every time he did his piece, he explained the joke to the waiter. I was almost in hysterics and laughing as much as he was in the end; it was so utterly ridiculous. He tried to claim a kiss before I left - 'custom of house' - but there are limits.

I now felt I had reached another significant point in the journey. My road again swung ninety degrees, to head south across the plain of Issus, where Alexander's Macedonians had defeated the mighty Persian armies of King Darius III in 333 BC; thereby opening up Asia and all of the Mediterranean to his unparalleled conquests.

From here on I was within the Crusader realms too, in the principality of Antioch, though I should not reach the once great city of that name for several days. First would come Iskenderun, the Alexandretta of antiquity, and a Crusader port; that is, I hoped to reach it if I were lucky enough to survive the murderous intent of the traffic, and its choking fumes.

The remains of castles had littered the shore for the last few miles. Amongst them was one older tower called Baba Yunas - Father Jonah - for it is round about this spot that the whale is said to have spewed forth that reluctant messenger of God. It would have been a significant place for the early pilgrims, whose numbers began to be swelled from this

TURKEY

Antakya
(Antioch)
Aleppo

S Y R I A

Latakia

Krak des
Chevaliers
Hamma

Homs

Palmyra
(Tadmor in the
Wilderness)

Tripoli

Nabak

L E B A N O N

Beirut

S e a

Syrian

Damascus

Tyre

Acre

Sea of
Galilee

D e s e r t

Dera

Bosra

I S R A E L

Jerash

J O R D A N

Jericho

Amman

Jerusalem
Bethlehem
Hebron
Gaza
Dead
Sea
Madaba

M O A B

Beersheva

Qatrana

Kerak

N e g e v

Krak de Montreal

Petra

Aqaba

Bettina's route
National boundaries
Ancient site
Crusader castles

Kilometres
0    50    100    150

point onwards by those who had joined the route from ships sailing via Cyprus. Among these pilgrims were Willibald, who had somehow found the fare to continue his long journey by sea; Arculf of the miraculous stories; and St. Jerome's friends, Paula and her daughter Eudocia. With this invisible pilgrim band about me and my ears again stuffed with cotton wool, I did survive, and duly presented myself at the office of the British Honorary Consul in Iskenderun.

At all stages of my journey I made courtesy calls on the consulates, as requested by the Foreign Office of H.M.G., which likes to think that a paternal eye is being kept on their citizens travelling in the more troubled areas of the world. It is a good idea because any urgent news can be passed on, as well as warnings of sudden local wars, or of other trouble spots to avoid. I would also like to think of them as a sort of oasis, where my fellow countrymen and women would be pleased to see me, and perhaps offer some old-fashioned, British hospitality, before sending me on my way refreshed. Unfortunately this is not a role which appeals to the staff of most consulates. By and large, they seem not to like their compatriots very much, and often resent them turning up in 'their patch'. I have some sympathy for this attitude in well-frequented, tourist places, especially those on the football hooligans' circuit, but in more remote parts I am very envious of other nationalities, who are mostly blessed with far friendlier consulates than ours.

Iskenderun was a glowing exception. Perhaps this is because it is only an honorary consulate, and Hanoud, the Honaray Consul isn't British; it is atypical, and, as far as my experience goes, all the better for it. There was great relief when I turned up, because there had been telexes and telephone calls about me, saying that I must be warned off going into Lebanon, as Muslim extremists in the North Bekaa were going through a spate of kidnapping any Westerners they thought might be worth holding to ransom.

Hanoud at once invited me to stay a night with her at her family home in a seaside town, south of Iskenderun. She did this out of kindness, because she knew from experience how lonely a traveller can be in a strange city. We soon found that we were in sympathy on many issues, however, and I was invited to stay on for a while.

The area, of which Iskenderun is roughly the centre, is called the Hattay, and is strangely situated, being in reality a giant-sized bite taken out of Syria. It was an area tagged on to Turkey only after a rather suspicious plebiscite in 1939. After the questionable take-over there had been a lot of confiscation of property, and a closing down of foreign missions. Many of the people of The Hattay speak Arabic, and unlike in the rest of Turkey, there are a good many Christians; most are Greek Orthodox or adherents of one of the complicated varieties of the Syrian Church, which I cannot at all sort out. Hanoud's Church was Protestant, of an evangelical persuasion, very rare for those parts. They had no church of their own, as their previous one had been commandeered by the government, and there was a legal wrangle of forty-years' standing still going on about it. In the meantime, they had been allowed a corner in the Syrian church for their services. I wished I could have been there on Sunday to join in their worship, for I hadn't attended any sort of church since Izmir, but with time, as usual, pressing, and the November rains threatening, I could not wait that long before setting out for Antioch.

After three days enjoying the unaccustomed luxury in Hanoud's company, I left early one morning to climb the two thousand feet over the mountain range which was known in ancient times as the Syrian Gates. Evans was weighed down by presents of all sorts of eatables, provided by Hanoud in case I perished of hunger before Antioch. She had already given me the best meal I had eaten since France. It was at a waterfront restaurant in Iskenderun and had consisted of separate courses of calamares, giant prawns, and red snapper, all beautifully cooked and costing more, I suspected than I usually spend in a week on my own. Evans of course was not fortified, as I was by all this generosity, and he made heavy weather of the climb, so I stopped quite frequently to eat some of the extra load.

With all the heavy traffic still about and behaving oppressively, I was worried about the descent to the Plains of Amik . At the top of the pass, however, there was a massive military manoeuvre taking place, and all the traffic was stopped. For some reason I was waved on, and as I moved out to overtake the long string of stationary lorries, I did a very stupid thing by going down and around a corner without first seeing my way clear. For long minutes it seemed I was fighting brakes which wouldn't grip, while a lorry tore up the slope towards me between the two rows of stationary trucks. I couldn't see any way that we could avoid a head-on collision, and I felt a deep sense of shame at having been so stupid. It all happened in a split second of course, and I still don't know how I squeezed through a non-existent gap, to finish up totally unscathed. I think it must have been a miracle, and none of my doing. After that the road was quite clear, and I sped down and down, and on to Antioch in time for lunch.

If I could have chosen one city to have seen through the eyes of Willibald or Paula, it would have been this one - Antioch, the third greatest city of the ancient world in Roman times, and continuing in its grandeur right through the Byzantine period, and after its capture by the Saracens remaining still a legend. To Christians it was especially holy because St Peter had established the first bishopric there, and the name Christian had first been applied there to the followers of the teaching of Jesus. I would have chosen to view it through Paula's eyes in preference to Willibald's because a bad earthquake in the Sixth Century had some-what dimmed its glory. Still, when the First Crusade closed in about it, it must still have been an awesome sight, filling the huge area between the River Orontes and Mount Silipus. It wasn't possible for the Crusaders to invest it entirely, its extent was too great.

Bohemond, as land hungry as Baldwin had been, had already decided that Antioch should be his portion. He was the son of the notorious Norman pirate-adventurer Robert Guiscard, and, according to Anna Comnena, was nothing more than a pirate himself. Even she admitted his striking good looks, however, and this, combined with his ability to lead men and to conduct complicated strategy, made him a formidable figure. Raymond of Toulouse, the richest prince of the Crusade, loathed Bohemond, and there was constant friction between his Provençal knights and Bohemond's Normans. Raymond hoped that the Byzantine Emperor would arrive in time to claim his property back before Bohemond could get his hands on it.

However, it was to Bohemond that the city fell; by treachery finally: for he had delayed a combined attack by the assembled hosts for fear the city should be spoiled by the looting of a victorious army. He wanted to gain it intact and, after nearly a year of siege, the gates were opened to him on the night of the second of June 1098, by an Armenian who had converted to Islam, but who was now having second thoughts. Within a few hours the Christian armies had killed so many Turks that it was not possible to walk in the streets without stepping on corpses.

The Crusaders had barely established themselves in Antioch before Kerbogha's huge army, fortuitously delayed by their siege of Baldwin's newly-acquired Eddessa, hove into view: It was now the Crusaders' turn to be besieged; and that within a city made dangerous with the rotting corpses of all the slain Turks. It was touch and go for the Crusaders, but their enemies were even less able to agree amongst themselves than were the Christians, and in the end, the city and the lands around were safely in Bohemond's hands. He extended his holdings to include Cilicia and, with this strong kingdom and Balwin's Edessa at their backs, the rest of the Crusade marched on to Jerusalem, with Raymond of Toulouse still at odds with the other princes for supporting Bohemond.

There is nothing at all left of the Latin state. It lasted for 170 years, until it was taken and totally destroyed in 1268 by the dreadful Marmeluke, Baibars. Even the great River Orontes, which in 1098 ran red with the blood of the slain, is now just a muddy trickle, its waters syphoned off for irrigation purposes. Antioch has become Antakya, a small, very ordinary, Turkish town. Other than to mourn its passing, only two things make it worth a visit: the mosaics from the ancient site of Daphne, housed in a new museum, and one of the first Christian churches in the world. This simple little cave-like place of worship had been provided with an escape passage through the rock, so dangerous was the practice of Christianity in those early days. The Crusaders built the small shrine, but it remains essentially simple, and I found it very moving. It was a particularly important place in the growth of the early Church, as it was the first community known of, in which Greeks were included along with Jews. Peter, Paul, and Barnabus had all worked and taught there, and many of the early doctrinal problems must have been prayed about and worked out in that small cave. I suddenly realized something that thinking about the Crusaders had put out of my mind - that I had arrived at the first official place of pilgrimage in the Holy Land.

# Chapter Fourteen

*Arryved ben this Cristen folk to londe,
In Syrië...*

Chaucer

With the sea route - the ancient Via Maris - now blocked to me because of the troubles in the Lebanon, I had no choice but to head eastwards to the border with Syria. I would then be able to turn Southward again on the inland route, the Via Nuova, a Roman road, but also an ancient way, where a trade route between the Babylonian cultures and Egypt had existed for at least four thousand years. Probably it was the line of Abraham's wanderings too, on his way from Ur of the Chaldees, to the land of Canaan. Accordingly, I spent the last of my Turkish money on a small gold cross to replace the leather pilgrim's one which I had lost in Iskenderun, and so, feeling not so much re-armed as bearing my proper credentials, I set forth on Evans for Syria.

I was not looking forward to this crossing; not all travellers can be wrong, and I had heard nothing good reported of the Syrian border officials. I went through my pilgrim's itinerary with especial diligence that morning, and what stayed in my mind like a talisman was the phrase about being accompanied by 'Thy co-operating graces, so that by the aids of Thy mercy we may rejoice for the success of our journey'. I also determined to 'stay loose' and not allow myself to be riled by the tyranny of petty officialdom. As always, my resolves came to nothing, for patience is not one of my virtues, and it was left to the 'co-operating graces' to see me through.

The nearer we came to the border, the rougher and more barren grew the land. Barbed wire fenced in the road for the last few miles, and tall towers, manned by armed Turks, kept watch over the desolate unpeopled scene.

Leaving Turkey was a mixture of kindliness and frustration. The guards at the first barrier pressed me to glasses of tea, admired Evans, and made me feel altogether approved of. The guard at the final post had me almost spitting with fury, as he sent me back for the third time, because he didn't think Evans's page in the passport was in order. Between these two points, I had fought my way through the milling crowds of truck drivers, in order to get to the windows and have my passport stamped: Turks don't queue. I had satisfied customs that I was not smuggling out any marble statues or carrying drugs, until finally every nicety had been observed, and there was nothing to stop me leaving the country, except this recalcitrant, bone-headed individual on the gate. Eventually, on the fourth rebuff, passport control sent a small boy of about eight to the gate with me, carrying a message for the guard, who then, most reluctantly, and with very bad grace, let me through.

There is something faintly sinister about having left one country and not yet being admitted into another. You are in no man's land, a place of extreme vulnerability, where you do not officially exist, and are no one's responsibility if you were suddenly to disappear. I was in an area which looked as though several bombs had exploded in it, and bulldozers had tried to fill in the craters. It went on for a mile or so, through a narrow defile with Byzantine remains and broken-down cars and trucks. There had certainly been fighting here, but when that was, and about what, I had no idea; and I had no desire to get off Evans and poke around, as the ground might very well have been mined.

The Syrian border post looked quite modern, and had instructions in several languages about how to proceed through the various formalities. What it did not mention was the piece of blackmail which had first to be attended to. Fortunately the Foreign Office had told me before leaving England that you needed a hundred dollars in cash to get into Syria. Several other currencies are also acceptable, as long as they too are in bank notes. These dollars have to be changed at a special low rate, before anyone will even look at your passport. I'd had time to adjust to the idea of this open blackmail and had already written off the amount I would lose on the exchange. People in transit, who are not even going to be twenty-four hours in the country, also have to change this amount of hard currency, which for young travellers on a limited budget can be quite a hardship.

One would imagine that the border bank would be highly delighted at this lucrative and captive trade, but nothing could be further from the truth. I went into the dirty, wooden hut, which I would have mistaken for a garden shed had I not been told otherwise. Remembering my resolve to stay calm and reasonable, I said 'Good morning' brightly, waving my crisp green dollars to show that I was on a peaceful and legitimate errand. An unshaven individual behind the counter, in a repulsively dirty shirt, was punching holes in sheets of paper. He snarled at my greeting, and turned his back on me. I tried again, 'Could you change my dollars please?' He turned round slowly, his eyes on my face as he operated the punch, his lips curled in a sneer. I thought he was making his meaning quite clear; it conveyed total disdain, together with a frustrated desire about how he would really like to respond.

'You wait five minutes,' he snapped.

'Why should I?' I retorted, resolve forgotten. 'You're not busy and I'm a customer.'

At this there was more movement behind the counter and another man, rising from a camp bed, came to the counter, seized my crisp, clean dollars, and flung down a few greasy notes in front of me, all without a word. I felt that they were both restraining themselves from spitting at me.

The rest of the formalities went relatively smoothly. There was no one in the large passport hall, but even so the officials felt obliged to inspect their nails, and pretend that they hadn't seen me. Work was beneath their dignity, it seemed. I restrained myself from asking if they could hurry it up as I wanted to get to Aleppo today, not tomorrow. Eventually one of them ambled slowly over and stamped my passport without really looking at it. He was interested only in whether I had the exchange note from the bank. Customs didn't even pretend to turn around when I presented myself, but merely waved an arm in dismissal, which was just as well, as I'd already come near to fisticuffs with an evilly-disposed youth outside the passport hall. He had maliciously threaded a garden hose through Evans's front wheel. Perhaps it was a joke, or an obscure form of protest about something, or perhaps he didn't like bicycles. I had been forced to uncouple the hose from the tap in order to get Evans free, at which the youth had run up screaming abuse, fists flailing.

When I recounted my border experiences to other travellers, they said I got off lightly. Some had been made to wait up to five hours for the bank to open; when they had got their money changed it had been flung on the floor and trodden on. Others, travelling in coach parties, said it was common for the officials to deal with three quarters of the passengers and then shut up shop, sometimes until the next day. All agreed that they had met nothing else in Syria to equal the repulsive attitude of the border personnel.

Free of officialdom, I pedalled away smartly, to ride off some of the aggression which had been aroused by my first hour in Syria. It is a very strange area between Antioch and Aleppo - the Land of Dead Cities, though most of these lie further to the north. Once it had been a fertile densely-populated land, but after the destruction of the Byzantine and Armenian civilizations, their irrigation works were broken up by the Mongol invaders, and the trees which bound the soil died, and the area soon became pure desert. The pilgrims and Crusaders who came this way would not have recognized it.

Not far from the border, the modern road I was on crossed the Roman road which Trajan had built at the beginning of the Second Century AD. It was twenty feet wide and built of well-cut blocks of limestone. It stretched away, in an almost perfect state of preservation, as far as I could see in both directions, over the rough, stony ground. There is something peculiarly evocative about ancient roads. With no effort, the mind peoples them with the passing pageant of the ages: Roman legions marching in disciplined ranks under the aegis of their eagles; Crusader armies, jangling with chain mail and weaponry, a forest of banners fluttering above their caparisoned horses. Evans and I did not fit into this scene. Travel in these parts, if you were not mounted on a horse or a camel, always meant walking; wheeled vehicles were very rare, and this did not change until 1864 with the coming of the railway.

Every pilgrim passing through this area from 420 AD onwards would have turned aside here to visit St Simeon Stylites while he was living on his sixty-foot pillar, and after his death they would have come to pray at the site and to chip away a piece of the pillar, to keep as a relic. Simeon Stylites epitomizes the extreme asceticism which, later, was such a feature of medieval Christianity in the West, and which is difficult for a more cynical and sybaritic age to understand. It sprang from a deep conviction that man was separated from God by the appetites of his body, and that to overcome this barrier to total communion, he must subjugate the flesh by mortification. By all accounts St Simeon's life suited him, and he achieved that aura of sanctity which marks the truly holy. Pilgrims took back such glowing accounts of him that the Pope became worried about the influence he was having, and dispatched a legate to bid him descend from the pillar. As Simeon immediately concurred and came down, the Pope concluded that he was a true child of the Church and a saint to boot, and gave him permission to return to his perch. There was quite a vogue for sitting on columns after that, all through the Middle East from Constantinople to Egypt.

The church which was raised over Simeon's column and finished in about 490 is quite lovely and in a surprisingly good state of preservation; much better than most buildings of the same period in Turkey. I especially liked the decoration on some of the capitals and architraves, which was a particularly fluent carving of acanthus leaves blown in the wind. Only a small section of the famous pillar remains, however, and is now behind a protective railing in the central octagonal court.

There were some villages on the route to Aleppo but these were all in stony areas where it was difficult to see how life was sustained. The housing looked very poor too, and it seemed a depressing contrast to the rich lands of coastal Turkey. The dirt was also noticeably greater, and in spite of everything seeming so backward and depressed, there was an abundance of modern effluvia about, in the shape of paper and plastic wrappings, so that at times the fields seemed to be growing crops of rubbish. One thing, however, was very much better than in Turkey; and that was the road surface. It was like glass; and this made an immediate difference to my comfort, and was easier on Evans also.

Once into the outskirts of Aleppo, I discovered that the Arab drivers were as pushy as the last lot in Turkey had been, and that they seemed to have an even lower opinion of bicycle riders. If we were to survive, I reckoned I would need more than just my wits about me. By the time I reached the centre of Aleppo, I was feeling quite harassed and in an anti-Syrian mood. The noise too was worse than anything I could have imagined; every driver of every vehicle kept his hand permanently on the horn, and every bicycle rider tinkled his bell, until I began to wonder if this was the site of the Tower of Babel. Fortunately the hotel I was headed for appeared as if by magic before I went completely mad.

Anybody who was anyone and passing through Syria since 1900 stayed at the Hotel Baron. The royalty of Europe, heads of state, titled nobility, authors, aviators, archaeologists all stayed there, as also did some quite ordinary travellers like Evans and me. It is a fine building with about a hundred rooms arranged on three floors. Arabic-baronial would best describe the style, I think. When it was first built it was outside the city walls, and guests could shoot duck from the verandahs. Now busy roads hem it in on all four sides, and its solid magnificence has grown somewhat threadbare.

Even so I didn't know if I could afford to stay there, but having put it to the young man at the desk that I was a bicycle traveller just arrived from England, anxious to sleep where Lawrence of Arabia had rested his head, he was so taken with my enterprise that he offered me special terms, as long as I didn't mind doing without a private bath. He was the grandson of the man who had built the Baron, and an ex-bicyclist himself. As a very young man, he said, he had wondered what it would be like to cycle to England - the idea was as imbued with great romance for him as riding through the Middle East was for me. He had decided, however, that it was not possible to get to England because there were so many mountains in the way. Perhaps his bicycle was a heavy town type, for he himself looked quite strong enough to have made the journey. He was most impressed with Evans and had him carried up the wide, imposing staircase to my bedroom. You can always tell the quality of an hotel by the attitude the personnel have towards bicycles.

I was invited to lunch with his parents, Krikor and Sally Maxloumian, and that was the beginning of three memorable days in Aleppo, listening to the anecdotes of Krikor who, as a boy, had been around when Lawrence of Arabia was a young scholar, working on his thesis about Crusader castles. Lawrence, I gathered, had been thought rather an arrogant young man. Both Krikor and Sally were very kind to me while I was stayed at the Baron, inviting me to meals, and generally making me welcome. By a curious coincidence they had been in London when the book about my travels in the Himalayas had come out, and had also read a newspaper account of my proposed journey to Jerusalem. On the strength of this I was invited to sign the special guest book, which contained such names as Agatha Christie, Freya Stark, Lindberg, and of course Lawrence - exalted company indeed.

Aleppo is the most attractive city in Syria, which is not saying very much. What charm the Syrian cities undoubtedly possess is seriously jeopardized by the awful traffic and the massive rebuilding which is taking place everywhere, as though an enormous amount of foreign aid had suddenly poured into the country. This means that constant swirling dust is added to the other irritants of traffic noise, fumes, and litter.

Traffic ruins even the souks of Aleppo, which otherwise would have no equal anywhere. There are about ten miles of these souks, all under their ancient heavy roofs, which shelter them from the burning heat. They sell every conceivable commodity, and around their peripheries are the Khans, like miniature fortresses, where the foreign merchants used once to secure themselves and their goods at night, with their camels and donkeys stabled in the enclosed courtyards. Hardly a camel remains in Syria now, alas; it is an unending stream of cars and vans which now pin people to the walls of passageways which are only just wide enough for them to force a way through. I found it impossible to admire the exotic spices, perfumes and jewellery under such pressured conditions.

The citadel of Aleppo is more restful, and when one is lucky enough to find it open, it is a good place to escape from the bustle of the town, although a lot of building work was going on there too. It is said to be the largest citadel in the world, and since the Ninth Century it was a complete and impregnable town in itself. Built at the top of a hill, on the rubble of previous strongholds, the supporting mound was smoothly faced with great blocks of worked stone. This was the strong city of Muslim resistance, and if the Crusaders could have taken it, events might have turned out differently for them. As it was, the citadel of Aleppo became the scene for some of their worst humiliations. Many Crusaders were imprisoned in the grim dungeons of the keep. Baldwin II, King of Jerusalem, spent two years there until he was ransomed by his strangely named Armenian wife, Mophia. One of the Counts of Edessa, Joscelin II, was less fortunate; he was first blinded, and languished in the citadel for nine years until he died there, in 1159.

Reynald de Chatillon spent sixteen years there, between 1160 and 1176, because no one was prepared to ransom him. It was a great pity that he ever did get out, because he was the most appalling man that fought on the Christian side. So evil was he, that he is almost a caricature of the 'arch-baddie'. When Reynald indulged in the common custom of the times, of tossing prisoners to their deaths from the castle battlements, he had specially constructed boxes placed around his victims' heads so that they should not lose consciousness on the way down and so lessen their sufferings. The list of his infamies would fill a book, and by the time the fate of the Kingdom of Jerusalem was sealed, at the battle of the Horns of Hattin, in 1187, he was the Crusader most hated by all Muslims. Even Saladin, that most gentlemanly of Saracens, could not restrain himself where Reynald was concerned.. When he was brought to his tent after the battle, Saladin seized a sword and killed him out of hand.

Cruelty was of course a feature of the age, as it is unfortunately of every age, but in those days most people seemed openly to delight in watching ghastly things being done to others. In Aleppo in 1119 the inhabitants were treated to a spectacle to rival anything the Roman Emperors had provided for their citizens. The remnant of a crusading army, which had just been totally routed in an horrendous battle known afterwards as the Battle of the Field of Blood, was dragged triumphantly into the city. There they were tortured to death on the streets, while one of their number, whose courage and proud bearing had impressed the Turcomans, was kept alive to listen to the screams of his dying comrades.

I did my tour of the citadel with a Scot who was also staying at the Baron. He was of the Bahai faith, and so able to take a detached view of all the nefarious dealings of both Christians and Muslims. He was a welcome companion, not least for the protection he afforded me; it is certainly easier to go sight-seeing accompanied by a male person in Arab countries. We went together to the archaeological museum too. This had not long been built, and it housed some marvellous things, particularly of early Mesopotamia. It was beautifully designed and built, but some of the exhibits were almost impossible to see because of the filthy state of the glass behind which they were housed..

Dirt and squalor were features more apparent in Syria than in Turkey, and I decided it had more to do with the national attitude to work than with poverty. There always seemed to be plenty of personnel available, mostly just standing around holding onto brooms, but I think menial tasks are beneath the dignity of such impressive looking people. The men particularly, in their long gowns and Arab head-dresses, would look out of place wielding the brooms, vacuum cleaners, and dusters which so many of the public buildings urgently need. It is not so easy to see what the women are like, because they mostly go around with black chiffon scarves completely covering their heads and faces, but they seem no keener to work at menial tasks than their men. The women cleaners at the Baron were on duty for long hours, but I think they spent more time watching that the guests didn't escape without tipping them, than actually doing the work for which they were paid. Labour regulations in Syria make it difficult to get rid of unsatisfactory workers, I gathered, even where theft is involved, which must make it nightmarish to attempt to run any service industry.

I was aware, however, of considerable poverty in Aleppo, where every rubbish bin had someone going through it, and where, in the dry moat of the citadel, which was used as the city dump, as well as a public lavatory, there were many scavengers at work. Although there was nothing like the quantity of beggars to be seen as in Pakistan and India, there were enough around to make one continuously aware of their presence. Pitiful deformities were publicly exhibited too, like one young woman loping along the streets on her hands and one good foot, while the other withered leg and foot dragged on the ground behind her. It all made me aware that I was truly in the East here, in a way I had not been in Turkey.

My most enjoyable times in Aleppo were spent with Krikor Maxloumian, chiefly because, as an Armenian, Krikor was able to further my new-found interest in the old Armenian kingdoms. I couldn't have found anyone more suitable, as he was passionate both about the history and about the present condition of Armenia.

I remember more of the things he told me, and the gramophone records of modern Armenian Church music he played me after dinner, than of what we saw.

One day he took me on a visit which began at his old school. It was in a fine old Armenian house in the Christian quarter of the city. On the outside, it was just blank walls, with not a single window, just a narrow, easily defended entrance. Like the Khans it had been built for defence; in this case to defend the Christians living there from attacks by their Muslim neighbours. Through the entrance we passed immediately into an impressive eighteenth-century residence, with the once elegant rooms opening out of a sizeable, open central court. Seventy years as a boy's school had not totally changed the interior. The women's balcony, from which they could watch, unseen, what was happening below in the main salon, was still there, though I was shocked when I was told its purpose, for I had not realized that Christian women were also subjected to a form of purdah as late as the Eighteenth Century.

I remember less of the church we visited, which had the usual, rather jolly Armenian icons, each with its share of little votive figures and shapes cut out of gold and silver foil - thanks for prayers granted, or hopes for future blessings. It was while we were looking at these that Krikor told me about a modern Armenian hero, who had been known as 'the man with the bag of gold'. The story concerned the period after the terrible forced marches of the Armenians driven out by the Turks in 1915. Only a very small remnant survived, and the majority of those were young orphaned children who were taken in by Arabs in the villages, to be reared as an investment in future labour. The man with the bag of gold had spent many years going around the Syrian villages, buying any Armenian child he could find. Most of those recovered were brought to Aleppo where they were adopted by the local Armenian community.

Our last visit of the day was to the home of an old gentleman of eighty-nine, probably not a great deal older than Krikor who, if he remembered Lawrence as a young man, could not have been born long after the turn of the

Twentieth Century. The old man was the honorary Italian Vice-Consul, and lived in a sixteenth-century Venetian merchant's house, which his family had occupied since 1800. It was probably the oldest inhabited house in Aleppo, and was tremendously interesting with its small panelled rooms, opening out of a long central passage, most of them with barrel vaulted ceilings. It was as full of unrelated treasures, from all ages, as a well-endowed small-town museum; and frail though he was, the old gentleman was clearly delighted to give guided tours of his treasures. If I could have chosen to live anywhere in Aleppo, it would have been here, for it was an oasis of peace and quiet in that excessively noisy city, and possessed the rare treat of a lovely, narrow, walled garden at the rear. Its main attraction, however, was the approach to it, which was by way of a circuitous route though the convolutions of the souks, which made it seem not only a very secret place, but one not altogether real or to be taken for granted. Perhaps on another attempt to visit it, you could seek endlessly through the souks and not find it. .

After three days in Aleppo I felt sufficiently adjusted to Syria to continue the journey. Certain features still worried me a little, but I found nothing alarming enough to make me want to take a train. One of the things which troubled me most was the huge photographs of the President, Lieutenant-General Hatez Al Assad, which were everywhere, sometimes rows of them together, like sinister strips of giant postage stamps. There were two poses: in one he smiled and in the other he didn't; and both were sinister. The `Big Brother' aspect of these larger than life-size photographs was extremely sinister, which I suppose was the intention, Syria being at present kept on a particularly tight rein, largely because of the emergent Muslim extremists in the country. As the year was 1984, the Orwellian association was particularly strong Another disconcerting presence was the children, who all seemed to be dressed in quasi-military uniforms. By the age of twelve these were no longer even quasi, but the real thing, and this held good for the girls too, right down to the boots: Syria seemed populated by mini-soldiers. But, strangely enough, I didn't see a single full-sized soldier the whole time I was there.

When I told the Maxloumians that I was leaving, and that I would be breaking my journey in Hamma, it produced some degree of consternation, and attempts were made to get me to change my plans. No one would exactly tell me why Hamma was to be avoided; it appeared to be a taboo subject, but nonetheless they were adamant that I must not go there. So to spare embarrassment, I pretended to agree to take a bus if I found I could not manage the whole 160 miles to Homs, which was the next town on my route after Hamma. I had no intention of avoiding Hamma, however, as it had various unique treasures which I was determined to see.

Over dinner on my last night at the Baron, Krikor told stories of the last war, when first the German, and then the British army had taken over his Hotel. I'm not sure which regimental H.Q. it became, but the sort of high jinks Krikor described seemed typical of what went on in the leisure time of many British regiments. Fox hunting was one such indoor pursuit, designed to channel the energies of young officers in a harmless direction. The fox was a co-operative waiter called Peter, the whippers-in were of field rank, and the pack was the subalterns. The whole hotel was the field, but what was done to the unfortunate Peter when he was finally caught was never revealed. Certain party nights, said Krikor, tended to be even more alarming to the uninitiated, as the tradition of this particular regiment, when celebrating the anniversary of some obscure battle, was to hurl all the furniture out through the windows at the close of the evening's festivities. I would have thought that armchairs, desks, tables, and chairs crashing down from the second-floor windows would have been lethal as well as alarming. Krikor, however, had no complaints at all about the revelries. The regiment always paid for the damages like gentlemen; they were 'just boys enjoying themselves'.

The last I saw of Krikor was when I staggered downstairs at one a m, to change my room yet again. The Baron has one insurmountable problem which it shares with all the other hotels in this, the tourist part of town: diabolical noise. The traffic of course goes on almost all night, but far worse are the night clubs, cheap little places which have mushroomed up all around. They play very loudly-amplified, Arab pop music which continues until three or four in the morning. All the hotels have complained about it, I was told, but either the Minister of Tourism is very open to bribery, or he truly believes, as he claims, that most Western visitors come to Syria only to enjoy this particular cultural experience.

There was an interesting sequel to the enforced money changing at the border, which I realized only when I came to settle my bill at the Baron. By taking away the bank exchange form at passport control (this is done to everyone), the Syrian money is of use only as small change. You may not pay hotel bills, travel agents, etc. in Syrian currency, unless you have the bank proof of exchange; nor may any Syrian accept foreign currency in payment. The banks do open occasionally, though not very often. If you are quite rich, all this is probably not too great a hardship. If your means are limited as mine always are, there is a problem. It seem a curious attitude for a country that has as much natural attractions for tourists as anywhere in the Middle East. I saw only a fraction of what was there, but the archaeologist in charge of Palmyra told me that the number of wonderfully preserved cities and temples, and other ancient fragments in the Syrian deserts exceed anything to be found in the Western Hemisphere. The slightest encouragement and visitors would flock there, but Syrians have a schizophrenic attitude to tourists: they like the revenue but they fear potential spies moving about, finding out secrets.

This was true even in the Eighth Century, as Willibald discovered when he spent several weeks in a Syrian prison, on suspicion of spying. In two days I would myself be in that same city. In a country as full of secret police as Syria, maintaining a low profile was obviously desirable; but I thought there were severe limits as to how far this could be achieved. Where almost no-one rode a bicycle outside towns, a lone female on Evans was sure to be noticed. I could only hope that the secret police would consider me too insignificant to bother about.

# Chapter Fifteen

*For sawcefleem he was, with eyen narwe,*
*As hoot he was, and lecherous as a sparwe*

*Chaucer*

Harvest time was long past when I started off on the long straight road to Hamma. The fields had been ploughed, and as yet grew only acres of plastic waste. Much of the land appeared to be marginal and there were also stretches of desert. The villages were a curious mixture of flat-roofed box-like houses and traditional beehive dwellings - tall, mud-faced, and beautifully proportioned. The mounds of evil-smelling rubbish which surrounded them seriously lessened their attraction.

Even the smallest village had a police post, and notices in English pointed the way to them. I found this useful in getting rid of the young men who came roaring out on their motorcycles when they spotted me passing. Possibly they were merely curious, but several motorcycles, each with two or three young men riding them, buzzing all around us was not a desirable situation. It was dangerous too, as they egged one another on to ride ever closer, in the hope that I'd get nervous and react. I did; I told them in word and gesture to 'clear off', and when that had no effect I told them, pointing towards the sign, that I was going for the police. They seemed to understand that gesture, and made off immediately with backward looks of extreme dislike.

I don't know what I would have done had the men persisted. After all I had heard of Syria's police, both secret and otherwise, I doubt I would have sought help there. The country was still new to me and I did not know what to expect. Syrians I had met in Aleppo were full of warnings and fears for my safety. No one dared speak openly, it seemed, and only gradually was I able to piece together something of the background to the present feelings of fear and insecurity.

Two years ago the dissension and lack of political stability, which seem always to have characterized Syria, had resulted in one of the periodic eruptions of violence. A group of religious extremists, calling themselves the Muslim Brotherhood, had attempted a take-over. Their main stronghold, Hamma, was immediately surrounded by Syria's considerable military might, including tanks and heavy artillery, and the insurrection was over in record time, with half of ancient Hamma reduced to fine brick dust.

Other Syrian cities had also had their pockets of Muslim Brotherhood sympathizers, and these had been flushed out with the same brutal efficiency. This was the cause of all the rebuilding in Aleppo, but there had been nothing there on the scale of the fighting in Hamma. Little of this had appeared in the world press, which was not surprising, considering how difficult it is for foreign journalists to obtain visas to enter the country even in untroubled times. But in Syria, and even in Turkey, the name of Hamma appears to strike a chill in people whatever their sympathies are.

Reprisals upon the people of Hamma had included televised marches to publicly demonstrate their allegiance.

Presumably they would have carried banners too, emblazoned with the executed leaders of the uprising. This is common practice in Syria; all sorts of groups, from school children upward, are expected to stage marches and to carry banners on which the current villain is depicted with a rope around his neck. A 'villain' is anyone of whom the government disapproves, or who is considered to be threatening Arab unity. President Sadat of Egypt was the subject of such marches when he established diplomatic relations with Israel. These marches are televised for the education of the people. Every night I was in Syria, at about six o'clock in the evening, if I was anywhere near a television set, I could see an hour of carefully edited marching sequences of seemingly endless battalions of young men and women, boys and girls, all goose-stepping belligerently with their banners.

It was not surprising that I felt somewhat wary with all this fresh in my mind, and for the first four hours I didn't dare stop. Once my water bottle was empty, however, I had no choice in that burning heat but to pull into the next café. It was a very dirty place, and, with all the piles of rotting rubbish I had seen along the way covered with clouds of flies, I thought I had better start taking preventive medicine to ward off any of the nasty enteric bugs which would be just waiting to infect an unresistant Western stomach. I am very glad I took this decision, because, in spite of some of the extremely insanitary conditions in which I found myself in the next few weeks, I stayed perfectly healthy.

The temperature was way up in the nineties and the sun blazed out of a clear blue sky, but this sort of dry desert heat suited me. On the delightfully smooth and almost flat road, I made the ninety-five miles to Hamma by three-thirty p m, feeling by that time as dehydrated as a dry bone. Finding water took precedence over any worries about possible danger. Just where I finally put foot to ground was, of all unlikely places, a tourist office. I went in and found that I couldn't speak until I had been lubricated with several glasses of water. The man in charge said there were only two hotels 'suitable for tourists' and directed me to them. He had no tourist literature or any helpful advice about local places of interest, and I couldn't quite see why he was there.

The two hotels were side by side, above some shops; to get to them meant first climbing a long flight of steep stairs. A local shopkeeper and several small boys seemed eager to watch over Evans while I prospected for a room. I wasn't long at the first hotel as a surly individual practically closed the door in my face, shouting, 'Full, full, go away.' At the second I was more pleasantly received, for the young owner, Hassan, was currently learning English and professed himself charmed by my accent. He told me that, except on the BBC World Service, you seldom hear English spoken in the Middle East other than with an American accent.

Although this hotel was also full, Hassan said he would find me somewhere to sleep; the roof was as yet unoccupied, and as he had to sleep in the hotel himself that night, he could make himself responsible for my safety. There seemed little point in looking further, as I was told every space in Hamma was cram full of engineers, rebuilding the shelled and shattered city. So having showered and left my luggage at the hotel, I set off to explore the town on Evans, promising to call later at Hassan's home, to meet his family.

The River Orontes (the same as ran red with the blood of the Crusaders in Antioch) also flows through Hamma. Since Roman times, and before most of its waters had been syphoned off for irrigation, the river powered the unique, giant water-wheels of Hamma - the famous and unique norias. These wheels are as much as seventy feet in diameter, and their purpose was to raise the water of the Orontes to the Babylonian-style rooftop gardens, and also to feed aqueducts. Until very recently they were still in use, and people said that the noise of them slowly turning was like the sound of distant aircraft, or wild beasts roaring. The muddy trickle of water which was all that was left in the river bed when I was there did not seem capable of turning anything at all, and the great wheels were silent. Even so, they were an amazing sight, and there were very many of them, for the Orontes snakes to and fro in great loops through the city.

I felt too intimidated by the atmosphere of brooding hostility to try to see anything else of Hamma. With so much of it in the process of being levelled, there seemed little point; instead I went to find something to eat. Hassan had told me that there were very few restaurants functioning, but I found a place which cooked chickens on a spit. Leaning Evans against the window where I could keep him in sight, I went in. Immediately a youth came out of the café and picked up the cycle, and I went out again in a hurry to prevent him making off with it. Why, after this short exchange, I should find myself stuck with the youth's company for the next half-hour, while I tried to eat my chicken, I could not quite understand, but so it was. I hope he was not typical of Syrian youth, and did not reflect generally held attitudes, for what he had to say was quite sickening.

It was a litany of hatred against Israel and America, and a promise of vengeance and the ultimate annihilation of both countries. It would have been ludicrous had there not been a voyeuristic lingering on the atrocities he claimed to have seen in the Lebanon, and the number of soldiers he thought he had himself shot there. At the beginning of this monologue, I had attempted to ask him why he thought the

Israelis and Americans were so evil, but he could only see that as a self-evident truth. How Syria could conquer both nations was also self-evident; Allah was on the side of Syria: Jehad, Holy War, no less. I could have been listening to a Muslim of the Crusader period, rather than a young man of the Twentieth Century. We did not part as friends, because I refused to let him pay for my food or to have a ride on Evans.

It was getting dark after I left the restaurant so I made my way to Hassan's house as I had promised, encountering a certain amount of aggression from young boys on the way. It was a small traditional Arab house, with three rooms leading off a narrow, open courtyard, a kitchen on the opposite side, adjacent to a washroom and an Asian lavatory. On the high, blank wall, a night-scented climbing plant grew, and the whole place was attractive and spotlessly clean. Hassan lived with his mother, his young wife, who was shortly expecting their second child, and his pretty two-year-old daughter. As none of the others spoke English he felt free to discuss them openly, as we all sat together, drinking delicious Arab coffee and eating sliced melon.

'It is my mother I love. My wife is just a business arrangement to have my children,' said Hassan matter-of-factly 'I could not live without my mother and my daughter too, but I can always get another wife,' he added, when, embarrassed, I felt moved to protest. The wife was not much more than a child herself, and it didn't seem much of a life for her, with the old lady taking all Hassan's affection and tenderness, while she was being treated little better than a servant. She certainly didn't look happy.

Hassan then suggested that I should stay the night in the house as his guest, rather than in the hotel. I readily accepted; the thought of being the only woman in the hotel, and without even a room, had not been particularly inviting. He said he would be relieved if I stayed, as he hated leaving the women alone at nights, especially now, when the baby was due. He was not expecting a perfect child, he said. The doctor had warned him there was the likelihood of some abnormality, but whatever came would be welcome. During the fighting in Hamma his wife had been so badly frightened she had lost the child she was carrying then. He told me these things in the same matter-of-fact way in which he discussed his relationship with his wife.

While Hassan and I talked, his mother, who had welcomed me by presenting me with one of the fragrant flowers from the climber, prepared herself for prayers. After a rapid, ritualistic wash at a tap in the courtyard, she placed a white cloth over her head and a white shapeless garment over her clothing. Spreading out her mat in the courtyard, she faced towards Mecca, and went through the ritual prostrations. Hassan followed, after a more thorough wash, and the donning of a long gown. It was all conducted without self-consciousness, as naturally as any other daily activity, but the young wife didn't participate.

I went back with Hassan to get my luggage, and he escorted me in both directions, as it clearly wasn't safe to be alone on the streets, which were unlit and full of milling crowds of men and boys. Then he hurried off, eager to be back in his hotel which was his pride and joy, and which he was determined to develop into one of the best hotels in the rebuilt Hamma. It wasn't an easy life, he said, since no one was willing to do menial work. If you wanted any job done properly, even washing the stairs, then you must do it yourself. We had said goodbye before he went as I would be gone before he returned the following day.

Back in the house, the mother sat with me while the poor young wife, who never smiled, moved heavily about preparing a meal. I thought she looked ready to give birth at any moment, and I was embarrassed to have her waiting on me. Occasionally her frustration showed in the sharp blows she gave the child, who went to her grandmother for anything denied her by her mother. We ate, sitting on cushions on the floor in the courtyard, a simple meal of rice and vegetables. The child, who had been slapped again for not eating, fell asleep on the old woman's lap.

The following morning I rode on to Homs, which I found to be the least lovely of all the Syrian towns I visited. Willibald had had a trying time there too. It was called Emessa in his day and, together with other companions he had met on the way, he had been imprisoned, on suspicion of being a spy. I thought how strange it was that countries seem to keep the same quirks and characteristics for so many centuries. Many pilgrims have mentioned troubles with police, customs, and permits in Syria, from the Fourth Century onwards.

Willibald had found a lot of kindness among individual Syrians too, just as I had done. While he was in prison, people had sent in food for him, and a rich merchant had arranged for him and his friends to be taken out for a bi-weekly bath and a wander through the bazaar, where they were instructed to ask for anything that took their fancy, which the merchant would settle up for later. They were even taken to pray at a Christian church so that their Muslim benefactor might acquire merit from the exercise of charity, which shows how tolerant Islam could be, 375 years before the Crusades.

I have less pleasant memories of the place than I imagine Willibald had, for he and his friends were soon released, and sent on their way with official permits, whereas I found it an ugly, noisy town, and this feeling wasn't helped by my meeting there with an unhappy British woman, married to an unpleasant, bullying Syrian, from whom she felt unable to break free because of their three teenage children. She would never see them again if she left the unhappy marriage, for in Muslim countries the man is always given custody of his offspring. It would be some comfort if I felt that my visit had given her any pleasure, but I think that the humiliation of having a stranger see the rudeness and disdain with which her husband treated her, must have outweighed the benefits of a new face and sympathetic ear.

It was a great relief to leave Homs behind, with its massive rebuilding programme and hideous industrial pollution, and take the old Baghdad trade road to Palmyra. To get to this most romantic of ancient cities meant going a hundred miles out of my way in an easterly direction, a journey through the clear air of the Syrian desert, which was welcome in itself, apart from the marvellous city at the end of it. Palmyra did not feature at all in the Crusades, nor would I think that any pilgrim bound for Jerusalem passed anywhere near it. Its glories were over by the beginning of the Second Century A D, after it was captured by Rome. Not to visit it, however, would have been unthinkable, as it is one of Syria's loveliest treasures.

There was a trading post there even in the days of Solomon, when it was known as Tadmor in the Wilderness, and before that the earliest of the wandering patriarchs watered their flocks there. It assumed its importance when the trade route from India and the East started to come up the Persian Gulf and on to Baghdad, instead of by the older way, via the Red Sea and Petra. Silks, jade, spices, and all the luxuries of the Orient lurched through the desert on the caravan route to the Mediterranean, and the substantial oasis of Palmyra made it an important stopping place on the way. Its greatness and romance are therefore rooted in trade, as are most civilizations - something which the English seem to choose to ignore, considering trade to be not the proper employment of gentlemen. A powerful kingdom grew up around Palmyra and, as Graeco-Roman culture came in from the West, a marvellous city took form in the desert, alongside the oasis, the work of yet another extraordinary woman who was its final independent ruler. This was Queen Zenobia, an educated, cultured woman, who both understood tactical warfare and had the ability to lead men in battle. So great a conqueror did she become that under her Palmyra's rule stretched from the coast of North Africa to the Caucasus. When eventually Rome moved against her, she held off the legions for several years before she was captured by the Roman general Aurelian in 106 A.D, and was led into Rome in golden chains. She disappears from history at that point, but she has as her memorial a city that very few rulers have been able to equal.

All knowledge of the existence Palmyra, the city in the desert, was lost to the West for centuries. It was discovered again by chance when some merchants came across the ruins in 1678, and brought back enthusiastic tales of its fabulous, fallen grandeur, and it has stirred people's imagination ever since.

When I caught my first glimpse of it from the lip of the shallow trough in which it lies, I could see why Rose Macaulay had described it as 'like a garden of broken daffodils'. There is a delicacy about the ruins which is reminiscent of natural growing things, a matter of colour and proportion. Corinthian columns of a deep creamy yellow rest in profusion upon the desert sand. Many are standing too, in lengthy colonnades, or supporting triumphal arches and temples. To the left of the fallen city is an Arabic castle, overlooking the site from a high spur of a ridge; and to the right is the vivid green of the palm trees in the oasis.

There are two hotels. The one known as the White Elephant, because no one stays there, has been built at a huge cost. It has a vast number of stars and can cater for hundreds of rich people at a time; but rich people don't seem to want to stay overnight, in Palmyra. Perhaps a film company will take it over one day, when making a desert epic; they would be able to quarter a complete Roman legion there, or Lawrence's Bedouin army. The other hotel is called, rather obviously, The Zenobia, and was originally built as a government rest house, and then turned into a hotel in the Twenties by an East European countess and her (reputedly) complaisant husband. It is said that she had a passion for Arab men and used the hotel as a selection ground. There was a tremendous scandal when she ran off with a married Saudi Arabian, who had been *en route* for Mecca. Apparently, the Countess was so smitten, that, disregarding her marriage to the Count, she committed bigamy by marrying her Saudi (he of course being Muslim could have several wives) and accompanied him to Mecca. King Ibn Saud was outraged at the thought of an infidel woman entering the sacred city and is said to have had the man executed and the Countess thrown into prison. It would have been a salutary tale, had the Countess mended her ways when she was released, and returned contritely to the Count. But of this, or of what the Count thought about it all, I have not heard.

The Zenobia had a certain shabby attraction; simple but good-sized bedrooms and antiquated bathrooms. The sheets were the only items that were really clean. Even so, surrounded as it is by the ruins, and with a pleasant garden full of Corinthian capitals, it would be an excellent place to stay, if the Arab staff didn't consider guests to be such a strain upon their life style. As it is, the best chairs, the shadiest table in the garden, and all the nicest things are all reserved for their use and, unless they are feeling particularly energetic, guests are made to feel that demands for service are in very poor taste.

I stayed for two days and could have easily spent a week without seeing it all. One of the temples, the Temple of Bel, is supposed to be the largest ruin in Syria; that alone was worth weeks of study, though just to walk across its vast courtyard was a daunting prospect in the afternoon heat. I found it much less taxing in the narrow valley to the north of the city, which housed the necropolis, and where it was possible to find shade. Here were the unique, tall, square Towers of the Dead, where the embalmed bodies were once stacked neatly on shelves, as many as five hundred to a tower whose entrances were painted and decorated with statuary.

Best of all was just to wander about Palmyra in the cool hours of early morning, enjoying the colour and the shadows of the graceful columns, with only the birds for company.

There was no escape from passing through Homs yet again. The second time I had the chance to see the industrial pollution on its western outskirts, as I made another side-trek, this time in order to visit the most famous castle in the world: Krak des Chevaliers, the stronghold of the Knights Hospitallers. The scenery changed abruptly at Homs, from the pale yellow sand of the great Syrian desert to the rich arable lands of Western Syria; a disorientating transformation even at the speed of Evans.

Krak was visible from a great distance, for it is set upon a very steep hill at a height of 2300 feet. When it was built, it dominated what was enemy country for miles around, and was called many different names by the Saracens, including 'a bone in the throat of the Muslims'. By Christians it was known as 'the key of the Christian lands'. It could hold a thousand horses and five thousand men, and could withstand a siege for an almost unspecified time. Its storage potential was enormous, and it had at least thirteen separate wells, and further water supplies within the walls. A string of such strongholds stretched throughout the narrow strip of Outremer, from Northern Syria to the Negev desert, seldom more than a day's ride apart. It was largely these castles which enabled the Crusaders to hold out against superior forces for nearly two hundred years. Whenever a castle was defeated, it was always the jealousies and internal problems which was the cause, for the castles themselves were virtually impregnable.

Of all these castles of Outremer, Krak was the greatest, the epitome of the medieval fortress-builder's art. When it finally came into the hands of Baibars in 1267 it was through surrender not conquest. As so many historians have written, if only the military orders of Templars and Hospitallers could have co-operated with each other and with the Kings of Jerusalem, what a different outcome there might have been to the Crusades, for they were the only permanent standing army in Outremer. As it was, however, the position was impossible. Answerable only to the Pope, and with the ludicrous power to make separate treaties with the Muslims, the military orders could be said to have actually hastened the inevitable downfall of the kingdom.

I was thinking hard about the Knights as I rode the last few miles towards their castle, for it helped to take my mind off the terrible steepness of the road. Even so the gradient proved too much, and I had to walk a lot of it. A village clusters up to the walls of Krak, and very small Arab boys raced me up the road when I was riding, easily keeping up with me.

Even within the walls, there was no way that I could quietly walk about on my own, and begin to work out what the various towers and rooms of this enormous citadel had been used for, not because I hadn't a guide book - I had a very good one in fact - but because there was no way that the importunate young Arab men hanging about the castle, were going to let me. A woman on her own was a rarity that they were not prepared to miss out on. After refusing the attentions of I don't know how many, the biggest bully of them all simply announced that he was taking me around; short of hitting him, which I didn't think was a good idea, there was nothing I could do to shake him off. Even when I lurked for what seemed to me like ages in a noisome lavatory, he was outside waiting for me when I emerged.

My suspicions about him were completely justified. He was indeed 'as hot and lecherous as Chaucer's sparrow' and my memories of Krak are all coloured by trying to escape being mauled about by him. Since so much of the castle consists of dark underground passages, this was not easy. Having inspected the oil storage vaults with difficulty, I eschewed the wine vaults and underground stables. Views are the thing at Krak, for the castle is a series of concentric fortifications and it is possible to gaze down into moats, courtyards, towers, and inner and outer walls from the embrasures. These narrow places also provided opportunities for my horrid escort to corner me. After one particularly forceful attempt at a steamy embrace I screamed at him, and it had a most salutary effect for a brief moment. He backed right off, but then I had to listen to all sorts of denials and protestations of innocence. He even told me he was in the secret police, with the unspoken implication that I had better mind my step, and by the time he finished defending his motives, he had talked himself into a mood of belligerence, as if I had deeply wronged him. His parting shot was: how dared I complain when he had charged me nothing for the guided tour?

I had no sooner got away from this odious individual and was walking around the outside walls, wheeling Evans, when a youth of no more than twenty came straight up and tried to put his arm around me, while pretending to point out something of interest. Fortunately Evans was between us and I was able to fend him off - leaving I was pleased to note, some black chain grease on his trouser leg. But I began to have serious doubts about my ability to cope with Krak unaided after that, and I went to the ticket office and told the man in charge what a miserable time I was having, and asked for his advice. He was a very calm and dignified old man who agreed that the young men were an awful nuisance. He invited me to take coffee with him, and afterwards he himself guided me around.

We went back up the long shallow stairway with a vaulted ceiling, along which the horses of the Knights were ridden to their stables, and which led through the eighty-foot-thick outer walls and up into the first courtyard. Up a steeper, open staircase we reached another, larger courtyard, with the church on the right and the great thirteenth-century council chamber on the left. Taking another staircase to a third courtyard, amongst towers of varying heights, we climbed to the top of the tallest tower of the inner ward. From here, without having to defend myself from amatory attack, I was able to look down on almost the whole incredible extent of the castle and its surrounding moat. It was a complete town, totally self-sufficient and, even with the decay of centuries upon it, tremendously impressive. I would not call it beautiful, but I could understand other people finding it so, in the sense that it was something as perfect of its kind as it was possible to imagine.

From this height, a vast extent of terrain could be surveyed, from the Mediterranean in the west to the desert beyond Homs in the east. I thought of how powerful and invincible the knights must have felt standing here. It was the sort of prospect given to Jesus by the devil, when he was undergoing his temptations in the wilderness. 'They were proud men,' said the guide, as though reading my thoughts.

# Chapter Sixteen

*In feith Squier, thou hast thee well y-quit,*
*And gentilly I preise well thy wit,*
*.. .Considering thy youthe.*

Chaucer

The Monastery of St George, where I spent the night, is within sight of Krak, and was standing there for at least six centuries before the Crusader castle was built. Being Greek Orthodox it had no role in the Crusader Kingdoms, which is perhaps the reason that it is still there today, providing shelter for modern pilgrims. The journey of eight miles or so up to the little side valley in which it stood, gave me a glimpse of an entirely different Syria from the one I had seen so far. It was an intimate countryside, of small fields, olive groves, and orchards worked by family groups. Two stout old ladies were picking apples and they stopped me to give me some; the apples were small like crab apples, but had a nutty flavour like Cox's. The taste, combining with the scenery, which was remarkably like parts of Wales, produced a sudden clear image of home, so sharp that for a moment I wasn't sure of where I was.

When I reached the monastery, I went through a gate-house into a high-walled courtyard and found a young monk who spoke a little English. There was no problem about my staying there, for there was plenty of room. I was given a fairly large cell in the guest wing, above the chapel. There were two ancient beds in it; both with high, curved, walnut headboards, lumpy flock mattresses, and an interesting assortment of quilts. There was no other furniture, pictures or texts in the room. The washing facilities were at ground level and very grim, consisting of a galvanized trough with a row of taps above it, in a narrow room full of overflowing waste buckets. As these facilities were used by both sexes, and there were several other guests staying at the monastery and no door to this washroom, there was no way I could wash properly, much as I needed to after the hard pull up to the castle. Still that was a small inconvenience compared to the pleasure of spending the night in a proper pilgrim setting.

It was an interesting building, though much of it was no later than the Nineteenth Century, when the monks rebuilt large parts of it themselves, including the chapel. Just three monks remain now, not nearly enough to keep the place in order. All the rooms centre on two courtyards. The outer one has the new church and offices on the ground floor, with the pilgrim accommodation above. Each cell opens off an outside gallery which runs around three sides of the courtyard. The inner courtyard is much earlier and considerably lower than the outer one. It has the fourth-century Roman church and hermit's cell beneath it and the ninth-century Byzantine church off to one side, under the outer courtyard. The rest of the building is for the monks; the three of them must rattle around in it rather, since it once housed around a hundred monks and novices.

The ninth-century church is the most interesting, with some superb icons, one of which was recently stolen by a French visitor. It passed through Sotheby's, I was told, where it fetched some astronomical sum, before Interpol got wind of it and tracked it down. It is back now, hanging in its old place with no attempt to protect it from other thieves.

Two young Syrian women were staying in the room next to mine, and one of them, who spoke English, invited me to have a cup of coffee with them. They worked in offices in Damascus, they told me, and they liked coming to the monastery for weekends, to walk about in the countryside; most people came for that reason, they said, but once a year there was a festival, when Christians of many different denominations have an ecumenical get-together which focuses on renewal and meaning. Syria's ten per cent of Christians have more denominations than any other country, just as there are more varieties of Muslims.

Later I walked to a restaurant with the young women, back down the hill under a marvellous night sky, dark velvety blue and thick with stars. The restaurant had a terrace overlooking a steep-sided valley, and with the absence of street lights and traffic, and a huge full moon low in the sky, it was a wonderfully romantic and restful place.

The lighting in the monastery was just sufficient to guide one to bed and no more. The other guests were all sitting outside their cells in the warm night air, chattering away like starlings. I thought I would never be able to get to sleep, tired though I was, but I must have felt very safe there, for I dropped off almost immediately, and slept better than I had at any time on the journey. In the morning I left my offering in the church box, since there seemed to be no other way of making payment.

Damascus was the next objective, but it was too far to reach in one day, even with my usual early start. A hundred miles away, and some forty miles before Damascus, there was a town called Nabak, which I was assured had an hotel, so it was towards this goal I was headed. At first the day went well, and I made good progress back again to Homs, to rejoin the Via Nuova. There, two strong doses of industrial pollution, from the western and the southern outskirts of the city, made me feel as though my lungs had been cauterized. Both Evans and I were covered in a thick layer of white ash.

I stopped at the first café I came to, which had several long-distance buses outside it, and queues of people were waiting to be served at the counter. I hadn't eaten since the previous day and, after cycling forty miles on an empty stomach, I expect my blood sugar was fairly low, and my patience was probably shorter than usual. Whatever the cause, I found myself embroiled in an incident in the queue, where I was telling off the Arab behind me for making a nuisance of himself, and an Australian youth in front was telling me off for being so touchy, and yet another Arab was taking my part and trying to pour oil on troubled water.

It was all over in a moment, and the Australian apologized. He was feeling very fed up because he'd come all the way from Iran on the bus and had had a bad time at the Syrian border. His last $100 was now in Syrian lire which he would have to convert again before he crossed into Jordan later that day. He was on his way to Israel as fast as possible in order to get work on a kibbutz for the winter. I told him about my problems with the Arab men, and he said that, now he'd thought about it, it made sense. Nearly all the men on his bus, he said, were Iranians bound for Damascus to pick up women. He said that they had talked about nothing else all the way from Iran, and he had the impression that Damascus must be full of brothels. Iran is supported by Syria in her war with Iraq, on account of Iranian oil, so Iranians in search of the sort of pleasures denied them by their Ayatollah, are made welcome in Syria.

My next encounter of the day with Arab men was a very different one. I had stopped at a shop on the edge of a village to buy drink, and after consuming several bottles of Coca-Cola and mineral water, the shopman beckoned me to a seat behind the counter, where I could drink the last bottle in comfort. While he chatted with a crony, a small boy played with empty bottles on the floor, and an occasional villager came in for some small purchase. The shopman then made me coffee, and insisted that I rest for a while before continuing my ride. He could not have been more courteous, and before I left he selected a large bunch of locally grown grapes, washed them, and presented them to me as a gift.

The land had grown increasingly desert throughout the day as I moved southwards. To my right behind a long mountain ridge was the Lebanon, and there seemed to be no time that I could not hear the sound of heavy guns from behind it, in the far distance. The more I saw of the desert, the more I liked it. It breathed a kind of peace which seemed odd coupled with the gunfire, but that is how I found it. Perhaps it is the impermanence of even the contours of the land, as the sand is perpetually reformed by the winds, which makes deserts seem so curiously restful; there is so little for the senses to fasten on and so the mind is free to turn inwards. No wonder prophets and holy men took to wandering the desert areas of the world, in order to be in closer contact with God. No wonder too that cultures like the Jews kept alive the idea that the nomadic life carried a blessing lost in the settled life of cities. The Rechabites, a tribe of Israel, had refused to live in anything other than tents, right up to the time of the exile, because they believed Jehovah wanted them to remain a nomadic people, alive to His voice.

I too would have liked to sleep out in the desert, under the stars, but I didn't quite dare to, mainly because I knew I wouldn't be able to get Evans through the sand to a spot far enough away from the road to feel safe. So I rode on to Nabak, which I reached in the late afternoon, and booked into the only hotel, which was not a nice place. It had dormitories rather than rooms; that is, they were ordinary rooms, but with as many beds as possible stuffed into them. A boy of about ten was in charge, and as there were several rooms free. I chose the least repulsive one, cleaned it up as best I could (there was no bathroom), and went out to find a meal.

When I returned, the boy had been replaced by a thickset, middle-aged man who started to scream at me in Arabic the moment I came in. Fortunately a young man who was also a guest there, and had earlier helped me carry up Evans, spoke good English, and came to my defence. The screaming individual was the owner, and he, apparently, was wanting me to pay for all the beds in my room (ten I think there were), which would be about the price of a suite in the Hilton. The young man said that I was not to do this, as it was quite illegal, and he told me to go to the room I had selected while he reasoned with the man. I had already heard Arabs arguing in various situations, and had found the noise level rather startling. But this argument, conducted just outside my door, sounded as though several people were being murdered in extreme agony. I locked the door, and someone immediately came and hammered on it, screaming like a banshee. I stayed put and the next moment someone was climbing into the room via the balcony, while someone else was simultaneously breaking down the door with an axe.

Somehow I found myself in the hall with Evans, taking refuge behind the young man, while the owner finished dismantling the door with his axe, at the same time directing various of his minions to remove my gear from the room, all with no abatement of the screaming. Unfortunately, I had unpacked everything, and had washed out my clothes, so there were piles of possessions for his grinning helpers to carry into the hall, and I had to keep darting out to rescue fragile items, like my camera or reading glasses. Otherwise I stayed firmly behind the young man, for I am a coward where violence is concerned, and I was by now convinced that this man was a psychopath. A macabre touch was added by all the other male guests sitting impassively on chairs around the walls as though nothing untoward was happening. The young man was visibly shaking with anger, and plainly something had to be done. I jammed all the loose possessions into the panniers, which wasn't easy as I was shaking too, only with me it was fear, not anger.

All I wanted was to get out of there, with Evans and my equipment intact. This was not enough for my young bene-factor, however. He, quite rightly, wanted justice. No sooner had we carried the loaded Evans into the street than he insisted that we go to the police. We were both practically in tears from all the tension, and he kept saying over and over that the man was a 'bastard', and that I must not judge Syrian men by him.

I had doubts about voluntarily entering the portals of an institution of which I had heard so many unsavoury rumours, but I really had no choice. My young man marched straight in and told his story, while I sat there trying to look respectable and intelligent, which is a difficult feat when people are discussing you in a foreign language. The police were perfectly polite and efficient; someone was sent to fetch the hotelier and he was interviewed in another room. From the screams which issued forth I did wonder if they were questioning him under torture, but I was soon called in and found this was not at all the case. He was merely trying to protest his innocence with the same degree of passion as he had demolished the door to the bedroom. The police, however, told him that he had to take me back and give me a room to myself for the night, and at the proper price. Everyone seemed satisfied by this except the hotelier and myself. He obviously didn't like losing face, and I was reluctant to return to a room with a demolished door and a balcony by which anyone could climb in.

A civilian who happened to be in the station at the time, and was an interested spectator of the scene, solved the dilemma by inviting me to spend the night at his house. He had noticed my gold cross, and being himself a Christian proposed taking me home to spend the night with his young daughters. I trusted him immediately but, although the invitation had been made in the presence of the police, it was not enough for the young man. He now felt responsible for my welfare and had no intention of leaving me, until he was assured that I was in safe hands. I was quite bowled over by this. Such courtesy seemed so at odds with the rough scenes that had preceded it; no medieval lady could have had a more gallant squire. With the young man (whose name I never discovered) on the back of my new benefactor's motor-bicycle, and with me following on Evans, we rode off to another part of town.

We went first to a brother who owned a jewellery shop where I 'changed hands' yet again, as it was decided that there was more room for me in the jeweller's house. My young man went away, satisfied that I was indeed safe with my fellow infidels - I just hope he had some idea of how grateful I was for his support. I was then plunged into a bewildering world of new faces, of which a fifteen-year-old girl, Fadia, was the only one who spoke English. She was the daughter of the first brother and a lively and intelligent girl. She said that her parents' home was not nearly as nice as her aunt's house, where we now were, but that she would really have preferred me to stay with her, so I promised to remain over the sabbath, attend their church service, and sleep at Fadia's flat the following night.

I had fallen in, not with a family but with a whole clan. One patriarch, his nine sons and six daughters, together with their families, numbered upward of seventy people and constituted the entire church, apart from the priest.

For all the service meant to me I might as well have gone to a mosque, a long-drawn 'A-m-e-n' was the closest sound or happening that was even faintly familiar. But sitting around beforehand and afterwards, at the patriarch's house, observing something of the richness of interchange between all these closely related people, was fascinating. Very few of them spoke English, so I was free to observe while the coffee and the sweetmeats were passed endlessly around.

Fadia's house was like a moral lesson on the theme of 'you don't need riches to be happy'. All was warmth and harmony and respect for one another, in spite of the lack of material comforts; while at the jeweller's house, there had been a frayed and overworked wife, trying to cope with too many rooms stuffed too full of possessions, and having little time for the two young sons who were constantly being nagged for petty misdemeanours.

Fadia had a sister, Bernadette, who was thirteen, a brother, Fardi, who was eight, and the baby, Susu, a clever six-year-old, already reading and writing well. The children were left a great deal to their own devices and seemed competent and independent. They washed their own clothes; the older girls cooked and, for all the time I was there, little Susu got on with her school work, sitting on the floor, totally engrossed. Their living space was two rooms, a kitchen, and a bathroom in process of being finished. The girls had one room for their bedroom and the parents pushed the floor cushions together in the sitting room to make their bed at night; Fardi slept in with them, I think. Susu did too, the night I was there, as I slept in the girls' room, in Susu's bed.

We spent most of the morning visiting relatives, who lived in a varied collection of houses, from apartments in modern concrete blocks like Fadia's, to two-floored adobe houses, set in a warren of narrow, twisting alleys. I found these older houses endlessly fascinating; no two were alike, but all were simple, with courtyards and whitewashed, uncluttered interiors. There were bright woven rugs and cushions on the floor to sit on.

In the afternoon we stayed in, and lots of Fadia's and Bernadette's school friends came to visit and to try out their English.

There was one thing I had to be very careful about, not to mention my destination. I had been warned about this before leaving England. The least suspicion that one was heading for Israel or had ever been there, would get one immediately deported. Even in this friendly place, among fellow Christians, the attitude of implacable hatred against Israel was just as marked. I had already been asked for my feelings on the subject, and had managed to turn the question around. 'Yes, we all hate Israel,' said the gentle Fadia. 'It is a very bad country.' It is hard not to be able to be open with people who have become your friends.

On the morning I left, I was escorted by Fadia's father on his motor-bicycle to the Damascus road, various members of the family waving me goodbye from their windows as we passed. After solemnly shaking hands, and promising to take great care, I sped away downhill, full of excited anticipation, towards the city which is claimed to be the oldest in the world. Damascus, set in a huge oasis, like an emerald in the surrounding desert, had always attracted people because of its fabled riches.

The Second Crusade had also moved up on Damascus in eager anticipation. They invested its walls on Saturday 24 July 1148, forty-nine years after the capture of Jerusalem, when the Crusader Kingdoms were beginning to feel the pressure of a great new Saracen leader, Nur Ed-Din, the uncle of Saladin. There were many towns it would have been desirable for the Crusaders to capture in order to consolidate the Christian position in the Holy Land. Damascus was not amongst them. It was a neutral city, eager to live in amity with the Franks, so as not to impair trade. Aleppo would have been a much better target, as it was a Muslim stronghold, and so Count Raymond of Antioch urged. Greed however took precedence; a city as rich as Damascus was too great a temptation to resist. The matter was settled when King Louis decided that his wife, Eleanor of Aquitaine, was having an illicit affair with her uncle, Count Raymond. Dragging the protesting Eleanor away from Antioch by force, he determined to do whatever was opposite to the advice of the only really competent tactician that the Crusaders possessed at that time.

The huge expense and effort of bringing the two armies all the way from Europe, not to mention the suffering and deaths on the march through Turkey, were thrown away in a worthless and unsuccessful siege, which they were forced to abandon five days later, when treachery and incompetence had rendered their position untenable. As the glorious army marched ignominiously away, the legend of invincibility which the Crusaders had established over the previous years was shattered for ever. Islam took heart and Damascus was forced into Nur Ed-Din's power, no longer neutral, but an implacable enemy.

Initially I did better than the Second Crusade. At least I entered the city, and with the help of a kind citizen. I was approaching through the usual contaminated outskirts, when a taxi started to cruise alongside. The driver eventually responded to my gestures of `get lost', but to my surprise parked further on and tried to flag me down. I ignored him. A little while later, I came to a confusion of roads, like Spaghetti Junction, and was forced to stop and consider. At which point the taxi reappeared, and the driver, who could quite well have said, 'Serve you right', instead offered me his help, and even said he could understand my hostile attitude, men being what they were. Rather than direct me to the British Consulate, he escorted me all the way there, a distance of several miles, during which time he turned down quite a few fares.

Perhaps my subsequent disappointment with Damascus would not have been so acute if I had not first visited the consulate. The indifference with which I was received was bad enough, but to overhear some loud-mouthed oaf yelling the joke of the day to a colleague - 'Have you heard?' he bellowed. 'There's some stupid Englishwoman trying to cycle through Syria' - made me feel thoroughly rejected and cheapened by association.

When John Ball preached his famous sermon on Blackheath, at the time of the Peasants' Revolt, 'When Adam delved and Eve span, who was then the gentleman?', he talked about fellowship being life, and the lack of fellow-ship, death. Hell, he said, was where man's cries for help could no longer be heard. In that sense these unfriendly British consulates are deathly, even hellish places, and I never at any time on my journey felt such a profound sense of loneliness as when I had been in contact with one.

Damascus was significant for pilgrims because of its association with St Paul. It was within sight of the walls that his conversion occurred, and into the city, down the 'street called Straight', that he was led, blind and helpless. There is still the Roman arch at the end of the street which was there in St Paul's day; the street itself is as straight as a knife from one end of the old city to the other. I felt closer to Willibald here than anywhere else so far, because he would not have found it so very different, apart from the cars, that is. He doesn't have much to say about Damascus, just that St Ananias was buried here. He was more interested in praying at the church of St Paul's conversion, which I think is no longer there.

I went to the Chapel of Ananias, which was a cave converted into a simple Franciscan chapel, near the Roman arch. Afterwards, I went to the house where St Paul was let down the city walls in a basket, to escape from the Jews who were seeking to kill him because of his change of heart. It must have been an odd experience for St Paul to be so dependent on other people for once. He seems such a proud, independent man usually, though after his conversion he obviously strived to achieve a proper Christian humility. Pride dies hard, however, and it is the little flashes of it that he reveals, from time to time, which make him seem so endearingly human. His 'I am a citizen of no mean city' and 'but I was free born' speak directly to something essential in human nature, the same something in me that felt it had been done violence to in the consulate office. I suppose it's our sense of worth.

The Ommayad Mosque is the central monument of Damascus and very unusual and impressive, with much of the earlier Roman structure showing through. Originally it was a church built to contain the head of St John the Baptist, which many Muslims believe is still there. John is a prophet of their faith, as is Jesus, for whom one of the three minarets of the mosque is named. It is believed that He will come down from Heaven to this spot on the Day of Judgement. I would have stayed longer in the mosque had I not been forced to wear the heavy, black, hooded garment which weighed a ton and was terribly hot. Without it no Western woman is allowed to enter, even into the courtyard.

From the Ommayad Mosque to Saladin's tomb is only a short way and this I had to see in order to pay my respects. For, apart from a very few of the Crusader princes, there was no man in the whole history of the Crusades who behaved with more integrity and resolution than Saladin. A devout believer, he was appalled by the Crusaders' behaviour in the Holy Land, especially by knights like the infamous Reynald de Chatillon. His whole life was dedicated to driving out the Christians completely from the East, and after he took Jerusalem on October 1187, he went on to sweep the Crusaders from all their possessions, except for a handful of strongholds on the coast.

The Third Crusade was mounted directly against Saladin, but the only leader of true worth in it, Richard Coeur de Lion, was no real match for him. Courage, charm, and skill in military strategy Richard certainly possessed, but this was coupled with arrogance, cruelty, treachery, and gross stupidity, especially in his dealings with people. Saladin had all Richard's virtues, except his dazzling good looks, but few if any of his failings. He was in every sense the better man, and his victory was as inevitable as it was deserved. Many Christians of his day, including many leading Crusaders, honoured him; they said had he but been born a Christian, they would have followed him to the ends of the earth. There surely cannot be many men who have received such an accolade from their enemies.

If I had been a pilgrim in a saner age, I should now have been able to retrace Paul's footsteps through Galilee, towards Jerusalem. With the present implacable state of international barriers, however, I had to part company with Willibald and my other pilgrim forerunners, and continue southwards along the line of the outer edge of Outremer, into Jordan, and make my crossing into Israel at the Allenby Bridge. In one of my telephone calls home I had been told that the Foreign Office had now secured permission from the Israeli military authorities for Evans to cross over into Israel by this route, so that was one uncertainty removed.

At my hotel in Damascus, the management took a certain interest in my journey, and complimented me for the adroitness with which I manoeuvred Evans in and out of the lift. I thought I was rather good at this too, since it was quite tricky and necessitated rearing him up to balance on his back wheel as though he were a skittish war horse. The lift was the only method of ingress to the hotel, so it was a case of 'needs must'. Before I left, the manager suggested that I should visit a German woman doctor he knew, who was working at a hospital near the border. He said she would find a bed for me there, as he doubted there would be anywhere else to stay. He also informed me that I would find that the road surface would be so bad that it would slow my progress. Syria's relations with Jordan were currently strained so the road leading to the border was not kept in repair, as a sign of disapproval.

I thought this was meant to be a joke, but soon found it was no more than the truth. The state of the road was terrible with a diabolical surface, full of holes and cracks. By the time I had covered the ninety miles to the hospital, I felt positively bruised and battered.

The doctor, Mieke, was a woman of my own age, and quite happy to have me stay for as long as I wanted, as European visitors were rare. Her English was excellent and she was only too pleased to hold long  conversations, the venue for which was most often the operating theatre or one of the wards. I wasn't sure if Mieke wished to shock me, or if she genuinely had got so used to the methods of the locals, who passed in and out of the wards and operating room almost as casually as if they were at home.

I didn't have time to get used to it, but by carefully not watching the moments of incision, and concentrating on what was being said, I was able to take an interest in the proceedings, and not do anything shameful, like  fainting. The staff were friendly and the male orderlies and nurses were so keen on establishing their equality with the doctors that I thought they were probably difficult to instruct.

The standard of hygiene was dismal, even in the theatre, where the patients had to walk in and climb onto the operating table, which was covered with a strip of plastic which still bore the blood and stains of the previous day's operations. What really shocked me, however, was the condition of the nurses' wash room. Mieke, whose quarters were next to the nurses' dormitory, had to share their facilities and I cannot think how she could bear it. It was basically an adequate room with a shower, three lavatories, a row of four basins, and some wall urinals, all white tiled and in working order. Every morning the room was cleaned out by orderlies, and by two o'clock in the afternoon it was disgusting again. The problem was that the nurses washed their clothes and did their cooking in there too, and every particle of rubbish was just thrown on the ground. I reckoned the Augean stables would have seemed like a palace after that place. In all fairness, the living conditions in the hospital were very low, even for the doctors, but I would have thought that they would all have been more comfortable had they practised a little rudimentary cleanliness.

It was in Mieke's room that I first came across Palestinian propaganda literature, and that made me feel considerably more sick than the blood and the dirt had. Many of the incidents the professionally produced booklets dealt with were true events, which had been reported internationally, mostly they were about atrocities perpetrated by Israelis against Palestinians. But the style of the pamphlets could only be described as obscene, for they took the facts and distorted them in a way which did as much violence to the victims as to the guilty. They were designed to be read by simple people, and were expressed in totally black-and-white terms, with a drawing out and a prolonging of the horror, and an almost voluptuous lingering on every dreadful detail. I thought they were specifically and skilfully produced to provoke the maximum amount of hatred in the reader.

I don't know what Mieke's real feelings were. She told me that such literature helped her to understand her patients, who were nearly all PLO, or had sympathies with the Palestinian cause. I wouldn't want to have such pamphlets around the place for I felt they were a corrupting influence; and I couldn't help wondering what all this concentrated hate literature was doing to the young people of Syria. What chance had they against such a cynical manipulation of their emotions?

I received a Christmas card from the gentle intelligent Fadia on my return to England, and the postage stamps bore a picture of one of the recent massacres in a refugee camp in the Lebanon.

# Chapter Seventeen

*Match me such a marvel save in Eastern clime*
*A rose-red city, half as old as time*
Dean Burgon

Sitting on the carpeted floor of an old Arab house, among the ruins of Bosra, having lunch with a village family was a welcome contrast to watching bodies being opened up in the operating theatre. I had spent the morning wandering around the remains of this ancient Roman town in the company of two delightful young men, Mohammed and Adnan, both English literature students at Damascus

University; it was in Adnan's house that I was being entertained. It was a low building sprawling around two sides of a large garden, the other two sides were enclosed by high walls. There was a well in the centre, several trees, and brick-edged flower and vegetable patches. Hens scratched about in the dust, and dogs sprawled panting in the shade. There were about a dozen people of various ages present, from Adnan's parents to a small grandchild just beginning to walk. No one else, apart from the boys, spoke English, but by smiles and gestures I was made to feel welcome.    I was impressed by the gentle courtesy with which everyone behaved towards each other. This was something I had observed in the wards of the hospital too; there was a warmth and graciousness about the people here and a respect for persons, which was very attractive, and quite different from what I had seen in other parts of Syria. This southern part of Syria was a strange area, of black volcanic soil, very fertile in places, but with a lot of poverty too, and, seemingly, more backward than the rest of the country.

Bosra itself had been the capital of the Roman province of Syria, and a substantial city had been built here in about 106 AD, to serve as the main trading post of the area, before Palmyra rose to prominence. Everything had been built out of the local black basalt, which makes the town seem a trifle sombre.    Nonetheless it has outstandingly beautiful remains, including the great colonnaded main street, more than half a mile in length, lined with sunken Roman markets and the bases of huge temples with soaring Corinthian pillars, all in the same black basalt. People live and work in and among the ruins, but there is a policy to remove them and rehouse them elsewhere. I hope they don't do that, because to see vegetable stalls set up among the black pillars, children playing, old men smoking and chatting on the temple steps, gives the place a life and colour which it needs and is an important part of its charm.

The main attraction of Bosra is the theatre enclosed within the citadel. The latter is an Arab structure, first built about 700 AD, and added to and modified over the years.

What makes it unique is that it used the solid structure of the theatre as its core which made it immensely strong. At the same time the enormous Roman theatre has been wonderfully preserved throughout the centuries.

Three times the Crusader armies marched on Bosra and each time they retreated without exchanging blows. It was a useful place for Muslim armies to seek shelter when danger threatened them, on their marches from Egypt to Northern Syria. The bravest and most pathetic of all the Kings of Jerusalem, Baldwin IV, did once reach the walls of Bosra, accompanied, as he invariably was, by the Patriarch of Jerusalem and the True Cross. No king could have had a more appropriate banner, for Baldwin's short life was very much a calvary. A leper from childhood, he had inherited an equally diseased kingdom at the age of thirteen, when his leprosy was already far advanced. For the next eleven years he did his best to hold the crumbling kingdom together, battling not only with the weakness of his hideous affliction, but also with a scheming mother, a headstrong sister and treacherous advisers. There were times when he had himself carried to the battlefield on a litter, too ill even to turn his head. Had his wishes for the succession been respected, it is conceivable that the end of the kingdom might have been averted, but, even on his deathbed, he probably knew that his mother and sister would overrule his wishes.

He died in 1185 at the age of twenty-four, spared the final defeat and the loss of Jerusalem. That occurred four years later, when his worthless successor, the consort of Baldwin's sister, Guy de Lusignan, stupidly led what was left of the Christian fighting forces into Saladin's trap, at the battle of the Horns of Hattin. From the battlements of the citadel I could see the towering bulk of Mount Hermon about eighty miles away in Israel. A little to the left is the site of the catastrophic battle. Thinking of that final battle, and of all the courage and adventure that had established the Kingdom of Jerusalem, brought to an end after less than 100 years, in an ignominious defeat, made me feel sad at such a waste. It was a relief to leave the citadel and go to look at the village.

We wandered through the streets of old houses with their sunken courtyards, where the animals had been stabled on the ground floor and the people had lived above them, going in and out by outside staircases. The design of these houses went back unchanged to Roman times, and there were countless streets of them, all emptied now and the people moved elsewhere: they had an abandoned, mournful air. Mohammed said that his family had lived in one of them, but the government had made them move. No one had wanted to leave their homes; they couldn't see the point, and, moreover, the buildings would fall down with no one to care for them. I supposed the idea was to turn them into a tourist site like the main colonaded Roman street.

They boys had kept what they considered to be Bosra's greatest treasure until last; it was an early Byzantine church which had been turned into a mosque in the late Seventh Century. Here, with pride and reverence, I was shown the footstep of the Prophet Mohammed's camel, set into the rock. It had been venerated for centuries by the Muslim pilgrims passing through, on their way to Mecca. They miss it out now that the road to Mecca no longer passes through Bosra. It occurred to me yet again that going on pilgrimage by bus, train, or aeroplane cuts one off from all sorts of experiences and delights, which pilgrims of a less technological age had enjoyed.

I was glad to have had this idyllic last day in Syria with the hospitable people of the Hauran Plain, but it made my entry into Jordan the following day all the more depressing.

I didn't have any particular problems entering the country, except for a lot of silly young soldiers, who kept stopping me as I neared the customs control, demanding to see my passport. After half a dozen of them had done this, I just said 'No', and as no one shot me I decided they had merely been exercising their chauvinist tendencies.

A little way past the border, I spotted a money-change office on the other side of the road, executed a smart U-turn to reach it, which unfortunately was straight through a patch of oil, and Evans and I were down, sliding almost under the wheels of a passing truck. I couldn't immediately extricate myself, as I was still attached to Evans by the pedal clips; also I was overcome by disbelief. Only twice in my life had I been toppled ignominiously from a bicycle, and both occasions were in the distant past. By the time people came milling around, however, I was already on my feet and assuring everyone that neither Evans nor I had suffered serious injury. Evans, well protected by the four panniers had lost one small area of paint. I was slightly worse off with a skinned left arm and knee, and was in need of a good clean-up as well as tea and sympathy.

I got none of those things. The small crowd lost interest as soon as they saw I was only a walking wounded. When I asked if there was anywhere I could wash, they just shrugged and walked off. So I cleaned up as best I could by the side of the road, using the contents of my water bottle and splashing on lots of iodine. Then, bruised and shaken, I struggled on towards Jerash against a strong headwind, feeling that Jordan wasn't exactly the welcoming country I had been led to expect from reading the brochures.

The countryside had changed abruptly at the frontier with the sudden appearance of hills; not that I could see much of them, as a sandstorm accompanied the wind, adding to my difficulties. By the time I reached Jerash I was not in the best of spirits, and the moment I stopped, I could feel my left arm and leg begin to stiffen. I thought I had better try to find somewhere to stay so that I could rest up for the day. Jerash promised to be a good place to spend some enforced leisure, as it was one of the most extensively excavated cities anywhere in the world, and I had looked forward to exploring it thoroughly. It was not to be, however, for according to the man in the tourist office there wasn't anywhere to stay in Jerash except his house, in which he was prepared to let me have a room at a price. But as he would be away for the day, it would be available only after about seven p m. I told him about my having fallen off Evans and needing a bath, but he merely shrugged and turned his back.

I met some friendly people in Jordan, whom I remember with affection, but I have to say that many of the people I came across were very like the rather sullen, uninterested individual in the tourist office. As a result I did not find Jordan anything like as enjoyable as Syria. Part of the trouble was that it was organized for tourists who arrived by aeroplane, stayed at expensive hotels, and went from place to place in air-conditioned coaches, with guides. Do-it-yourself travellers didn't seem very well catered for. A further problem was that it was horrendously expensive, as there was an artificial rate of exchange so that £1 was worth only half its value.

The real underlying problem however - the cause of all the hostility, veiled and unveiled - was, I felt sure, the Palestinian problem. When a country is as full of refugees as is Jordan, that is bad enough; but when those refugees are your own people, and the land from which they have fled, or been driven out, is part of your land, it must make for a very complicated set of emotions.

I shall have to return some time and see Jerash properly because I obtained no more than the most cursory impression of it on that occasion. After doing little more than walking through its extraordinary and wonderful main street, I accepted a lift to Amman with a couple of British businessmen who were trying to sell Jordan a railway, and who took pity on my dishevelled and, bloodstained condition. I saw them once or twice afterwards for dinner, and they are one of my few good memories of Amman, which ranks as almost the lowest point of the journey. Unfortunately, I had to wait about there for a few days in order for the consulate to start the process whereby Evans and I could cross over into the Promised Land. This required diplomacy on two scores. The first was relatively easy; it meant informing the Israeli authorities of the precise time and date of my crossing. Although permission had been given, confirmation was needed if I was not to be stopped at the bridge by the Israelis, and this meant telexes to Tel Aviv and back again via London - long-winded but foolproof, or so I was told.

The second piece of work was obtaining the bridge pass from the Jordanian authorities. This was normally quite straightforward when it involved only people; a couple of photographs and some money were all there was to it. As far as Jordan is concerned, the West Bank still belongs to them, so you are visiting only occupied territory, not Israel. If you had been to Israel of course you wouldn't be allowed into Jordan at all, so it is strictly one-way traffic. It is really all meaningless face-saving, combined with not missing out on the tourist trade, but both sides cynically maintain the fiction. It was the Jordanians who had first informed the Foreign Office that Israel doesn't allow bicycles over the Allenby Bridge. It would be indelicate to tell the Jordanian authorities that Israel had given special permission for this particular bicycle, as how could the Israelis give permission to enter an area which didn't belong to them? I suppose consulates exist to exercise this sort of diplomacy, and I was thankful to leave them to it.

Once I had appeared, events could be set in motion, and I could wait for a week or so, kicking my heels in Amman, or I could spend the time seeing something of the country. Needless to say I chose the latter. I decided to continue south on the oldest of all Middle Eastern trade roads which led from Babylon to Egypt, and whose course I had been in fact been following since entering Syria. From Amman onwards though, it is known as the King's Highway, because of the biblical reference in Genesis 14 to the 'Kings of the North' who had travelled down it thousands of years ago to attack the Kings of Sodom and Gomorrah and their allies. There was not an inch of the King's Highway which was not steeped in history and, about two hundred miles away, it passed close to one of the most romantic and famous spots in the world.. Petra, the 'rose red city', was somewhere I had dreamt of visiting since I first knew of its existence.

I left while it was still dark. As dawn broke, I was riding through the Old Testament lands of Moab, my spirits rising with every mile I put between myself and Amman. I had left a lot of my luggage behind and on the lightened Evans I had ridden the twenty miles to Madaba before anything was open, and so I sidetracked to Mount Nebo, one of the traditional burial places of Moses. From here I could see the view which Moses showed to the Children of Israel after their forty years in the wilderness. Before me was the wide panorama of the Jordan Valley, with the Dead Sea below and the Judaean Hills behind - the Promised Land. Even at that stage of their journey, gazing over this same view, the trials of Moses were not over. While Joshua and the army had prepared their weapons, some of the Israelites refused to take part in the invasion of Canaan; they wanted to stay in Moab, they said, because it was such good cattle country. Unity of purpose it seems has never been easy to achieve.

I retraced my tracks to Madaba to see the most famous map in the world, the sixth-century Byzantine mosaic of Palestine, showing Jerusalem with its gates and the Holy Sepulchre. It is kept in a modern Greek Orthodox church where it covers a great part of the floor. The little town of Madaba is full of glorious mosaic floors which have been wonderfully preserved, and are now probably the finest collection anywhere. I took the time to see a few of them before continuing on through the  Mountains of Moab.

The one discordant note in the otherwise lovely day was the unfriendliness of the young male Moabites. In every village I rode through I was pursued by jeers and stones until, finally, in an uninspiring town called Rhiban, matters came to a head. I was so mobbed and jostled by jeering boys just let out of school, that I was forced to get off Evans as I was trying to cycle up the steep main street. There was a police post at the top and I was so angry that I marched straight in, full of righteous indignation, and demanded protection. The policemen didn't hesitate; I had the distinct impression that they were used to such complaints. I was accompanied back to the road by two policemen armed with short lengths of plastic hosepipe. The young Moabites had quite wisely scattered in the meantime so I was invited back for tea, and the schoolmaster was sent for to proffer apologies. I was more interested in finding out why their young were so aggressive, but the schoolmaster couldn't manage 'why' questions, he could only say that he knew the boys were 'bad' but they had ways of 'training' them.

'Come back in five years,' he said, 'They will be different, you will see.' I hope so, as do other travellers who have been similarly harassed in Jordan.

I met my first wadi in the hottest part of the day, a profound gash in the earth's crust, about 4000 feet deep; a desert place, which had touches of green here and there, where some hidden source of water nourished a few plants. I sped down growing wonderfully cool as I did so, and was just starting on the climb out of it, in bottom gear and concentrating on finding my rhythm, when a car stopped me, eager to carry us both to the top. I mimed that Evans wouldn't fit into his boot, but he persisted until I got off and demonstrated this fact to him. He was a very kind and tender-hearted man who seemed deeply shocked that someone should try to pedal up such steep slopes. Actually, they were just about the limit of what I could do, especially in that heat; and if anyone else had stopped me, I probably would have given up the struggle and stuffed Evans into their vehicle somehow.

In the late afternoon I came suddenly upon the enormous ruins of the Crusader castle of Kerak, towering above the road at the summit of a hill known to the ancients as *Petra Deserti* - the Stone of the Desert. I booked a room for the night in the government rest house alongside the castle, though not before I had run the gauntlet of further gangs of aggressive young Moabites, impeding my entry into their ancient capital. I was glad to have arrived in time to explore the fortress, for though not as well preserved as Krak, it was still possible to see what a mighty fortification it had been. Built in 1142, it was one of the oldest of the Crusader castles, and became the great family seat of Oultrejourdain, where the châtelaine lived more splendidly than in any royal palace of Europe.

It was when the property fell to Reynald de Chatillon through marriage that it became the chief object of Saladin's attentions, and whenever the opportunity arose he besieged it. By this time the list of Reynald's perfidies was truly horrifying. He had made a most vicious and unprovoked attack on the Christian island of Cyprus; his soldiers streaming all over it for three weeks, burning, looting, raping, and killing in an orgy of destruction. In 1182 he had attacked the pilgrim route to Mecca, planning to take the Holy City itself and scatter the bones of the Prophet. Although he had got no further than Medina, he had sickened everyone by burning and sinking ships full of helpless pilgrims. Even worse from the Cruaders' position, he broke the precious truce with Saladin by attacking the rich caravans which passed so temptingly close to his castles. He even captured a pilgrim caravan taking Saladin's sister to Mecca, and that was the final straw for Saladin who took a solemn oath to destroy him.

In 1183 when Saladin arrived to besiege Kerak yet again, a wedding was being celebrated between the twelve-year-old Princess Isabella, one of the possible heiresses of Jerusalem, and the seventeen-year-old Humphrey of Toron. The mother of the bride sent out dishes from the wedding feast for Saladin. He in return asked which tower the young people were housed in, and gave orders to his soldiers that it should not be bombarded. While everyone was behaving with true medieval chivalry, the Leper King had himself carried from Jerusalem to lift the siege, and once again Saladin had to wait for his revenge, though not for too long. Four years later he had the satisfaction of hacking off Reynald's head, after the debacle of the Horns of Hattin, the disaster for which Reynald's advice was directly responsible.

Kerak was never taken by force. After Reynald's summary execution, it became the property of Humphrey of Toron, who was taken prisoner after the fall of Jerusalem. He was offered his freedom in return for the surrender of Kerak and his other castle, Montreal, and was released from prison to arrange it. The garrison, however, refused to surrender and Humphrey, with true honour, returned voluntarily to prison. Saladin, who respected such honourable behaviour gave the young Humphrey his freedom as a gift and returned to the siege. It was a year before the garrison submitted. They had sold some of their younger women to Bedouin for food and turned out the rest, with the children and other non-combatants to fend for themselves, in order to preserve the food supplies for the fighting men. It was only when the last horse had been eaten that they gave in and surrendered to the Saracens.

The following day I rode through scenery which was as spectacular as any I have ever seen. One of my greatest regrets on this journey was that I hurried through this part of it in such a rush. It was wilderness country, not flat expanses of wind-blown sand, but wildly-riven hills and wadis; infinitely varied and with no two views alike. The road turned and twisted, as it had from time immemorial, the water holes and wells determining its course. The occasional small towns were built by oases and their foundations were as old as anything made by man.

At some point, I passed from biblical Moab into Edom, which seemed altogether less aggressive - as the Children of Israel had also found, according to the Old Testament. Everybody in those days, however, seemed to be fighting one another, and exulting over the numbers they had killed, or lamenting over the bodies of their own dead. The Psalms are full of obscure boasts like 'Moab is my washpot; over Edom will I cast out my shoe'. And the kings of Moab had their boasts about the number of Israelites they had slain inscribed upon stone pillars. So it was really only a matter of the degree of hostility then.

When I stopped at Shaubak in the late afternoon, I found no bands of hostile boys, but an agricultural college from which several young men came out to invite me in to take refreshment with them. There was nowhere to stay in the small town, but as it was too late to make Petra by nightfall, I accepted the invitation to sleep at the home of one of the students, Yosef, whose father was a porter at the college, and who had a house on the campus. The family seemed to be just four persons; the parents, Yosef, and his younger sister; and only Yosef spoke English. It was a simple very small house but fairly modern, and the people sat on chairs, not on the floor.

By the time we had eaten an evening meal of bread, olives, cheese, and eggs, night had fallen and, to my relief, for I was deathly tired after the long hard ride, I saw that Yosef and his family were as ready to go to bed as I was. They all vanished into inner rooms and I was left in a sort of enclosed verandah with dozens of potted plants. I fell asleep just as soon as I had crawled into my sleeping bag.

I was away at daybreak on the last twenty miles, eager to get to Petra now that I was so close. The land became wilder and more mountainous with every mile, and lowering clouds covered the sun, which I had not seen dimmed for several months. The scene took on an air of desolation. Finally, just as the heavens were about to open, I reached the summit of a high ridge on the edge of Wadi Musa and was beckoned over to a souvenir shop to take coffee with the owner as the first drops fell. The thunder of rain on the tin roof stopped abruptly as we finished our coffee and I went outside to see the last of the squall sweeping away across an extraordinary landscape.

At the head of a steep, wide valley rose range upon range of fantastically riven mountains, none of them particularly high, but so jagged and pinnacled and split by crevices that not even the Black Cuillin of Skye could compare with them. Their colours too seemed not of this world: purple, navy blue, and dark red, edged with the yellow, harsh blue, and pink of the clearing sky. Somewhere behind those unreal pinnacles lay the hidden city of Petra.

I had already decided that, like earlier travellers before me, I was going to sleep in the ruins of Petra, not in the hotels outside. With only two days to spend there, I did not want to waste my time trekking up and down the four miles of the Siq; also, I wanted to be there to see the place by moonlight. So after getting permission to do this from the archaeologist in charge, Evans and I entered the inconspicuous crack in the cliffs and proceeded down the Siq, the unique passage which kept Petra a secret city until the Nineteenth Century.

I found myself in a narrow twisting chasm between steep, flat-faced cliffs, several hundred feet high. The Nabataeans who first built the city diverted the river which over the millenia had shaped this passage, thus making a perfect approach for their city.

About fifty feet from the exit, the black uneven walls of the Siq suddenly become the frame for a massive temple front in glowing, pale-pink sandstone. It didn't make any difference that I knew what was coming, that I had previously seen pictures of it, and had some idea of what to expect. It still burst upon the consciousness with a great shock of disbelief, as I began to get some notion of the immense scale of it.

A little further, and I was standing in an enormous open bowl in the heart of those jagged mountains. In the centre was a huge shapeless mound of broken masonry which was the city, as yet barely touched by the archaeologists. Houses, palaces, temples, baths, theatres, everything that pertained to the living is just rubble. It is the city of the dead which remains. Every cliff face is carved with elaborate façades in high relief, behind which are the burial chambers.

Everything is carved out of the solid living rock, including the statuary and ornamentation, nothing is added on - which is why they have survived the wars, earthquakes, and other disasters which have completely erased the free-standing buildings.

The style of these vast mortuary monuments is unified, but strange; an eclectic mixture of Greek, Mesopotamian, and Egyptian, with a few other styles thrown in - for the Nabbateans were great travellers. But it is the colour that makes it so especially haunting. Although Dean Burgon, who wrote 'a rose-red city half as old as time', never saw the place, he hit upon the perfect description for it: rose-red it is, with a little green, blue, yellow, and pink also; but in the early morning and as the sun sets, it glows with a perfect and unforgettable rose-red radiance.

Earlier travellers, such as Agatha Christie and H V Morton slept among the ruins in a well-organized camp; but that has been replaced now by the four-star hotel outside the siq. Travellers who wish to follow in their predecessors' footsteps must do so in less comfort. The first night I slept in the compound of a Bedouin family. The Bedouin have lived in the ruins for centuries, some of them in their traditional tents, and others in the smaller tombs built in freestanding rocks. The head of the family whose facilities I shared had three wives, so there were quite a few small children around; thin, poorly-clothed, and very grubby, they were nonetheless an appealing bunch. They saw me as a welcome diversion, and hauled me off for my first exploration of the ruins. They fought over who would hold my hands, though I must admit that I would have preferred for them to keep their hands to themselves, as they were absolutely filthy: with no sanitation and virtually no water in Petra, I dreaded to think of the assortment of bacteria they were passing on to me. We ate supper, almost in the dark, I doing my best to manage the rice with fingers and pitta bread, and my host pushing succulent pieces of chicken to my side of the communal plate.

After supper the compound began to fill with men, all sitting around the open fire, on cushions on the dirt floor.

One spoke some English, and he sat by me to explain what was going on. Apparently my host's sister had quarrelled with her husband, and had left him and come to stay with her brother, bringing her baby son with her. Her husband wanted her to return, and had come to discuss the matter, together with all the male relatives of both families. As the marihuana went round, voices got higher and speeches longer, and it went on and on interminably, while I kept falling asleep, and then waking up and watching the stars twinkling far away, but twice as big and twice as numerous as in England. Eventually everyone went away, except for the errant wife, who remained unreconciled (I was told that divorce is common among the Bedouin). I crawled into my sleeping bag and lay down on the mattress they had spread for me on the dirt floor which was strewn with the various bones and debris of supper. The rest of the family were jumbled together in an adjacent cave, and this was where they had at first proposed I should also sleep. I was thankful it was not raining so that I could stay in the fresh air under the stars. My head was just out of reach of the tethered camel, who stamped about and made strange noises all night.

It says a great deal for the magic of Petra that I was able to contemplate another day there without the possibility of even the most rudimentary wash; there is water, but very little, and the Bedouin keep its whereabouts a strict secret. I wandered around with Evans, taking photographs, and the Bedouin men who bring the tourists through the Siq on their horses came and chatted to me, and the ones who had souvenir stalls gave me tea. European women are popular with Bedouin and several of them have Western wives, including one from New Zealand, who was introduced to Queen Elizabeth when she visited Petra recently. I was told that the Queen had been somewhat nonplussed by the introduction. Bedouin normally buy their wives. Fifteen is the age they prefer, but such girls are very expensive, I was told; even an Egyptian one costs around $100.

I received several proposals of marriage as I wandered around, and at one point, a deputation rode up to make me a formal offer on behalf of one of their number - a very small, rather elderly man. I explained that I already had a husband, but they thought that didn't matter as he was not around to claim me. I was rather at a loss for any other defence, until one of them asked if my husband could ride as well as their candidate. I replied truthfully that I thought not, but that he was much taller. They seemed to think that was a huge joke, and did not renew their offer.

The keeper of Petra's shop invited me to leave Evans locked up in his store room, which was a great help as a bicycle was of no use to me among the ruins. Free of him I was able to explore some of the side valleys, and climb to the tops of the cliffs where the 'high places' were. These are the ancient altars of sacrifice, for the worship of the dark gods of antiquity - the Baalim. Every hilltop in this Old Testament land once had its altar to its own particular Baal - a local god who could guarantee the fertility of the crops, the animals, and the people, in return for blood sacrifices. They were places far older even than Petra, where the people of the land had ritually slain their children as acts of propitiation.

The chief high place of Petra is above the Siq, an extensive platform on the levelled summit of the cliff. Two obelisks stand by the altars, and they and the channels for draining off the blood of the victims, and the pools cut into the rock for ritual ablutions are all as sharply incised as though they were abandoned only yesterday. The place gave me a new insight into the continual thunderings of the Old Testament prophets concerning the Israelites' apostasy: 'backsliding', 'whoring after strange gods', 'playing the harlot on every high place'. Israel had a concept of God which was immeasurably higher and finer than the other cultures around her; a God both universal and beneficent; a God who demanded obedience to a high moral code rather than blood sacrifices. Unfortunately, human nature seemed to prefer the excitement and the drama of the Baal worship. Even when Israel had its own centralized temple at Jerusalem, the worship still centred on the continual   slaughter of animals, as though Jehovah was the local Baal of Jerusalem, to be propitiated with blood, while Hosea, Amos, Isaiah and the other prophets preached on through the centuries that it was not burnt offerings, but 'justice' and 'righteousness' that God wanted. Jesus was preaching much the same message 800 years later.

Brooding over it all from this high place, nearly 2000 years further on still, I wondered whether there had really been any progress at all towards Amos's vision of 'justice rolling like waters and righteousness like an ever-flowing stream'. The cruelties which have been perpetrated in this century are as ghastly as anything done in antiquity, and the inequalities seem just as great. There are still people starving all around the world, while the West suffers from the diseases of superabundance; and the dispossessed live out their lives in refugee camps, their numbers increasing year by year. It seemed to me that the Baalim had just as much pull as they ever did.

Petra was far more enjoyable away from the disturbing high places that provoked dark thoughts. There was no vertical surface anywhere which did not have tombs cut into it, each with its elaborate façade, and each different. Some were small, like little villas, others were almost as large as St Paul's Cathedral. That night I was to sleep in a cave near to the largest of them all, one known as 'the monastery'. The cave was owned by the shopkeeper who was looking after Evans, and the cave was an hour's walk away, along a steeply-ascending valley of marvellous rock scenery and carvings.

When I reached the high plateau my Bedouin host was sitting in a little souvenir-cum-teashop in a natural cave, facing the huge barbaric façade of the monastery. This was his second shop, which I suppose made him something of a tycoon. After he had made me a glass of delicious mint tea, he showed me a staircase around the side of the monastery, which the builders had made and by which I could climb to the enormous urn at the top; it was very exposed up there, like being on the golden ball above St Paul's. He also showed me the jug handles cut into the rock for fixing ropes to, so as to lower the blocks of stone. The colossal designs had to be worked out first, and then the cutting was started, working from the top, downwards, without scaffolding and knowing that if you made an error there could be no sticking it back on again. There were several such errors, monuments abandoned by the builders after their chisel had slipped, or the sandstone had fractured along the wrong line.

I decided that these Nabbatean tomb carvers of Petra had been as compulsive as gamblers; happy only when hacking away at a cliff or planning some new gigantic project; but then one could could say the same about most artists, or writers, or of anyone who has a passion for one thing above all others.

The Nabbateans were an Arabic people who built up a trade monopoly in the Third Century BC. They had a string of cities right across Arabia to the coast, at Gaza and grew very rich - which was why they had lots of leisure to travel around and study the art styles of other cultures, before coming back to Petra to practise in a habitat ideally suited to it.

That night, while another of the early-winter rain storms lashed the hillside, I sat on the floor of my host's cave, with his wife and eight children, our shadows thrown onto the roof and walls by the light of the single oil lamp. My host, unusually, had only one wife. The children were aged between one and fourteen, and one of the boys, who was about six, sang songs right through the meal. From the fervour and the gestures, I would have guessed that they were Palestinian fighting songs, even had I not been told so. The only girl was the beautiful year old baby scuttling on all fours around the cave, and the object of affection for all the brothers who quarrelled perpetually over who should hold her, until they were quelled by a word from their father.

As I grew used to the dim light, I could make out more details of the cave, which was lined all around the edges with boxes and suitcases for storage. Lines stretched between the jug handles carved into the rock supported quilts and spare clothing. Cooking was done on a primus stove and everything was neat and homely and relatively clean.

When the rain had stopped, I was escorted to my night's lodging, a very small free-standing tomb, rather like a hermit's cell. There was a pile of quilts and cushions on the floor, a few jug handles, and a shelf cut into the rock. If it had only had a water source near by, it would have been a perfect place for a retreat. I lay watching the patch of velvet darkness full of stars which marked the doorway, and there seemed nothing eerie in the thought that this had once been someone's burial chamber. At hourly intervals all through the night, I awoke as one or another of the cat population of Petra crept in to see who had invaded their territory.

# Chapter Eighteen

*This worlde is but a thurghfare ful of wo*
*And we ben pilgrimes passing to and fro*
Chaucer

I rode the Desert Highway back to Amman, and that I am still alive to tell the tale is because a brand new road is taking shape alongside the existing two-lane one. On this I could pick my way among the slow-moving construction and tar-laying machines for quite long stretches, and so escape for a while from the lethal passage of madly-speeding truck drivers. It was a fast route, which is why I chose it, but the danger from the trucks and the high winds blowing across the flat sandy wastes, tossing Evans about like chaff, was a high price to pay. The warm hospitality I met with on the way was another compensation for the grimness of the journey.

The first night out of Petra I thought I was being kidnapped when a car forced me to stop and the driver leapt out and prevented me from proceeding. The passenger, who turned out to be his wife, a schoolteacher, spoke a little English and managed to explain that they wanted to take me to their village for the night. As it was just coming on to rain again it seemed a good time to find shelter. I went with them and became the guest of a Bedouin village, just across the valley from the Crusader castle of Krak de Montreal.

Like many Bedouin in Jordan these people had ceased to live in tents generations since, and had perfectly ordinary houses furnished with many of the trappings of modern civilization, such as refrigerators, televisions, and washing machines. They still preferred to eat sitting cross-legged on the floor, however, and the social structure of the village was very closely interwoven. I wasn't able to work out many of the relationships, which was not surprising as I think I must have met at least a hundred persons. When people were not pouring into whichever house I was in, I was being taken round to someone else's place. I got the distinct impression that it would be a social gaffe to miss out on meeting this Western woman who rode a bicycle. Everyone was most hospitable, and kept pressing food and drink upon me; they even took me by car to see the castle and I was intrigued to be told that thirty years ago it had been their village school.

Krak de Montreal - the 'Castle of the Royal Mountain' - is older even than Kerak, and was built by Baldwin I in 1115, as the chief stronghold of Oultrejourdain for keeping the Saracens out of Judaea. After Kerak was built, Montreal in its bleak territory, became more of an outpost, though in the last event, it held out a few months longer than Kerak. Not until most of its garrison had gone blind (from lack of salt, it was thought), did they surrender to Saladin. Now it is just a ruin and even the Turkish repairs and additions are almost obliterated. Only from a distance can its formidable outline conjure up the power and menace it once held.

For my last night in the desert, I thought I should be able to find some sort of hotel at the staging post of Qatrana, which has a multitude of cafés and garages to service the never-ending flow of trucks and buses. But after wandering up and down them all and finding nowhere to sleep, I was forced to present my Arabic letter of introduction at the police post, and as a consequence became the guest of one of the café proprietors. He lived in some degree of opulence, in a large bungalow on a piece of rubbish-strewn waste ground beside the railway. He had numerous children of all ages, and a wife who was confined to a wheel chair. His bungalow had many large rooms with terrazzo floors covered with colourful rugs. One large salon had Western-style furnishings, complete with chandelier, and another was traditional Arabic, with cushions on the floor. The only thing that seemed to be lacking was a bathroom. I had a bed made up for me in the Arabic room, and Evans was locked up in the Western-style salon, to keep temptation away from his younger sons, my host explained. Only my host spoke English, and that was just a word or so. Nonetheless, I was treated with great kindness and courtesy and made to feel really welcome, which under such circumstances is, I feel, no mean art.

Amman seemed no pleasanter than I had found it before my trip south. It was still a huge, formless metropolis, where I felt lonely in a way I seldom experience in more remote areas. My stay was further blighted by having to spend most of the time in the Ministry of the Interior and the British Consulate, trying to get the bridge pass for myself and Evans. Unfortunately the consulate office, instead of going ahead and arranging the matter by letter, had left it until my return from Petra, and it was now all a rush to get it done by the required date.

There were two beacons in the general gloom. One was a retired British Army Warrant Officer, William, the doorman at the consulate, the only person there who was at all friendly, and the other was the complement of a British double-decker bus, parked in Amman's central car park. The bus was taking fourteen people and their drivers to India, visiting various places of interest on the way, and was temporarily grounded in Amman to sort out visa problems.

All the passengers were in their early twenties and were conspicuous for their air of good humour and enjoyment, in marked contrast to the general apathy and surliness I seemed to meet all around. The bus party was using my hotel to buy baths, so I got to know them, and was invited to breakfast and a conducted tour of the bus.

By no stretch of the imagination could the bus be called comfortable. It was extremely cramped and to move about inside required skill and agility. It was, nonetheless a triumph of ingenuity, fitted out to supply sleeping, cooking, and living quarters for up to twenty people for an eight-week trip. The passengers did all the cleaning and cooking; and the sheer amount of co-operation and control needed to preserve harmony and to prevent the whole project degenerating into total disaster was what the trip was all about.

People went on the tour who would not normally travel alone, but who wanted to see something of the world, for as little money as possible. They told me that within a few days they had found that the travel itself had become secondary to the fascination of having to relate to the others on the bus, and that they were learning new things about themselves in the process.

Two Australians organized the tour and shared the driving. They were not much older than the passengers, though they had been escorting groups for a number of years. There was a carefully worked-out duty roster, which included the writing up of the daily log. This log was an important element because it meant that experiences were constantly being reviewed and assessed, and no one could remain uninvolved. It was plain to see that everyone was making considerable efforts to make the trip work, and were getting as much out of the enterprise as they put in. I don't think they would see their journey as a pilgrimage, but they were having the sort of shared insights which I am sure many of the early pilgrims would have recognized.

While I was with them, two Arab boys of about ten years of age rode into the car park on a skinny donkey and came to a halt in front of the bus. They had a young dog with them which they lowered slowly to the ground by the length of string tied around its neck. The act was purely for our benefit, the boys waiting for our reactions. They tethered the poor creature, which by this time had its tail between its legs and was shivering with fright, and began to throw stones at it. We could do nothing more than temporarily halt the torture by chasing the boys off, and everyone was sickened and frustrated. The organizers said that they saw similar incidents all the time in Jordan; they too found the village boys a big problem, and said the bus came in for a lot of stoning, which made me feel a little better about the way I had been treated; at least it wasn't personal. They had seen a change for the worse in Jordan, they said, over the years, and put it down to the increasing problems created by the huge numbers of Palestinian refugees. If it wasn't for Petra, they'd like to give the country a miss.

While the overlanders' bus hung about in the car park, waiting for visas, I hung about the Ministry of the Interior waiting for my bridge pass, which took two very fraught days and all but ended in defeat.

Things went badly for me the moment I arrived there and I did everything wrong in the handling of Middle Eastern officialdom. To begin with I went on Evans, a great mistake; for when I arrived at the gate for my appointment, I was stopped at gunpoint by the guard. He was no good at mime and could not understand that Evans could not be left outside the railings to be stolen by any passer-by. I was quite happy to leave him just inside the railings by the guard, and I did this while I went to square things with the receptionist. I was relieved to see this man nod his approval, and give every appearance of dealing with the situation.

No one, however, should ever assume anything, especially when dealing with Arab ministries. When I took a look half an hour later, I found Evans had been pressed into military service to teach the art of bicycling to soldiers who were probably bored with guard duties. I thought I dealt with this contretemps tactfully and efficiently too; again I was wrong. Two days later, having sped up and down thousands of stairs and hundreds of thousands of feet of corridors, driven on from room to room by curt, unsmiling officials, I still wasn't given the wretched piece of paper. The British Consulate then sent an Arab employee with me to find out what was amiss.

Sure enough it was all because of Evans, and I might still be on the wrong side of the Jordan if I hadn't had help, since the bureaucrats were not going to give me the pass out of spite. It was spite which I felt had a lot to do with my being an independent woman in a male-dominated society. Several people both in Syria and Jordan had told me that the Ayatollah's regime in Iran and the emergence of the Muslim Brotherhood had affected the emancipation of women throughout the Middle East; and that there were many movements afoot to return women to the totally subservient position they had climbed out of years ago. My experiences in Amman would tend to bear this out.

William, the ex-army doorman, had developed quite a rapport with me during the time I had spent kicking my heels in the consulate foyer. He was the only one who was at all interested in my journey, and he invited me to a meal in a Chinese restaurant on my last evening in Amman so that we could swop travel tales; he had spent years as a soldier in parts of the world I had ridden through. Had his wife not been away, he said, he would have invited me to stay at his home, new company being at a premium in Amman, where the conversation didn't often rise above the level of knitting patterns. It was a very good dinner, and it lasted for ages because we found so much to talk about. By the time we had finished there were only a few hours left before I needed to set off for the border and Jerusalem.

Confirmation that my arrival was expected in Israel had been received from Tel Aviv, via London, only the previous day. It was impressed upon me that I must arrive at the bridge when it opened at eight, in order to avoid the press of people waiting to cross, which could delay entry for twenty-four hours. With so many people involved in getting us over, and with the alarming mystique that had built up about the crossing, I felt that the thing had assumed the proportion of a drama; and I was anxious that Evans and I shouldn't let the side down.

Accordingly, at a little before five a.m., in the small pool of light shed by my front lamp, I rode away from Amman. A grey dawn was only just beginning to break as I reached the edge of the great trench of the Jordan Valley which I had last seen in all its startling savagery from the top of Mount Nebo.

The descent into this valley is an awesome experience; 4000 feet it plunges, and the last 1300 are below sea level. As Evans and I dropped down the desolate, bare slopes of the Mountains of Moab, around the continuous hairpin bends, the tops of the Judaean Hills across the valley were just beginning to catch the first gleams of the morning light. Below, to the left, in the greyness of the valley floor, I could discern a lighter area, which was the salty wastes of the Dead Sea. The exultation of the descent was mixed with a sense of awe over the savage scenery and the historical richness of the place. I found myself reciting the pilgrim's itinerary out loud (for by now I had it off by heart), and when I got to 'Be unto us, O Lord, a tower of strength. Let not the enemy prevail against us', I thought of Joshua leading the Children of Israel down this same road to march on the tribes of Canaan, the priests going in front, with the Ark of the Covenant upon their shoulders: that too was an awesome thought.

I stopped to take a photograph and immediately a lorry drew up opposite and the driver shouted at me angrily to put my camera away. A little further on there was a notice saying that photography was forbidden as it was a military zone. I could see that there was as much suspicion and hostility here as there had been in Joshua's day.

By the time I reached the level floor of the Jordan Valley it was seven-fifteen a.m., and the sun was shining on the rich crops of bananas and citrus fruit. The barren lands which had greeted travellers for centuries had been regenerated in this age into something resembling Jeremiah's 'jungles of the Jordan' where lions had been a common sight. This hot steamy valley had been one of the fertile places of history, thought to be the site of the Cities of the Plains, possibly as early as the Sumerian cities on the Euphrates. Intense volcanic activity around 2000 B.C. completely removed all traces of these cities, and drastically changed the landscape.

In spite of all the lush vegetation, the predominant feeling as I rode through was of tension. I rode on and came to a guard post where my papers were examined and I was passed through; on again, past soldiers in sentry boxes, along an empty road in a torn, dead land, until I saw ahead a little scrub growth and then clumps of tall reeds. There suddenly was the border, two small sheds, hidden around a bend in a mass of greenery.

The guard in charge didn't seem to like me. He liked my pass even less, but was pleased when he saw it hadn't the right stamp on it and he could direct me to go five miles back up to the road to get it put right. I returned, found the office, which was off the road, down a side turning. I got the necessary stamp but not before I'd listened to a lecture on the perfidies of Israel. Before I went, the man said, 'You tell them we need to pray in Jerusalem sometimes.' It was not the first time a Jordanian had given me this message to give to 'them', and always it was said as though I was somehow implicated and somehow responsible for their exclusion from the holy site of Jerusalem.

Back down the five miles I rode, overtaken by the occasional bus, but feeling horribly exposed in a landscape torn apart by craters, disused trenches, and gun emplacements. The guard wouldn't look at me; he took a cursory glance at the pass and raised his chin slightly, in the direction of the open gate, straight ahead.

The bridge over the River Jordan consists of about twenty planks of splintered wood, laid side by side. The river itself is hardly wider than a drainage ditch. There isn't any no-man's-land, unless you count the river, and once over that, I found the heavily-armoured Israeli guard post was a bus length and a half away. There were three soldiers on duty in a smaller hut, and they didn't see me coming until I had walked right up to them. I'm glad I walked because the gun emplacements in the guard post and on the roof were manned by armed soldiers, who I think would have had no hesitation in shooting me had I swept up on Evans. No bicycle had been allowed through this control point since the Six Day War in 1967, and Israelis tend to shoot first, when faced with the unexpected, and ask questions later. I could see straight away from the look of surprise on the guard's face when he turned round that something had gone wrong with the arrangements.

Perhaps a little of the aura of the pilgrim surrounded me at this stage. I certainly felt the elation of having arrived in the Holy Land after four months of journeying towards it. It was like a homecoming when you are sure of your welcome. I smilingly assured the guards that all was in order, they had only to use their field telephones, and they would find that telexes had been received. I sat with them in their guard box drinking coffee, and thinking how much more civilized it was here than on the other side, and one of them told me how he wished there was no such thing as war.

The field telephones were not very efficient, but eventually one of the guards got through and talked, and after that the friendliness was withdrawn. A telex had certainly arrived, but as far as they were concerned no military permission had been given. I naturally said that this was not so, quoted chapter and verse, and all that was relayed down the telephone, but all to no avail; I must wait until the matter was cleared up. This quite suited me. I'd had a long ride, and I was happy to sit on a bench and read or just think for a while. I did that for about half an hour, until a guard came and told me that I wasn't allowed to wait on the Israeli side any longer. I must go back to the Jordan side and wait there, and he would call me when the permission came through.

The Jordanians greeted my reappearance with a jaundiced look, but indicated a bench for me to sit on, out of the way of the buses, which were pouring through fairly steadily into Israel, while lorries full of produce were pouring into Jordan. Then a curious event took place for which I have no explanation: a small pick-up truck drove up on the

Jordan side, had a word with the guard, backed onto the bridge, where the driver and passenger got out and began to toss a load of new but dented aluminium cooking pots into the river. There were a lot of them and it took the Arabs about ten minutes to empty the truck, during which time one of the Israeli guards came up to watch, but did nothing. When they had thrown every last pot and pan into the river they got back into the truck and drove off. I did wonder vaguely if Moab was making a gesture on the 'washpot' theme but I didn't think anyone would tell me if I asked.

A little way upstream was one of the holy sites of Christendom, where pilgrims had bathed in the River Jordan, at the place where John the Baptist had baptized Christ. Afterwards the pilgrims would cut palm branches from the river bank to take home as a sign of having made the great journey. As far as I could see, the river bank was mined now on both sides and spread with tangled masses of barbed wire.

Half an hour after my return to Jordan I was told that I could not wait at their border either. I must go into Israel or get away from the sensitive area altogether. Back I went across the bridge, to explain the situation, still clinging to my belief that Israel must surely sort out the muddle soon. Once again 1 took up my quarters on the Israeli bench; the buses and the lorries went on flowing in both directions, and I found that I'd been at the border over two hours.

I was to be there five hours in all, and I believe that if I hadn't finally given in to tears of sheer exhaustion, frustration and hopelessness, I wouldn't have been allowed in at all. Various people tried to make me go away, including a perfect bully of an Israeli army officer. It was when I was quite unable to convince him that all the paperwork had been done by our respective embassies, and particularly by the military, in the person of the Mayor of Samaria and Judaea, that I took refuge in tears. This was the best thing I could have done, though at the time I didn't think so, and the bully was absolutely furious. 'You finish crying and get back over the bridge!' he yelled at me. Though this made me feel even more desperate, somewhere, deep down, it also made me realize that, as long as I remained in floods of tears, the Israelis were unlikely to throw me back into Jordan as a witness to their brutality.

I could have gritted my teeth, and retraced my route up the huge incline to Amman, I suppose. From there I could have made the long trek down to Suez to approach Israel from her southern border, and had I been refused permission in the first place to use the bridge, I would have done that. At this stage of the journey, however, I think all the trials of the last few days had completely drained my energies and the thought of returning to Amman seemed altogether more than I could bear. So I just sat there and wept, and I suppose it released all the built-up tensions better than anything else could have done.

Eventually, one of the guards came over with a plate of cold rice with five chick-peas in it, and two slices of dry bread on the side; somehow I knew they wouldn't expel me after that. Shortly afterwards I was told to get on Evans and I was escorted by army truck to the customs shed. Before I went, one of the guards muttered that he was sorry, but whether that was because the permission had been belatedly found, or because he was unhappy at the role he'd been forced to play, I don't know. I received no other apology or explanation.

There was still nearly an hour of searching of both Evans and me before we were free to go and ride through the war-torn strip of sand bordering the west bank of the Jordan. After that, we came in a little while to Jericho, and I wondered whether to stop and look for the stones which all the early pilgrims came there to see. These were the stones which Joshua made the Children of Israel bring up from the bed of the River Jordan to commemorate the crossing; I had been reading it up in the Book of Joshua, while I was waiting around in Amman. They had crossed dryshod for, as the priests with the Ark of the Covenant on their shoulders had entered the river, the waters had divided, just as the Red Sea had done for Moses.

I did stop in Jericho but I felt too emotionally battered to do any sight-seeing. I couldn't even quite believe that I was in the Holy Land; so after drinking several pints of liquid, I started on the long climb up to Jerusalem.

I remember little of the details of the first part of the ascent, because I was too intent upon trying to re-establish some kind of inner equilibrium as I rode. It is a strange and disturbing feeling to have been caught up in other people's quarrels and disharmonies. All the events of the last few days had really had nothing to do with me at all. I was merely a hapless traveller who, through no fault of my own, hadn't slotted into the system, and had in consequence been roughly treated. The really disturbing element was the small first-hand glimpse I had been given into the political cynicism and the bitterness, violence, and hatred present in this part of the world.

After I thought I'd been going for ages, I came to a notice which informed me that I'd only just reached sea level again, and had another 2000 feet of climbing still to do. It was all wild, rough country, the traditional haunt of robbers, and the setting for the parable of the Good Samaritan. Remembering this, I remembered too that this country had seldom been anything other than war-torn and full of bitterness and political treachery; and never more so than in Christ's own day, when he had told that parable of human kindliness, against a background of Roman occupation, fanatical religious sects, and a corrupt and power-seeking priesthood. It seemed that the nearer one was to the 'City of Peace' the less of that commodity there was around.

As the Jericho road nears the Kidron Valley, above the road and a little to the left, the walls and towers of Jerusalem come into full view. It is a sight so charged with the emotions of centuries that it is very hard to take it in. The sheer amount of significant history contained in so small a compass is too overwhelming. Even at bicycle speed it all happens too fast.

I stopped where the angle of the wall makes a ninety-degree turn at the foot of Mount Moriah, the traditional place where Abraham prepared to sacrifice Isaac, and which, centuries later, David bought from the Jebusites in order to build an altar for Yaweh. Since then it has been a holy place for Jews, Christians and Muslims, and for Romans also, for they built an enormous temple to Zeus here in the Second Century AD, after they had destroyed the great temple of Herod, which Christ had known.

A couple of centuries later, when Rome adopted Christianity, the pagan temple was allowed to rot and turn into a rubbish dump, for Christians held the place accursed, and would have nothing to do with it.

When the Saracens conquered Jersualem in the Seventh Century, soon after the rise of Islam, they cleared the site and built the first mosque; for it was already a holy city for Muslims, second only to Mecca and Medina. Mohammed had prayed all his life facing towards Jerusalem, and it was from Abraham's rock that he was believed to have leapt his charger straight into heaven.

The beautiful golden dome of the Mosque of Omar soon replaced the first simple wooden mosque, and is still there today, just as the Crusader armies saw it, mistaking it for Solomon's Temple, when they marched up to the walls of Jerusalem on the seventh of June 1099. Five weeks later Jerusalem was in the Crusaders hands, and the Dome of the Rock was filled with the bodies of slain Muslims.

On the right of where I was halted, was the Garden of Gethsemane, at the foot of the Mount of Olives, whose slopes were covered with acres of the white graves of the largest and oldest Jewish cemetery in the world. Within a stone's throw were so many sites of Christ's life and Passion that I dared not stop again, for fear of not reaching my destination that night. Instead I got back on Evans and rode on up the Jericho Road, past the Golden Gate and St Stephen's Gate, and where I came to the next angle of the wall, I turned west and rode on to Herod's Gate.

It was near this gate that Godfrey de Bouillon and his brother Eustace, with tremendous personal courage and tenacity, had breached the defences and gained the walls of Jerusalem. A week before the whole army had walked barefoot right around the city walls, in imitation of the humility of Christ, and in the hope of victory. It had been a hard siege, and they had all suffered great privations, and had been kept in a state of sustained enthusiasm and religious excitement by preachers and army chaplains.

When victory came, they celebrated it in an orgy of killing that left no Muslim or Jew alive in the city - man, woman, or child. The massacre was awful enough to shock people, even in those days of brutality and sudden death. When the killing was over, the Christian princes went up in procession to the Church of the Holy Sepulchre in tears of exultation to give thanks to God for His manifold and great mercies. What is more, they were confident that they had rid the earth of the enemies of Christ, and that He had fought on their side.

Western culture is so impregnated with romantic notions of knighthood and chivalry that it is hard to accept that these eleventh-century Crusaders were essentially little more than barbarians with only the thinnest veneer of civilization. They thought in black-and-white terms, and were moved as much by superstition as by reason. They did not see the dreadful mockery in the worship of a just and merciful God coupled so closely to so dreadful a slaughter. Nine centuries further on, with equally barbarous acts still being perpetrated, perhaps we have to accept that the veneer is no thicker.

I found a simple little hostel near the Damascus Gate, where I booked a bed and left Evans. Then I went into Jerusalem, and as Willibald had done and Paula, and all the other pilgrims whose routes I had followed and crossed and recrossed for so long, I went up to the Church of the Holy Sepulchre, to give thanks for my journey.

# Chapter Nineteen

*Our feet shall stand within thy gates, O Jerusalem*
Psalm 122

Jerusalem seemed to me quite wonderful on that first evening. Perhaps this had something to do with my defences being eroded by the events of the day, so that I was more receptive to the atmosphere of the place. It was also the only time that I found the Church of the Holy Sepulchre virtually empty, and that might have had a lot to do with the sense of peace and unity which I experienced there.

With hindsight, I think it is only by association that any sense of unity is possible, in what is really a thoroughly unsatisfactory building, chopped up as it is into so many chapels, with a different branch of the Christian Church jealously guarding each portion. As for peace, that was in very short supply - with flash bulbs going off in constant bursts of cold blue light, and people forever asking you to move, so that they could take their 'we were here' photograph, even in the Holy Tomb itself.

That first evening, though, I was conscious of being a part of a great company of pilgrims, reaching back through the centuries, to when the Empress Helena first identified the place as Golgotha in 326 AD. All of the innumerable pilgrim routes, coming from all directions met here, and the concentration of so much faith and longing in one small space was overwhelming. There was so much more here than the stones and mortar of a temporal city. Even the graffiti of the Crusaders, in the shape of the hundreds of small crosses they had cut into the walls leading down to the chapel of the True Cross, seemed not to be out of place. The church in London, from which my journey had begun, was modelled upon this one, and both were built by the Crusaders. No matter how curiously un-Christian their conduct, for the most part, seems to have been, they were an essential part of the story of Jerusalem, and I felt that the thread of my journey had become enmeshed with theirs.

I spent the remaining hours of daylight wandering around the streets of Jerusalem in a kind of delighted disbelief, hardly crediting what I was seeing. After all the tremendous sights I had been exposed to along the way, it could so easily have been an anti-climax - or could it? Basically, it was just another busy Middle Eastern town, with narrow streets and teeming, colourful bazaars, and yet it was totally unlike any of them. The sense of religious and  historical continuity alone was staggering. On this one  Judaean hill, Islam, Judaism, and Christianity had focused, as had happened nowhere else in the world. The city has been destroyed and rebuilt so many times, with the same stones used again and again, that all the ages seem present there at the same time. From Solomon's quarries deep beneath the city, where the stones had been taken for the first Temple, to the newly built Jewish quarter above, three thousand years of different styles exist side by side in a strangely unique harmony.

There was an extraordinary sense of disbelief too at actually being where the central events of the Christian faith were so casually present. In the middle of all the everyday bustle of a noisy Arab market, a street sign reads Via Dolorosa, and tablets are let into the walls of houses or shops, showing that these same winding streets were also the route of Jesus from the Praetorium to Calvary. I thought it was the most beautiful and disturbing city I had ever seen, but after that first evening I never again thought of it as peaceful.

The hostel I had found, called, rather grandly, the Palm Hotel was in the unfashionable Muslim quarter, just outside the Damascus Gate. It was an old Arab house, imaginatively decorated and managed by two young Canadian immigrants, Michael and David. They kept a pretty little red and grey bird which flew freely around the place and perched in a large indoor tree, across the foyer from the kitchen. It was a good place, cheap and clean, and guests could cook their own food, which, in a country where the inflation runs at something like 400 per cent, makes a lot of sense. I was glad to have found it, and not least because Michael and David represented almost my only meaningful contact with Israelis. It was also a useful base from which to explore Jerusalem and a friendly place to return to from wanderings further afield.

Like Willibald and most of the early pilgrims, Jerusalem was to be my centre for visiting some of the sites of the Holy Land. In the eighth-century gazetteer compiled for pilgrims to make their round of the Holy Land there were well over 2000 Old and New Testament places scattered throughout the Middle East, from Northern Syria to Sinai; a serious pilgrim would visit them all, which was why a Holy Land pilgrimage lasted for years. Jerusalem was the spiritual hub of these journeys, to which the pilgrim returned, again and again, until the pilgrimage was completed. By that time, most of the central events of both New and Old Testaments had taken on a deeper significance because they had been seen and pondered over in their geographical context. For the pilgrim all these strands led back to Jerusalem, to Golgotha and the empty tomb.

With just a few weeks left before I needed to return to England, I could not hope to go everywhere, but I thought I would like to see something of Southern Israel and then spend a short time in the North, in Galilee. With much of Evans's load left behind at the Palm Hotel, my bicycle felt quite skittish as I rode off towards the Negev. I had been warned to take great care where my route ran through the area of the West Bank, which would be for the first two days or so. Such warnings hardly seemed necessary; the hostility and bitterness in the country were only too apparent. Even if every Arab I met had not been eager to talk about the inequalities and hardships they feel they are subjected to, their permanent air of smouldering resentment would make it quite obvious that this is a country bitterly divided.

The resentment is not confined to the Arabs, nor is the violence. I had been only a day in Jerusalem when the sound of a loud explosion announced the passage of a rocket ploughing through an Arab bus, killing or maiming most of the passengers. Four Israeli soldiers had fired it, in reprisal for the killing of two Israeli students by Arabs a week earlier. The violence of modern urban life, the bombs, the faceless killings have become such a feature of so many cities that such incidents hardly make the headlines any more. They are just as inhuman wherever they happen, but is seemed infinitely more terrible here because of it being where Christ died for unity and forgiveness.

I found little opportunity to exchange views with Israelis, except with new immigrants. Israelis seemed to be totally preoccupied, like their forebears at the time of the return from the Babylonian captivity, when in the Book of Nehemiah they are shown rebuilding the walls of Jerusalem with one hand, while bearing their weapons in the other. This idea struck me the first time I took a bus and saw all the youngsters in their casual military uniforms, using their powerful automatic rifles much as other people might use their elbows to clear a path for themselves. There was a pervasive attitude everywhere, too, of the rightness of their position, again rather like Nehemiah, when he said, 'I am doing a great work and cannot come down.'

Bethlehem was my first stop on the journey south from Jerusalem. The tomb of Rachel is just on the outskirts, a small simple building with a square catafalque around which a few women were standing, praying quietly, their foreheads against the stone. I couldn't tell if they were Arab women or Sephardic Jews, for many of these women dress alike and look the same to me. Then I went on to the second most important shrine in Christendom, the site of the birth of Christ.

The church which has been raised over the stable is the same magnificent Byzantine structure that Arculf described when he was here in 670, and which Willibald visited in 724, mentioning the altar which had been built over the spot where Jesus was born. The Church of Constantine, which St Jerome and Paula had known, when they lived here in their respective convents, had burnt down in 527.

There could not have been a greater contrast between the atmosphere at Rachel's tomb and the atmosphere in the Church of the Nativity; where the one had been all a place of peace and quiet reflection, the Church of The Nativity was filled with strident bustle. The entrance to the church is through a doorway so low that everyone has to bend to enter, and it is called, appropriately, the Door of Humility. This, however, had no salutary effect on the hordes of noisy tourists who seethed about the place. When Paula first visited the scene of the manger she had been cultivating the 'eye of faith' which St Jerome was so very keen about. He said that with this `eye of faith' Paula actually saw the Infant Jesus lying in the manger at Bethlehem. What I saw was Maisie from Milwaukee being immortalized on celluloid, with all her fellow coach travellers queuing up giggling while they waited to be immortalized too, crouching under the alter in the place where, traditionally, Mary had given birth to the Christ Child. It occurred to me to wonder if Paula could have risen above these unseemly distractions; I certainly could not.

It has become a great problem, this use of cameras in holy places, in museums and art galleries too, or any place where the peace and quiet are constantly shattered by flashes and clunks. It seems that photographs have taken the place of holy relics, but I don't know which is worse: having the sites removed physically, chip by chip, as was the earlier tradition, or having their atmosphere totally destroyed in this more insidious manner.

South from Bethlehem, the countryside is very beautiful, with high wooded hills and fertile valleys. It is all West Bank territory and very tense. I suppose the Arab boys must have thought I was an Israeli, or perhaps they hate all Westerners because of their own unenviable situation. Whatever the reason, I came in for quite a lot of hostility and stone throwing; and for the first time on the journey I felt really frightened, not just annoyed. That night I had planned to sleep in a youth hostel not far from Hebron, but when I arrived, just before nightfall, I found that it had now been taken over for special Jewish only groups, and the Israeli in charge refused to take me in. No Israeli in this area would dream of being out alone after dark; the perimeter fences are high and people patrol with guns. I put it to the Israeli that I had not ridden five thousand miles to risk death so unnecessarily, by being turned away from the only available shelter on the West Bank. After a great deal of such persuasion, I was allowed, without much show of good grace, to stay.

It was an interesting experience because I met a large group of British teenage Jews who were also staying there. They were spending a year in Israel, learning Hebrew and living on a kibbutz, in what appeared to be a very concentrated induction course. They were treated like royalty, given a surrogate family, and taken on lots of outings, like this one. They were a pleasant group, lively and intelligent; and they were quite aware that the object of the exercise was to encourage them to become Israeli citizens. Some of them thought that they probably would do so because life seemed so much more purposeful for Jews in Israel, 'more of a challenge' they said. The climate was so much better than in England too, they added. I was very impressed with them and thought that if Israel was able to call on an unending flow of such youngsters, reared and educated at no expense to itself, it had a strength and advantage that few other countries could match.

The following day I arrived at Hebron, a town which seemed much more like a setting for *High Noon* at the moment when the gun battle is about to be fought, than the site of the Tombs of the Patriarchs. The Israeli military presence was particularly heavy and obvious, with an armed guard on every rooftop. I seemed to be the only visitor, and the back of my neck felt horribly exposed for the half-hour I spent there.

The name Hebron means 'family', or 'friend of God' in Arabic, and is the setting for the Abraham story in Genesis, where Sarah overhears a mysterious stranger saying that she will have a son and she laughs because she is long past child-bearing age. I thought of this story as I visited the mosque which is built over her tomb; the atmosphere would certainly have been lightened by a little laughter.

Abraham, Leah, Isaac, Rebecca, Jacob, and Joseph all have their tombs in Hebron. Joseph set out from here in his coat of many colours, on a short journey, which was to end in Egypt, while his brothers brought back the bloodstained coat to his father Jacob. In the tense and horrible atmosphere of Hebron it was impossible not to think of similar bloodstained relics of Israelis and Arabs brought back to grief-stricken parents today. It was a relief to think about David instead, for it was here that Samuel had anointed him king. But then, that led on to thinking about David giving the seven sons of Saul to the Gibeonites, to be hanged as an expiation for Israel's guilt in having tried to exterminate this Amorite tribe after Saul had promised they should be left in peace. This story also seemed to have remarkable present-day parallels, and I got so gloomy thinking about them and about the dark and bloody deeds of the Old Testament, which seem to go on and on to the present day, that I thought I had better get on Evans and put some distance between myself and Hebron.

I found the Negev desert a great relief from the continual pressure of being in the present day Holy Land. It seemed a place apart; a beautiful sandy wilderness with, here and there, the ruins of ancient cultures which did not set up disturbing trains of thought. I felt I could have been happy there for a long time, wandering about like the Bedouin; and yet, Jerusalem drew me back inexorably.

On the return journey, I stayed at a hostel where I met an American woman, Marion, who was also wrestling with the disturbing realities of present day Palestine. She had been working for a year as a United Nations doctor in one of the Palestinian refugee hospitals in Lebanon, and was having a holiday in Israel before she returned to the States. It was the hostility of the Arabs towards her that she was finding so difficult. She had visited the refugee camps around Gaza, to see conditions there for herself, and she had travelled on the Arab buses. As she spoke Arabic she thought she would be able to communicate with the refugees, and that, when they knew her story, they would accept her as a person, an individual who cared about them. The Palestinians, however, could see her only as a member of the hated American race, a people who they felt were as much responsible for their present plight as Israel. She had come in for some very heavy abuse and felt the unfairness of it all very deeply.

When I got back to Jerusalem, I thought I would spend some time on serious sight-seeing, but Jerusalem is not like any other city. It does not have particularly fine buildings and great art treasures like Istanbul or Venice; its uniqueness lies in its historical and religious associations — a city of events rather than of places. Wandering around the streets is often more meaningful than doing the tourist rounds, for the historical reality, breaking through the normal everyday life, is all the more powerful for being unexpected. What draws people back to Jerusalem is the feeling that even in the meanest little alleyway one is walking streets that Christ and his disciples walked. The fact that the clothes and the domestic details of everyday life are probably not all that different to what they were 2000 years ago adds to this sense of contiguous history.

The finest building in Jerusalem, the Dome of the Rock, is the one place which I consciously avoided. The mosque is indeed exquisite; someone once claimed that its mathematical harmony has never been equalled and I could well believe it, and yet the atmosphere of the whole area was redolent of anything but harmony. No Jews will go there, except for the armed Israeli soldiers keeping a perpetual watch from their high vantage points. The parties of tourists, escorted by Arabs with walkie-talkies and dark sunglasses, are lost in the vastness of the spaces of the great platform.

The Dome of the Rock is situated in the middle of this enormous open terrace which Herod created around the top of the sacred Mount Moriah between 20 and 12 BC, in order to provide a platform for his great Temple. This was the Temple Mount of the Jews, called by Muslims 'the Noble Enclosure'. Inside the Dome, at its very centre, is the rock where Abraham offered up Isaac; the message in this choice of site is clear. Unequivocally it makes the statement that Islam has superseded Judaism. It gives a similar message to Christians in its dedication inscription, which begins, '0 you People of the Book, overstep not bounds in your religion', and it goes on to spell out the errors of Christian theology, part of which reads, 'Believe therefore in God and say not Three. God is only one God. Far be it from his glory that he should have a son. The inscription dates from 691 AD, but I think it sums up the unchanging and implacable nature of Islam, which has a greater conviction of its own unarguable rightness than any other world religion.

Below the Noble Enclosure is the 'Wailing Wall', which Israelis would now prefer to be called the Western Wall. It is part of the great Herodian retaining wall for the terrace above, and it is where Jews have traditionally come for the best part of two thousand years to mourn the destruction of their Temple. Unlike the eerie silence above on the Temple Mount, there is always a great bustle here at the Wailing Wall. Scores of Jews pray there very openly, in a great variety of styles: a few stand silently, their foreheads against the huge blocks of the wall; others, clothed in a variety of the traditional black garb of the Orthodox Jews, bob back and forwards continuously, as they chant in an age-old liturgical mode, their long earlocks flying backwards and forwards giving them such an odd, distinctive look.

Outside the praying area is an open piazza. When the Israelis captured East Jerusalem in the Six Day War, they bull-dozed the houses of the Moroccan Quarter which stood there in order to create this open space, which is now the heart of Jewish Jerusalem. Jews from all over the world congregate there, and Israeli families come to celebrate their sons' bar mitzvahs. So there is always the sound of dancing and rejoicing, and the noise of women making the strange Asiatic ululations, as the boy is danced around on his father's shoulders, bearing the symbols of his religion.

For a Christian there is really nowhere in Jerusalem that does not continually remind one that this is the city where Christ suffered His Passion, Death, and Resurrection. Such a place can be tremendously meaningful, but it is not comfortable. It isn't an atmosphere where a cosy Christianity can remain unchallenged. It is a city that makes difficult demands upon the individual, and after a few days I was glad to leave it again, and ride north to Galilee.

I stayed in a hospice overlooking the shores of the Sea of Galilee and was amazed that I had it almost to myself; for the weather, which had threatened to deteriorate, recovered, and it was sunny and perfect for swimming in the warm, soft lake water. This area, like the Negev, also seemed a place apart from the turmoil of the rest of Israel: a gentle, pastoral landscape of tremendous beauty, which was somehow as it should be and where it wasn't difficult to picture the events of Christ's life and teaching.

Of all the sites, the one which drew me most was the stony beach where the events described in John 21 are said to have taken place. It is all about the last appearance of the Risen Christ to his disciples, and John's account is so full of detail and so charged with meaning that I found it a very moving experience just to sit there all alone and read though the passage. When I think of that spot now, what comes into my mind is not so much the miraculous draught of fishes, or Peter leaping into the water, and his subsequent emotional turmoil, in which he finally met the demands made upon him; but the Risen Christ on that lonely little beach, making breakfast for his friends.

From the Sea of Galilee I went on to Acre, cycling up the steep hill past the battleground of the Horns of Hattin where the Crusader armies had perished at the hands of Saladin on a boiling hot day in July 1187. They died in an agony of thirst within sight of the lake, unable to spring the trap that they had so blindly walked into.

In some ways I got more of a flavour of the Crusaders in Acre than I had anywhere else on the journey. This had been their main port, captured by Baldwin I in 1104 with the help of a Genoese fleet, anxious to secure trading concessions in the area. Although it had fallen to Saladin after the battle at the Horns of Hattin, the Third Crusade, under Richard Coeur de Lion, recaptured it four years later in 1191. Richard ruined his reputation in the process, by a most callous act of cold-blooded butchery. The garrison had surrendered to him and he had agreed terms for their release, but when a slight hitch occurred in the exchange arrangement, he had them all killed out of hand: 2700 men, with their women and children, were despatched in front of the outposts of Saladin's army, who tried desperately to come to their aid.

A hundred years later Acre was lost again and this time for ever. In reality the Crusader Kingdom of Outremer had ended in 1187 with the fall of Jerusalem, and for this last hundred years they had been merely hanging on to a few coastal cities, mainly for the sake of the rich trade. The simple faith of the First Crusade, which had had the strength of purpose to win Jerusalem, was a thing of an already distant past. Europe was busy with its own affairs, and only a few isolated Western princes, like St Louis, had any desire to wrest Jerusalem from the Infidel.

While the net was drawing ever tighter around the remaining strongolds, Venetian, Paduan, and Genoese merchants were busy selling weapons to the enemy to be used against their fellow Christians.

When Acre fell to the Marmeluke army of Al Ashraf in 1291, it was a shambles. There were not enough ships to take off all the defenders, and Crusaders who had fought with tremendous courage while there was still hope sold their honour cheaply in defeat. Knights Templars amassed fortunes, selling passages to safety. Priests and soldiers fought with the women and children for places in the boats. Thousands were left to be slaughtered by the Marmelukes, and even so, there were enough left to glut the slave markets. The price of women was never so low;. From the harems where so many of them finished up, it could be said that they exerted a more lasting, if more subtle, influence on the Muslim world than their turbulent menfolk ever had. The other cities quickly succumbed and Al Ashraf wasted the land and the towns, cutting down orchards, detroying the acqueducts and irrigation conduits, burning and dismantling the works of hundreds of years of civilization, so that nothing should remain to enable the Franks to achieve a footing there ever again.

In spite of all Al Ashraf's efforts and the intervening centuries, Acre is still the substantial shell of a Crusader town, jutting out belligerently into the Mediterranean. Many of its walls and towers still remain, and everywhere there are medieval fragments. The most impressive of these are the Halls of the Knights, an underground city, which was the basement of the Church of St John and the quarters of the Knights Templars. These magnificent vaulted chambers with their secret passages to the advanced guard posts and their enormous pillars have survived unchanged since the Twelfth Century. One can only guess at the splendour of the buildings they once supported.

I felt I'd said a final farewell to the Crusaders at Acre, but this was not so. In my last rushed days in Jerusalem, when I searched in vain for a place to spend a quiet half-hour away from the clamour which was growing daily more strident as the Christmas season approached, I found the Crusader Church of St Anne. It is tucked away in the Muslim quarter by St Stephen's Gate, and is without doubt the most beautiful church in the city, as well as the most silent and peaceful. Romanesque in form, it has a high domed roof, and is built of the creamy coloured, local limestone. There is almost no interior ornamentation or furnishing, apart from a simple altar and a few plain wooden pews. According to Byzantine tradition, the crypt enshrines the house of Joachim and Anne, the parents of the Virgin Mary, and close by is the pool of Bethesda where Jesus healed the man who had been ill for thirty-eight years. Under the Romans, in the Second Century, the pool was incorporated into a sanctuary of healing dedicated to Asclepius. The Byzantines replaced this temple with a large church dedicated to the Blessed Virgin, which in its turn was destroyed by the mad Caliph Hakim in 1009. For some reason, the Crusaders did not attempt to build their church upon the former ruins, though they did construct a small chapel among the debris with a stairway for pilgrims to go down to the pool, which was by this time thirteen metres below the surface of the city.

In 1192 Saladin turned the Crusader church of St Anne into a Muslim theological school, which flourished for several centuries until it fell into disuse and slowly decayed. It remained in this sorry state until 1856 when the Ottoman Turks presented it to France in gratitude for help in the Crimean War. Its former glory was restored by the White Fathers, in whose charge it has remained ever since.

It is the one place in Jerusalem where all the elements of pagan, Jew, Muslim and Christian come together and it proved a most appropriate haven in which to sit and think over my journey, so nearly at its end. I didn't want to leave Jerusalem without trying to make some sense of the experience. It had been so long and varied a trek that I knew it would take months to sort it all out; there were probably elements of it that would remain permanently unresolved.

There was no doubt that I had found the experience immensely enriching. Geographically, historically, and culturally I felt I now knew a small part of the world in a unique way. The wealth of what I had seen, in the wide range of natural beauty, and in man-made treasures, I would always have, and that alone would have made the journey worthwhile. But I had gained far more than that. Travelling so slowly, like the pilgrims before me, I had had the time to appreciate the smaller nuances of change from one area to the next. It had for the most part been a continuous unfolding experience, rather than sudden transitions from one culture to another.

The differences in people's attitude to me as the journey unfolded had been very marked. In Europe, no one took any notice of me at all, and I was waved through international barriers as if they didn't exist. The further east I went, the more exotic I appeared as a woman travelling alone, and the greater restraints I had felt upon my freedom. This was offset by the tremendous amounts of warmth and kindness 1 met with. For short periods I had been given opportunities to be accepted into other cultures, which was by far the most rewarding element of the entire journey. Had I not travelled alone, these opportunities would not have occurred in the same way; so I had to balance the loneliness, which sometimes afflicted me, against such riches.

Violence was the worst problem I had to cope with, not from the position of my own personal safety but in trying to reach some understanding of its expression in the lands I was travelling through. From the relatively safe and settled world of Europe, I had passed through progressively more troubled and turbulent countries, until, in the Holy Land itself, I felt I had reached the most violent and divided of them all. To be amongst people torn apart by the sort of hatreds which operate in the Middle East, and which have an historical basis stretching back thousands of years, I found a deeply disturbing experience. No amount of reading news accounts or seeing television reports had prepared me for the realities of such a situation.

Within this context of conflict and violence, I lost the sense of those early pilgrims, Willibald, Paula, and Arculf. Apart from the one moment in the Holy Sepulchre, they seemed to belong somewhere else, in a different time and place altogether. Perhaps this is because they are among the few who found true holiness.

thoroughly reprehensible lot they all were, but now, against the long bloodthirsty history of which they were but a small part, I was no longer quite so sure. It didn't seem that simple anymore. Somewhere along the way, I had had a glimpse of them as individuals, perhaps where they had carved their crosses into the walls of the Holy Sepulchre. It had been easy to see their corporate barbarism, treachery, and inglorious self-seeking, but the individual motivation which had led them to Jerusalem was buried with them and impossible to discover.

When I thought of the dreadful inhumanity the Crusaders had shown in the taking of the city it seemed ironic and yet somehow fitting that they should have built this austere and lovely church as a monument in which to pray for the Peace of Jerusalem.

# Appendix I

## Prayers at Mass and Itinerarium for Travellers

### Collect

Give ear 0 Lord we beseech Thee, to our supplications and dispose the way of Thy servants in the prosperity of Thy salvation, that amidst all the various changes of this journey and this life, we may ever be protected by Thy help. Through Jesus Christ etc.

### Secret

Be propitious, 0 Lord to our supplications and mercifully accept these oblations which we offer Thee in behalf of Thy servants, that Thou mayest direct them by Thy preventing grace and deign to accompany them by Thy co-operating graces, so that by the aids of Thy mercy we may rejoice for the success of their journey. Through Jesus Christ etc.

### Itinerarium

In the way of peace and prosperity may the Lord, the Almighty and merciful direct our steps. And may the Angel Raphael accompany us on the way, that we may return to our home in peace, safety and joy.

Lord have mercy on us

V:   Save thy servants
R:   *Who trust in Thee, 0 my God*

V:   Send us help, 0 Lord, from Thy holy place.
R:   *And defend us out of Sion*

V: Be unto us, O Lord, a tower of strength
R: *From the face of the enemy*

V: Let not the enemy prevail against us
R: *Nor the son of iniquity approach to hurt us*

V: Blessed be the Lord from day to day
R: *May the God of our salvation make
our way prosperous before us*

*V:* The crooked ways shall be made straight
R: *And the rough ways smooth*

*V:* God hath given his Angels charge concerning Thee
R: *To keep Thee in all Thy ways*

*V:* The Lord be with you
R: *And with thy spirit.*

O GOD, Who madest the sons of Israel to walk with dry feet through the midst of the sea, and Who didst open to the three Wise Men by the guiding of a star, the way that led to Thee; grant to us, we beseech Thee, a prosperous journey and calm weather, in order that, attended by thy holy Angel, we may happily arrive at that place where we are journeying, and finally at the haven of everlasting salvation.

O GOD, Who didst bring Abraham, Thy servant out of Ur of the Chaldeans, and didst preserve him unhurt through all the paths of his pilgrimage, vouchsafe, we beseech Thee, to keep us, ThyServants; be unto us a well-wishing in our setting out, a solace on the way, a shade in the heat, a covering in the rain and cold, a chariot in our weariness, a fortress in our adversity, a staff in slippery places, and a harbour in shipwreck, that under Thy guidance we may happily reach the end of our journey, and at length return to our home in safety.

Give ear, 0 Lord, we beseech Thee, to our supplications, and dispose the way of Thy servants in the prosperity of Thy salvation, that amidst all the various changes of this life, we may ever be protected by Thy help.

Grant, we beseech Thee, Almighty God, that Thy household may walk in the way of salvation and by following the exhortations of the blessed forerunner, John, may come safe to Him Whom he preached, Jesus Christ, Thy Son, Our Lord, Who liveth and reigneth with Thee in the unity of the Holy Spirit, God, forever and ever.

> R:     *Amen*
> *V:*   Let us proceed in peace
> *R: In the name of the Lord. Amen.*

# Appendix 2

## The anatomy of Evans

Evans was built by F.W. Evans of 71 The Cut, Waterloo, in London, out of Reynolds 531 C double butted tubing. Its dimensions are:

Down tube 21 inches
Top tube 20½ inches
Seat angle 75 degrees
Head angle 71 degrees
Brazed on fittings for rear carrier and bottle cage

| | |
|---|---|
| Wheels: | Sun Tour small flange, sealed bearing hubs, Super Champion rims, 14 gauge rustless spokes, crossing three |
| Tyres: | Specialized expedition. Nutrak heavy duty inner tubes |

| | |
|---|---|
| Bottom Bracket: | Nadax sealed bearing |
| Chainset: | Stronglight 45 outer ring, 28 inner |
| Block: | Sun Tour six (15, 17, 19, 21, 24, 28) |
| Rear mechanism: | Sun Tour Superbe Tech |
| Front changer: | Sun Tour |
| Chain: | Sedis |

| | |
|---|---|
| Pedals: | Sun Tour Superbe Pro |
| Headset: | Specialized |
| Brakes: | Weinmann 999 dual levers. Scott Mathauser brake blocks |

| Saddle: | Avocet anatomical W 11 |
| Lighting: | Sanyo dynamo |
| Mudguards: | Esge chromoplastic |
| Carriers: | Jim Blackburn, frame-fitting at rear, low-loader front. |

Handle bar padding. Grab Ons

| Luggage: | Karrimor Iberian rear panniers in red cordura. |
| | Front, Karrimor Universal 3 |
| Handlebar bag | Karrimor Bardale |

Not one single item performed badly, except the handlebar padding which constantly leaked black dye, and the valve seating of an inner tube, which sprang a leak

I was particularly impressed with the tyres which carried me without a single replacement or a puncture, all the way to Jerusalem

# General Equipment

A sleeping bag with an inner sheet.
(For Europe only, a tent, a self-inflating mat,
gas  stove and pan, mug, coffee)
Lengths of thin nylon cord for rigging
clothes lines and for general repairs.
Safety pins for hanging up clothes
A torch, spare batteries, matches,
slow burning candle Notebooks, pens,
guide books, bible, maps, passport and
other documents
Penknife, compass, spare sunglasses,
toiletries Camera, ten rolls of film

Clothes: Two pairs lightweight baggy trousers,
hree shirts, underwear, sun hat, waterproof
cape, socks, sandals, cycling shoes, cycling
 mitts, sweater, swimming costume, belt,
 handkerchiefs, spare shoe laces

Medical:     Plasters, crepe bandage,
                  insect repellent, burn cream,
                  eye ointment, iodine, antibiotics, aspirin

## Equipment for Evans
Spanners, screwdrivers, allen keys, a chain link extractor, pliers, puncture repair kit, spare cables, 2 spare inner tubes and tyres, oil-free lubricant, spare chain links, water bottles, pump, spare bulbs for dynamo